THE VENICE GHETTO

VENICE

A Memory

University of Massachusetts Press
Amherst and Boston

EDITED BY
CHIARA CAMARDA,
AMANDA K. SHARICK, AND
KATHARINE G. TROSTEL

THE GHETTO

Space that Travels

Printed in the United States of America

ISBN 978-1-62534-615-5 (paper); 614-8 (hardcover)

Designed by Sally Nichols
Set in Alegreya and Hypatia
Printed and bound by Books International, Inc.

Cover design by Kristina Kachele Design, llc
Cover photo by Federica Ruspio, *Reflection*, © 2020. Courtesy of the photographer.

Library of Congress Cataloging-in-Publication Data

Names: Camarda, Chiara, editor. | Sharick, Amanda K., editor. | Trostel, Katharine G., editor. | Venice Ghetto Collaboration.
Title: The Venice Ghetto : a memory space that travels / edited by Chiara Camarda, Amanda K. Sharick, and Katharine G. Trostel.
Other titles: Memory space that travels
Description: Amherst : University of Massachusetts Press, [2022] | "Interlinked Essays by members of The Venice Ghetto Collaboration." | Includes bibliographical references and index.
Identifiers: LCCN 2021016893 (print) | LCCN 2021016894 (ebook) | ISBN 9781625346148 (hardcover) | ISBN 9781625346155 (paper) | ISBN 9781613768907 (ebook) | ISBN 9781613768914 (ebook)
Subjects: LCSH: Jewish ghettos—Italy—Venice—History. | Jews—Segregation—Italy—Venice—History. | Venice (Italy)—History. | Venice (Italy)—In literature. | Collective memory—Italy—Venice.
Classification: LCC DS135.I85 V45 2022 (print) | LCC DS135.I85 (ebook) | DDC 945/.311004924—dc23
LC record available at https://lccn.loc.gov/2021016893
LC ebook record available at https://lccn.loc.gov/2021016894

British Library Cataloguing-in-Publication Data
A catalog record for this book is available from the British Library.

To Murray Baumgarten, the most generous of mentors, whose lifelong passion for the Venice Ghetto inspired the next generation of scholars.

Contents

A Note on the Essays

Venice Ghetto Collaboration

The Venice Ghetto Collaboration was formed by an interdisciplinary group of humanities scholars in 2016 after an immersive workshop in which we explored the legacy of the historic space at the five hundredth anniversary of its founding. This collection, The Venice Ghetto: A Memory Space that Travels, *comprises interlinking essays that investigate the space of the world's first ghetto both as a concrete place and as a global metaphor.*
www.veniceghettocollaboration.com

Foreword

JAMES E. YOUNG

As I write these words, the floating city of Venice is just starting to reopen after being turned into one large ghetto by the mandatory self-quarantine rules that forbade anyone from coming into or leaving Venice during the height of the spring 2020 coronavirus pandemic. During this lockdown, the murky waters of the canals turned crystal clear, having had no water traffic for almost two months. But now there are no tourists to delight in the clear and quiet canals, only the Venetians who now venture out, the memory of their containment and segregation—their decreed ghettoization—still fresh in their minds.

As the editors of this volume have so eloquently described it, the Venice Ghetto is both a memory and a space in the mind, both a concrete place and a global metaphor. And as the poet Marjorie Agosín would amplify, it is also "a portal, to what is good, and to what is evil, to what is remembered, and what is often forgotten. A portal of oblivion and of remembrance."[1] How fitting that the floating city of Venice is also, in the editors' felicitous words, "a memory space that travels."

But one day in the next century, the city of Venice, Ghetto and all, will also join the mythic Atlantis at the bottom of the sea. It will live on, of course, in cultural lore, in memory, in metaphor, myth, and parable; it will continue to be "a memory space that travels." But physically, it will be no more. In its long *durée*, however, on its way to the mythical realm, both Venice and its ghetto will continue to be defined by its place at the water's edge, appearing to float above the sea on now-ancient pilings and platforms for much of the year, even as it is also flooded several times annually, inundated by the high waters of storms and super tides.

In the introduction, Amanda K. Sharick and Katharine G. Trostel ask, "How do we resist thinking about the Venice Ghetto as a static site" dedicated to the past?[2] How to resist this static fixedness? By remembering that it lives, temporarily, at the water's edge, whose only constancy is change—and whose only certainty is eventual inundation, given human-caused climate change and the resulting rise in sea level. Its future rests in memory only, and this knowledge, if we let it, can unexpectedly animate the Ghetto's beautiful mosaic walls and synagogues with portent. The Venice Ghetto is latent with its eventual inundation, its oblivion, and its conversion into memory only.

The water's edge is also the city's edge, but of course, this "edge" is not a fixed line or even the actual edge of either land or water but the constantly lapping, surging, waning, and hence ephemeral line between them. As parable, a history of the Venice Ghetto at the water's "edge" is suggestive on at least two levels. In his sublime meditation on how memory and oblivion are reciprocally defined and shaped by each other, the great French ethnographer Marc Augé muses, "The definition of oblivion as loss of remembrance takes on another meaning as soon as one perceives it as a component of memory itself." Why is this so? "It is quite clear that our memory would be 'saturated' rapidly if we had to preserve every image of our childhood, especially those of our earliest childhood," he answers. "But what is interesting is that which remains. And what remains . . . is the product of erosion caused by oblivion. Memories are crafted by oblivion as the outlines of the shore are created by the sea." Or as he puts it even more succinctly, "Oblivion is the life force of memory, and remembrance is its product."[3]

At another level, we might also regard the high-water season as an annual reminder, a pre-memorial, if you will, of the Venice Ghetto's eventual permanent home beneath the waves. The high-water events thus also become annual reminders of our own certain mortality, of the fragility and eventual inundation of all of our great cultural creations. And that human resilience in the face of this terrible loss might only be found in its memory—and in its invocation as trope, as a part of our universal lexicon. All of us and our creations need to accept our fragile ephemerality over the long durée. Cultural memory of the Venice Ghetto thus serves as a portal to both its loss and our resilience in the face of such loss, what remains in the face of oblivion.

The Ghetto as a "memory space that travels" begins its travels the moment it becomes a meme or a trope—sometimes remaining figurative, sometimes literalized as policy, sometimes a post-factum descriptor of segregated, sequestered, and contained victim groups. If, as Murray Baumgarten suggests in this volume, the Ghetto serves as a portal into the lives of a people and a community, it also necessarily functions as a "literary trope and thought experiment," in Baumgarten's words.[4] Here he draws an arc between the Venice Ghetto, the Turin Ghetto, the Nazi Lager, and the Warsaw Ghetto. Each "ghetto" is now known in light of the others, "a memory space that travels" over time and space.

Here I am reminded that when first proposed and voted into law in the Israeli Parliament in April 1951, what we now call Holocaust Remembrance Day was then named "Yom Hashoah Umered Hageta'ot" (Holocaust and Uprising of the Ghettos Remembrance Day). From its inception, Yom Hashoah thus twinned the catastrophe of mass murder with a collective uprising of "the ghettos." Here the law's principal author, Mordechai Nurok, was referring specifically to uprisings in the Warsaw and Bialystok Ghettos during World War II. But in effect, Yom Hashoah Umered Hageta'ot was initially conceived to commemorate a collective uprising, as it were, of all ghettos over the long durée of the very term.[5]

As a result, the generic reference to "ghettos" here as places of resistance embeds the term *ghetto* with memory of both sequestration and uprising, concentration and resistance. The day itself would necessarily allude to and thereby include memory of all ghettos everywhere that ever sequestered Jews, going back on a mnemonic and etymological road to the first ghetto of them all, established by decree in Venice by il Doge in 1516. Played forward on the calendar, it could also include post–World War II ghettos and the uprisings within them, from North American urban centers to the *mellah* and *hara* of North Africa. This would be a "memory space that travels," indeed, over vast stretches of time, oceans, and generations, forward and backward.

Pierre Nora has famously suggested that "without the intention to remember, *lieux de memoire* (places of memory) created in the play between memory and history . . . become indistinguishable from *lieux d'histoire* (places of history)." That is, without the deliberate will to remember or the deliberate act of remembrance, buildings and streets, ruins and archives remain little more than inert pieces of the cityscape, empty shells of history. If it is also true that such places of memory "only exist because of their capacity for metamorphosis," as Nora believes, it becomes clear that by our own acts of remembrance and our own capacity to recognize the long durée of the ghetto's many and evolving meanings over time, we become the agents of the ghetto's metamorphosis from a place of history to a place of memory.[6] The editors of this volume have it exactly right: by conceiving of the Venice Ghetto as "a memory space that travels," they ensure that the Venice Ghetto lives in perpetuity as a place of memory, par excellence.

NOTES

1. Marjorie Agosín, interview by Katharine G. Trostel, October 23, 2015.
2. Amanda K. Sharick and Katharine G. Trostel, introduction to this volume, 9.
3. Marc Augé, *Oblivion*, trans. Marjolijn de Jager (Minneapolis: University of Minnesota Press, 2004), 20, 21.
4. Murray Baumgarten, "Primo Levi, the Ghetto, and *The Periodic Table*," this volume, 147.
5. James E. Young, *The Texture of Memory: Holocaust Memorials and Meaning* (New Haven, CT: Yale University Press, 1993).
6. Pierre Nora, "Between Memory and History: *Les Lieux de Memoire*," *Representations* 26 (Spring 1989): 8, 19.

Acknowledgments

The editors of this collection would like to acknowledge the many individuals and organizations that have made this publication possible.

First, we recognize the contributions of all of the members of the Venice Ghetto Collaboration—both past and present (www.venice ghettocollaboration.com).

The working group was formed under the leadership of Murray Baumgarten at the University of California, Santa Cruz (UCSC). The work began with a conference entitled, "Liminal Spaces and the Jewish Imagination" in February 2015. Thanks to the Siegfried B. and Elisabeth Mignon Puknat Literary Studies Endowment at UCSC, we were able to host a second conference in 2016 entitled "Liminal Spaces and the Jewish Imagination II: The Venice Ghetto at 500 and the Future of Memory." A special thanks also to the Santa Cruz Department of Jewish Studies and to the Institute for Humanities Research.

From June 28 to July 5, 2016, with the support of the Gladys Krieble Delmas Foundation and the Department of Jewish Studies at UCSC, we hosted an early career workshop in the space of the Venice Ghetto, which was a transformative experience for our writing and research collaborative. The editors would especially like to thank Shaul Bassi and Beit

Venezia for hosting our research collective, and Sheila Baumgarten—our project coordinator extraordinaire—for all her behind-the-scenes work.

A special thanks to James E. Young for his enthusiastic support of this project in all its iterations over the years. Our conversations with you helped crystalize the final shape of this collection.

We would like to acknowledge that this volume was made possible by the financial support of the Siegfried B. and Elisabeth Mignon Puknat Literary Studies Endowment at UCSC, the Diller Endowment in Jewish Studies at UCSC, and Ursuline College.

On a personal note, the editors would like to thank their families and loved ones for all their support throughout the different phases of the collection, especially during the COVID-19 pandemic.

THE VENICE GHETTO

INTRODUCTION

AMANDA K. SHARICK AND
KATHARINE G. TROSTEL

In 2014, Rita Dove, former U.S. poet laureate (1993–95), was invited by Shaul Bassi of the cultural organization Beit Venezia to create new poetry inspired by the five-hundred-year-old space of the Venice Ghetto.[1] Rooted in this site for a month as an artist-in-residence, she contemplated her personal connection to "the many variations of 'ghetto'" that "provided the seeds for [her] poems, which leapfrog centuries and continents."[2] In a poem entitled "Sketch for Terezin," Dove considers what it means to enter the concentration camp through acts of memory and recall, as she connects the Venice Ghetto to Terezin via the thread of memory. The end of her poem contains a message of hope—a way of liberating bodies from ghettoized spaces, a road forward that is carved from the domain of language. In this fictional geography, the tangible space of the Terezin concentration camp is infused with the realm of the imagined, made flexible through creative acts of engagement. Dove, as the poet and cartographer, holds these two ghetto spaces in productive tension and charts a new future as she walks

> a path free of echoes,
>   a promise of no perimeters,
>
> my foot soles polishing the scarred stones.
>
> (80)

Dove's footsteps trace the scars left behind by the collective movements of feet that came before her—an absent presence—while her own memories simultaneously leave a subtle trace as they polish, and thus reactivate, these vessels of memory. The stones hold the acts of memory making, the etchings of individual pathways, keeping a record of these collective remembrances evoked by place. Dove's poetry helps us unpack the frameworks of both oppression and the possibility of liberation found within the Ghetto: the building and dismantling of structures, the ebbs and flows, the experience of rootedness and diaspora. Memory allows us to hold these forces in tension. The space of the Venice Ghetto is not folded into or conflated with the space of Terezin; rather, Dove's poetry enables the reader to bridge both concepts as she creates an interlinked memory.

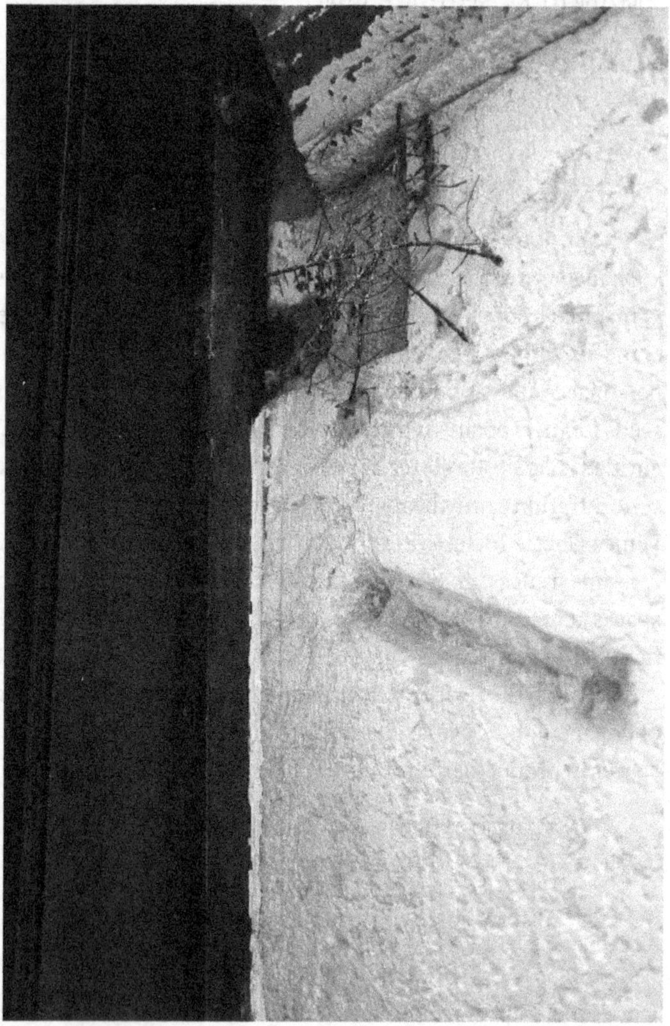

FIGURE 1. The indent where a mezuzah once hung in a doorway in the Venice Ghetto.
—Photograph by Katharine G. Trostel, summer 2016.

Much like the spaces depicted in Dove's poem, the Venice Ghetto is a place whose history is marked by present absences: the mark on the doorway where a mezuzah once hung, the scars on the stone where the gate once stood, the elaborate synagogues where a vibrant and diverse community has prayed for centuries, and the stumbling stones that mark the families who once lived in the Ghetto but were exterminated in the Holocaust.[3] Its relevance to the present and the future has yet to be fully explored. In *The Ghetto Inside Out*, Shaul Bassi and Isabella di Lenardo (2016) explain: "The key Ghetto stories remain hidden and unexplored, buried under a layer of seductive and powerful clichés, prompted by the now globalized

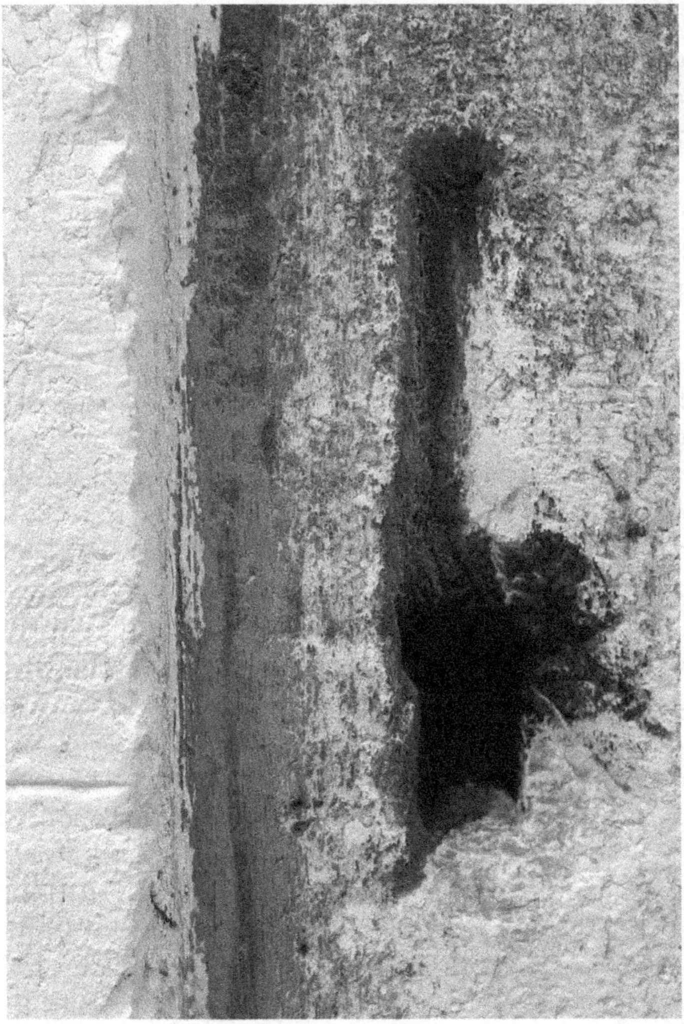

FIGURE 2. The indent where a gate once stood in the Venice Ghetto.
—Photograph by Katharine G. Trostel, 2016.

word 'ghetto.' . . . Nonetheless, precisely because of its resistance to interpretation, the Venice Ghetto at the same time poses important questions: while other parts of the city inspire mute admiration, these two adjacent *campi*, offering little in the way of beautiful facades and breathtaking monuments, prompt instead meditation and query, and raise issues of global relevance: What do we mean exactly by a ghetto? . . . We want to argue that this small area contains large lessons for the contemporary world, lessons that emerge from a patient excavation of its past and a critical examination of its present."[4] Our research collective attempts to situate the Ghetto as a cultural touchstone central to a vibrant present—a hub for exchange and creative production that will ensure a dynamic future.

In a 2016 interview with the University of Arizona Poetry Center, Dove again resurrects the image of the Venice Ghetto.[5] *Ghetto* is a term whose history had been buried, whose layers of meaning are carefully excavated through the space of her poetry. A native of Akron, Ohio, and an African American woman, Dove connects deeply with the word "ghetto" and the weight that it carries for her personally as the product of a postindustrial, deeply segregated Rust Belt city.[6] An image of Dove standing in the Spanish Synagogue in the Venice Ghetto at the five hundredth anniversary of its founding is one that Trostel often shows her students in Cleveland; it allows her to make an immediate connection between (what to them is) the distant past and the pressing present, urging them to think through carefully the weight of the word "ghetto" and the knotted histories it carries.[7] They read her poem "Ghettoland: Exeunt," observing how Dove tangles the double images now evoked for her by the word "ghetto"—an image of the world's first ghetto, the Venice Ghetto, constructed in 1516 and an image of the Rust Belt ghetto—a space that inherits this long-lasting memory of sequestration, exclusion, division, and segregation.[8] In her interview, she reflects: "I've been thinking about the word 'ghetto,' and how the concept of 'ghetto' has evolved over the years. I was asked to participate in a project aimed at commemorating the founding of the Venetian ghetto: This year marks the 500th anniversary of the first mention of the word in 1516, when the Serene Republic of Venice issued a decree banning all Jews to a portion of land designated as the 'ghetto.' The word has had many transformations, evolving through the centuries; from *shtetl* to slum to acting 'ghetto'; also the idea of ghettoizing thought, of ghettoizing emotions, and of course the glass ceilings imposed on race, gender, age—all of these things are part of my exploration and from which poems are still emerging."[9] As Dove brings to the surface, the word "ghetto"—prevalent in everyday American discourse when referring to neglected areas of our urban centers, a term that marks poverty and blight—comes from the Venetian context; according to Bassi and di Lenardo, it stems from the Venetian "terren del geto," an "area of the public foundry for casting ordnance."[10]

The history and movement of the word "ghetto" has been well traced by scholars such as Daniel B. Schwartz, Joe William Trotter Jr., and Wendy Z. Goldman. As Goldman and Trotter write of their 2018 edited collection: "One of the main contributions offered by [*The Ghetto in Global History*] is precisely the variation, contingency, and mutability of the ghetto as a word, concept, and lived experience. Rejecting an emphasis on static definition, it is our contention that the ghetto in global history is best understood dynamically and historically. Indeed, we have based the volume on the argument that the practice, etymology, and meaning of the ghetto have shifted over time in conjunction with its circuits of transmission and its changing contexts."[11] Our volume of interlinked essays, *The Venice Ghetto: A Memory Space that Travels*, moves beyond tracing the word's historical movement and instead considers how the memory of the Venice Ghetto travels in the realm of both the literal and the imaginary—as a space imbued with affective meaning. This collection explores the fluidity of the Ghetto as a place whose meaning is both anchored and dispersed. The unique composition of Venice is equally defined by its buildings' foundations and its water, the canals that circulate throughout the city and the lapping of the sea. The interplay between land and sea, past and present, is mirrored by the endurance of the ever-changing lagoon and the waves (natural and artificial) that shape the landscape. The metaphor of the wave, too, expands our project's engagement with memory as both individual and singular and as belonging to larger tides of collective and historical currents. The city and its Ghetto sit in this liminal position: on the water's edge.

RETURNING TIDES: CONDUITS OF MEMORY

Inspired by Dove's connection to late sixteenth- and early seventeenth-century Jewish Italian poet Sarra Copia Sullam, who once lived in the Ghetto, Bassi invited two other poets, Meena Alexander and Esther Schor, to "complete the experiment" of the Beit Venezia's writers-in-residence program in 2016 (16). The results were combined into a bilingual 2018

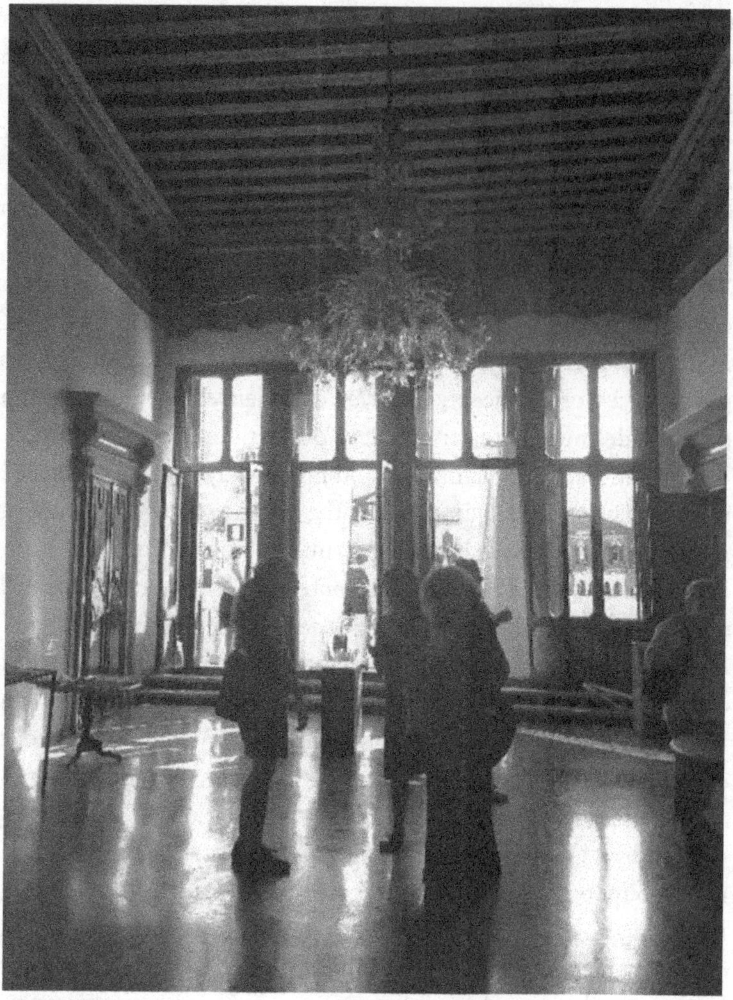

FIGURE 3. Palazzo Fontana Rezzonico. —Photograph by Amanda K. Sharick, June 30, 2016.

publication, *Poems for Sarra/Poesie per Sara*. "This book is a tribute to Sarra," Bassi writes, "a promise to continue our effort to nourish the tradition of the Ghetto as a foundry of ideas, always choosing poetry over silence" (16). These acts of creative production reactivate the space of the Ghetto as the poets serve as caretakers of Sarra's memories and draw inspiration and new life from "the few lines that survive" (14); in fact, Meena Alexander titles her section of the collection "In Praise of Fragments." Dove, Alexander, and Schor bear witness to Venice at its quincentennial and use poetry as a medium to bring together the signature features of Venice: its watery canals, stone streets, and distinct ghetto walls are woven together with the memories and stories collected from the archive, specifically Sarra's six-year correspondence with Genoan priest Ansaldo Cebà. Throughout the poetry collection, the environment of Venice becomes the portal through which to transport the contemporary poet to Sarra's time and Sarra's words to our own moment. Dove, Alexander, and Schor conjure Sarra by splicing and interspersing lines of inspiration from her letters into their poems. These overlapping voices pool on the page as the memory of the poet ripples across a new generation of artists, connecting the edges of the past to the present.

Schor's poems, particularly, carry forward an emphasis on the waters of Venice as the elemental and essential connection binding together both the place and the people of the Ghetto—past, present, and even the future. In "a canzone composed out of tears," Schor channels Sarra's experience of painful exclusion with tears that not only serve as one more tributary for the lagoon but also allude to a future that imagines the running together of all that is finite into the seemingly infinite yet ephemeral waves of the lagoon:

> All else in Venice, sooner or later
> turns to water:
> waves of song, lagoons of sound.
>
> (132)

The individual wave returns to the collective sea, its life a song amid many. On the edges of life and death, Jewish and Christian traditions, the land and the sea, the poem holds a new vantage point, that of the Lido, a thin barrier island that separates the lagoon from the Adriatic Sea and the home of the ancient Jewish cemetery. In Schor's poem "Lido," the island becomes a space for memory of those now "living" on the boundary of the lagoon:

> the sandy Lido
> holds them fast,
> ....
> In Elul,
> we'll carry his soul
>
> to this place—endearments,
> garlic breath, his face turned
> to our mother's voice

calling his name, . . .
. . . .
all that flows in us

through memory's
canals that flood
but cannot spill.
(128)

Here memory courses through the speaker's mind, activating a cyclical return at the end of each year during Elul, the twelfth month of the Jewish calendar. The flood of memory captures the affective traces—sounds and smells—that correspond to the connection of the speaker's uncle to others, which like waves of water are perpetually returned in new and infinite iterations. Yet the imprint of that which is gone or lost is revealed by the lapidary movement of waves of memory over time, just as the Lido is shaped—built up and washed away—by the crosscurrents of the Adriatic Sea and Venetian Lagoon. The gravitational force of the Ghetto creates unique individual engagements and collective energies that, like tides, pull different stories toward its center to imagine a future yet to be realized.

Memory, as with the water that defines Venice, becomes a central feature of *Poems for Sarra* and a conduit for creating new connections between past and future. In Alexander's poem "Refuge," Sarra sees the lifeless body of a Syrian refugee wash up on the shore after falling from an overcrowded fishing boat in the Mediterranean Sea. In the poem, she scoops him up and performs a ritual of mourning, marking his unmarked death by untying his shoes and setting them at his side as witnesses. Alexander follows the traumatic scene with questions about the future of memory: the fictional Sarra's wish is that the unnamed boy can symbolically live where another wave of unwanted bodies made their home in 1516, within the abandoned contours of a copper foundry. In discussing her creative process, Alexander notes that "I imagined Sarra, our shadow traces flowing together on the stones of the courtyard. There I completed the poem 'Refuge'" (22). The piece marks Alexander's desire to reanimate Sarra's legacy of "dialogue and exchange" in a contemporary global context (12). Her choice is future oriented as it envisions the potential of a new, more just world, "a house made of wind and water and sky" (50). Leaving the task of creating a refuge for the displaced in the hands of the reader, Alexander ends the poem with a question, "Who am I?"—one that prompts a reflection of the power of memory to create and re-create the world. Writing from within the geographic and temporal boundaries of the Venice Ghetto at five hundred years old, Alexander centers Venice as a crossroads of cultures and global currents across half a millennium. The Venice Ghetto as a memory space that travels witnesses both the returning tides of memory and the bodies of the forgotten, the overlooked, the silenced, and the refugee. It is precisely this power of place that our research collective seeks to investigate. The Venice Ghetto is a symbolic space capable not only of conjuring forth memories of the past but also of spurring an outpouring of creative work in the present; it allows us to think through twenty-first-century issues of identity, exile, marginalization, and segregation—the legacy of divides.

FOUR FRAMES FOR MEMORY WORK: VENICE GHETTO AS CASE STUDY

This book is organized as a collection of interlinked essays that together trace the refraction of the Ghetto across space and time. In doing so, we borrow Marianne Hirsch's idea of connectivity. Our contemporary moment, she argues, is marked by "multiplying" moments of historical violence, trauma, and structural injustice, stories and histories that have come to inscribe the surface of our present-day landscapes. Hirsch urges us to think through how we respond to these knots of history and memory: "What do these entangled responses do in the present? What do they demand of their viewers?"[12] The Venice Ghetto organizes memory in ways that necessitate a consideration of its multitemporality and multidirectionality and urges us to think about time in a nonlinear fashion: it is a touchstone for memory that is both rooted and global, both metaphorical and concrete. The Ghetto thus becomes a laboratory for thinking through the ways in which we consider how heritage sites "do" memory work. We explore the nature of this traveling memory space and also ask the question: How do we resist thinking about the Venice Ghetto as a static site and instead imagine the space as a heuristic for activating a framework of global interchange?

The chapters investigate the history, conditions, physical space, and lived experience of the Venice Ghetto, as well as broader questions about the legacy of the Ghetto, how and why the it became a paradigm, and how comparisons have been (and continue to be) drawn between compulsory, segregated, and enclosed spaces in cultural discourse, literature, and academic research. The physical place itself is key to Jewish Venetian memory where tangible traces of this vibrant past can be palpably experienced through monuments, archives, and museums. However, the space has also traveled in the realm of the imaginary, appearing as a literary image in novels and poetry across the globe. The original Ghetto gave its name to a space, a social policy of sequestration, and a stereotyping of a people; it has served as the blueprint for other cities' efforts to think through issues of segregation and inclusion. The word draws comparisons with such disparate places as the Nazi ghettos of World War II, the mellahs of North Africa, and the segregated and impoverished pockets of cities in the United States.

In thinking through the work of our collective, we have conceptually divided our scholarship into four categories. Our first grouping, "The Archive: Rooted Memories," focuses on the physical site of the Venice Ghetto, specifically examining the footprints left behind by the community made visible through studying the archival collections that shed light on its past. Included in this section is the scholarship of Chiara Camarda at Ca' Foscari University ("Hebrew Books in the Venice Ghetto") and Federica Ruspio, archivist for the Jewish Community of Venice ("The Ghetto's Archival Heritage").

Together, the essays included in this section ask vital questions that frame the act of memory work through the archives themselves. Books become witness to the mutable history of the archive and its multiple meanings for generations across time, but as the authors note, they capture memories that cannot be completely trusted because the network that allows one to re-create these historical ties has been lost. Unstable printing and itinerant printers of the period reveal the Ghetto to be a dynamic, highly mobile place where books somewhat defiantly escape its walls. Yet, despite having been made to circulate not only across places but also through generations, today the books serve as anchors rooted in their space of origin.

The essays ask us to think about the circulation of manuscripts, locally and globally. They pose a series of questions: How does the curation of the texts, their stories, and their memories shape the conditions of possibility for the future of the Ghetto archive in Venice—and for a Venetian public after the five hundredth anniversary? How do archivists place or situate themselves as guardians of this memory, battling record flooding and rising seas induced by climate change? To whom does this memory "belong," and how can we be thoughtful and ethical stewards of memory and its tangible traces? What footprints remain behind—imprinted on or contained by the books themselves—that can help us tell the story of the Ghetto's past, present, and future?

The second section of the collection, "The Blueprint: Global Archetypes (1516–2016)," examines the provenance of the figure of the Jewish merchant and the literary evolution of the Venice Ghetto's most iconic moneylender in Shakespeare's *The Merchant of Venice*, tracing permutations of Shylock from before and after World War II up to the seven-stage performance at the five hundredth anniversary of the Venice Ghetto. These many Shylocks, like the Ghetto itself, reveal that the famous Shakespearean figure serves as an archetype, a blueprint and barometer, of Jewish-Christian relations in the West. Beginning with the historical-social configurations of the Jewish settlement in sixteenth-century Italy, Andrea Yaakov Lattes, president of the Israeli Association for the Study of History of Italian Jews, traces the changing sociopolitical and religious landscape that creates the conditions for not only the Venice Ghetto but also all subsequent Italian ghettos. His essay fleshes out the historical contexts of the Jewish moneylender that gave rise to Shakespeare's archetype. Moving forward in time, Michael Shapiro, professor emeritus of English, considers how the blueprint of Shylock has traveled across centuries and reappears to illuminate contemporary Jewish experiences in the wake of the Holocaust in his essay "Disruptive Strategies in Post-Shoah Versions of *The Merchant of Venice*." Finally, in "The Ghetto of Venice: Clive Sinclair Discusses Venice, Judaism and Shylock," the late English author Sinclair reflects on the significance of the first-ever staging of the Shakespearean adaptation *The Merchant in Venice*—a performance that took place in the Ghetto on its five hundredth anniversary.

Together, the essays consider how the Venice Ghetto (and its most famous figure, Shylock) became a blueprint for understanding dynamic representations of Jewish experience. The authors trace how the Ghetto-dweller Shylock travels in the global sphere as his character takes on new meanings in new historical contexts. We see how Shylock, like the Ghetto itself, becomes a symbol for patterns of exclusion and difference—a kind of mobile signifier. The space of the Ghetto compels us to consider the categories of insider/outsider; the authors' examination of these various theatrical productions likewise asks us to think through how the historical context supports a narrative of "disruption"; the very structure of the Ghetto relies on the "necessary other." This is what drives the conflict in *The Merchant of Venice*.

The third section of the collection, "The Map: A Memory Space that Travels," looks at the way the Ghetto serves as a framework and map to understanding the complexities of modern Jewish identity in the twentieth century. The section traces how the Ghetto acts as a portal into and out of Jewish historical memory and experiences across the globe. In "Primo Levi, the Ghetto, and *The Periodic Table*," Murray Baumgarten, distinguished professor emeritus of literature and Jewish studies at the University of California, Santa Cruz, demonstrates that the metaphor of the chemist's laboratory illustrates how the elements of place-based memory bind individual and collective Jewish experiences, illuminating the Ghetto both as a haunting specter and space intrinsic to Levi's identity.

Like the Ghetto, the spaces of the Moroccan mellah are captured in "memorial" literature to reinscribe them with the memories of an irretrievable collective past. In "What the Mellah Was: Imagining the Moroccan Jewish Quarter," literary works connect multiple generations through the significance of physical spaces, both real and imagined, forging a sense of belonging through a shared history. In their cowritten essay, Emanuela Trevisan Semi, professor emerita of Hebrew, and Dario Miccoli, lecturer of modern Hebrew and Jewish studies, both at University of Venice (see https://www.unive.it/pag/13526), demonstrate how the historical and literary lens work together to shed light on the importance of site-based memory work.

The scholars look at the way in which the Venice Ghetto itself has been taken up in literature in contexts distant from the original site. They focus on how place can serve as a container for memory and how cartography can encode remembrance. Contexts mapped back on to other spaces—whether intentional or not—prove to be rich sites for interpretation (the Venice and other Italian ghettos from 1516 to the World War II Nazi ghettos or the diasporic conditions of the mellah). From a contemporary perspective, each ghetto's history is both haunted and shaped by our understanding of other spaces that have carried this name. The ghetto as a memory space that travels both highlights the challenges of modernity that pervade each iteration and is in service of discovering new potentialities and means of experimentation. The memory or literary maps are overlaid with various stories spanning space and time and become a guide to the way in which presents and pasts are intertwined and how new futures can be imagined—a kind of cultural wayfinding through the tangled, overlapping nature of historical antecedents and creative production.

The fourth section of the collection, "The Tourist: The Future of Memory," reflects on this question: After the five hundredth anniversary, what future possibilities emerge from interacting with the Ghetto of Venice? What is the value of memory studies frameworks for holding together competing pasts, layered histories, and contested futures? This section features two interviews with scholars who have grappled with ghetto spaces and knotted networks of memory through creative forms. The first interview, accompanied by an original creative essay and poetry, features a conversation with Chilean American Jewish poet and scholar Marjorie Agosín about her time as an artist-in-residence in the Venice Ghetto. The second interview centers a discussion with American Tunisian Jewish scholar and film director Margaux Fitoussi about her film *El Hara* (2017), which includes a candid interview with Tunisian author and theorist Albert Memmi. In both pieces, these artist-scholars reflect on the enduring impact of the Ghetto for audiences, tourists, and communities across the globe. Here we engage with the question of the "future of memory."

In Shaul Bassi's *New York Times* article "Waters Close over Venice," we are reminded once again of the fragility of memory and its material trace. Overlapping forces, both global and local, caused record-breaking floods to engulf the city in water with what "is all but a natural catastrophe, caused by the indiscriminate tampering with an ecosystem nurtured by Venice for centuries, the impact of cruise ships, threatening new and intrusive excavations of the lagoon and the rapacious investment in tourism."[13] The devastating effects of climate change force us to consider how the space of the Venice Ghetto requires scholars from all disciplines to think about emplaced memory work. The collection examines the fragility and resilience of memory, the impact of rising waters, the possibility of poetry, and the imperative to function as guardians and stewards of memory—rooted and global, static and traveling, archival and digital—in the twenty-first century. As Bassi reminds us in an interview with NPR that addressed this unprecedented flooding: "We need to imagine what climate change is going to be like. And for that, you need the artist, you need the intellectual, you need the poets, you need philosophers, you need the historians."[14] It is our hope that this interdisciplinary volume responds in part to this essential call.

NOTES

1. "The Venice Ghetto was founded in 1516 as a place of segregation. Against all odds, it became a cosmopolitan crossroads of different Jewish communities and an influential site of cultural exchange between Jews and non-Jews. This is the vision that inspires Beit Venezia (from the Hebrew *bait*—home), which aims to promote Jewish thought and culture and serve as a bridge between people of all cultures and religions. Beit Venezia invites both residents and international visitors to live, learn, and create in Jewish Venice. In cooperation with international partners we foster education, research and artistic expression. Our programs include conferences, lectures, residencies and performances." See "About Us," Beit Venezia, Centro Veneziano di Studi Ebraici Internazionali, http://beitvenezia.org/about-us.
2. From the introduction by Shaul Bassi to Meena Alexander, Rita Dove, and Esther Schor, *Poems for Sarra / Poesie per Sara* (Venice: Damocle, 2018), 108. Unless otherwise noted, references to poems by these authors and Bassi's introduction refer to this volume and will henceforth be cited parenthetically in the text.
3. Gunter Demnig, *Stolpersteine*, "Home," updated January 18, 2021, http://www.stolpersteine.eu/en/home.
4. Shaul Bassi and Isabella di Lenardo, *The Ghetto Inside Out* (Venice: Corte del Fontego, 2016), 29.
5. Sarah Gzemski, "An Interview with Rita Dove," *1508 [a blog where poetry lives]* (blog), University of Arizona Poetry Center, October 26, 2016, https://poetry.arizona.edu/blog/interview-rita-dove.
6. A part of Northeast Ohio in which Katharine Trostel grew up and in which she now teaches.
7. Mandel Center for the Humanities and the Italian Studies Program of Brandeis University, "A Lunch Talk with Professor Shaul Bassi: Reimagining the Ghetto through the Arts," flyer, December 5, 2016, photograph by Fred Viebahn.
8. Rita Dove, "Ghettoland: Exeunt," *Georgia Review* 70, no. 1 (Spring 2016), 24, https://thegeorgiareview.com/posts/ghettoland-exeunt/. Daniel B. Schwartz makes the case for why we can consider the Venice Ghetto the "world's first" ghetto while acknowledging that it certainly was not the first example of a Jewish quarter: "On March 29, 1516, the Venetian Republic ordered that the Jews of Venice be restricted to a small island on the northern edge of the city. Christian inhabitants of this area were compelled to vacate their homes; all outward-facing doors, windows, and quays on the island were to be bricked over; and gates were to be erected in two places, to be locked at sunset. The new Venetian enclave was hardly the first example in history of the 'Jewish street' or 'Jewish quarter,' which dated to the origins of the Jewish Diaspora in antiquity. Nor was it the first instance in which the Jews of a European town or city were compelled to live in an enclosed area separately from Christians, although segregation of this kind, especially in

Italy, certainly grew more common in its wake. Yet the establishment of an enforced and exclusive residential space for the Jews of Venice was a historical beginning in at least one crucial respect. It marked the start of a fateful link between the idea of segregation and a particular word: 'ghetto.'" Benjamin Ravid also makes the case for why we should consider the Venice Ghetto of 1516 as the world's first: "Jewish quarters have often been indiscriminately designated as 'ghettos' without any definition of what actually constitutes a 'ghetto.' I propose to establish a definition of the medieval and early modern ghetto as a compulsory segregated and enclosed Jewish quarter, on the basis of three decisive characteristics of the institution initially referred to by that name which came into being in Venice in 1516. Subsequently I demonstrate that most pre-emancipation Jewish quarters outside the Italian peninsula were not really ghettos, and that the loose use of the word ghetto has created much confusion with regard to understanding the nature of Jewish quarters." See Schwartz, *Ghetto: The History of a Word* (Cambridge, MA: Harvard University Press, 2019), 1, and Ravid, "All Ghettos Were Jewish Quarters but Not All Jewish Quarters Were Ghettos," *Jewish Culture and History* 10, nos. 2–3 (2008): 5.

9. Gzemski, "Interview with Rita Dove."
10. Bassi and di Lenardo, *Ghetto Inside Out*, 10.
11. Wendy Z. Goldman and Joe William Trotter Jr., eds., *The Ghetto in Global History: 1500 to the Present* (New York: Routledge, 2017), 3.
12. Marianne Hirsch, "Presidential Address 2014—Connective Histories in Vulnerable Times," *PMLA* 129, no. 3 (2014): 341.
13. Shaul Bassi, "Waters Close over Venice," opinion, *New York Times*, November 15, 2019, https://www.nytimes.com/2019/11/15/opinion/venice-flood-climate-change.html.
14. Sylvia Poggioli, "Rising Sea Levels and Mass Tourism Are Sinking Venice, Threatening City's Future," *All Things Considered*, NPR, November 28, 2019, https://www.npr.org/2019/11/28/783622529/rising-sea-levels-and-mass-tourism-are-sinking-venice-threatening-citys-future.

PART I

FIGURES 4 & 5. Facade of the Jewish Museum of Venice's entrance during the five hundredth anniversary, summer 2016.

—Photographs by Katharine G. Trostel.

THE ARCHIVE

ROOTED MEMORIES

CHIARA CAMARDA, FEDERICA RUSPIO,
AMANDA K. SHARICK, AND KATHARINE G. TROSTEL

There are several myths attending the archive. One is that it is unmediated, that objects located there might mean something outside the framing of the archival impetus itself. What makes an object archival is the process whereby it is selected, classified, and presented for analysis. Another myth is that the archive resists change, corruptibility, and political manipulation. Individual things . . . might mysteriously appear in or disappear from the archive.

—Diana Taylor, *Archive and the Repertoire*

We start with the concept of the archive, an image that brings to mind a physical storehouse of tangible documents holding the collective history of a particular people, place, and institution. The archive contains place-based artifacts, books, and primary documents that serve as witnesses to the daily (Jewish) life of generations past and present. By understanding how these material objects traveled multiple times throughout history—how they were circulated, utilized for daily life, sold internationally, neglected, forgotten, or left behind—and what losses occurred, we can interrogate the function of this memory in the contemporary landscape. The Ghetto's archive, expanding and contracting over centuries, tells a story of mobile memory. Its artifacts show that the archive is also an example of how the Ghetto and its inhabitants have continued to change, evolve, scatter across the globe, and return again. Its holdings, disseminated across time and space, are at once the anchors of this mobile community and at times the very means by which passage out of the Ghetto was secured during difficult moments given an object's monetary value.

This section discusses the current holdings of the Renato Maestro Library and Archive, which are adjacent to the Jewish Museum of Venice in the heart of the Ghetto Nuovo (see figures 4 and 5). At the five hundredth anniversary, the museum was under renovation with a temporary access entry, its modern, modular design covering the ancient facade and obscuring the entrance to the archive itself. We might think of the building as a metaphor for the archive and library—as representative of construction, renovation, and obfuscation. It highlights questions of access, circulation, and visibility. As the epigraph, authored by Diana Taylor, reminds us, we falsely think of the archive as the exemplar of permanent, static storage of artifacts and memory. Yet not even the building that holds these materials is static; the dynamic architectural facade allows us to think more deeply about the holdings that it contains.

The archive suggests a place of protection and preservation, a site locked away from the effects of time and space: a temperature-controlled room, the smell of ethafoam, and brittle texts gently lit under plexiglass. Yet the archive of the Ghetto is not a space apart from the broader concerns of the city or its place above or under the water. In 2016, these spaces were cordoned off from the public owing to much-needed renovation. In the fall of 2019, the *acqua alta* flooded this historic plaza of the Ghetto and narrowly missed damaging the Jewish community's library and archive. In 2020, the COVID-19 pandemic has similarly revealed a new vulnerability, one of a tourist-dependent economy that has simultaneously forced the closure of this research space so as to contain the spread of the virus. These factors firmly place the future of these materials in a network of local, national, and global forces. In other words, if an archive is always in flux, the Venice Ghetto archive reveals the underacknowledged underside of these dips and rises in interest: its existence relies on a constant reinvestment in and rearticulation of the importance of its contents for the present moment.

This instability and uncertainty prompt important questions for the practitioners of memory studies: Who serves as the stewards of these archival spaces? Should we bring renewed attention to this collection and entice a global network of scholars to interact with the holdings? To begin grappling with these questions, we must trace the archive and re-root it *in* the Ghetto—recognizing that these materials are site specific. The archive always prompts negotiation of issues of preservation and care. These considerations constitute major questions in the field of memory studies and help us outline one core tenet of this collection: the Ghetto has both local and global significance. (It's both a rooted space and the symbol of a diasporic population.) These questions also point us toward the benefits of dialogue across disciplines and what it might mean to practice ethical caretaking of primary sources still connected to living communities.

The first order of questioning centers on ownership, access, and audience: Who should have access to this archive? Whom are these memories "for"? The future of these archives, when viewed through the lens of memory studies, raises similar questions as those discussed in a 2009 article entitled "The Witness in the Archive: Holocaust Studies/Memory Studies," by Marianne Hirsch and Leo Spitzer. In this article, the authors unpack the impact of the changing dynamics of "secondary witnessing" introduced by video testimony, which, as eternally present acts, always show that memory, whether through testimony or archival documents, has the capacity to create new listeners across time and spaces. The listeners learn to "hear" silences in much the same way that archivists are trained to map footprints and absences. The Ghetto archive and its holdings become a dynamic space, an ever-present witness, encoding its memory in the affective remains of past "presents" or daily happenings of the Ghetto locked in the marginalia and ephemera of ancient books and documents. As we shall see in this section, the archivist and the librarian give us a view of the texts that position them as listeners, "inhabit[ing] . . . without appropriating or owning the archive."[1] Hirsch and Spitzer remind us of the effort it takes to walk the fine line between listening and appropriation, and in these essays that line is in constant negotiation, as the Ghetto's archive and its future remain precariously positioned between estate holders and national archives.

While part of the precariousness of the archive stems from questions of ownership, these questions are also part of a core tension of the Venice Ghetto that was similarly displayed and mapped during the five hundredth anniversary celebrations. As a national celebration, the official exhibits on the Venice Ghetto were placed at the center of the city, the Palazzo Ducale, where tourists and pilgrims of various sorts navigated through modern, interactive, digital displays of the Ghetto's archival remains. In this exhibit, the Venice Ghetto's Jewishness was part of a Venetian story that was also tethered to a sense of pride in national narratives of cross-cultural, linguistic, and social exchanges. By contrast, the localized memories of the Ghetto's library and archive remained closed to passersby, obscured by a temporary entrance to the museum. Unique in its holding, the historical remains of the Ghetto—its synagogues and material remnants of sequestered life which provide an internal perspective—remain anchored in place and accessible by appointment only. The place-based memories housed within the metal ironwork that encompassed the Ghetto's apartments tell a different story of the uneven nature of these cross-cultural exchanges. The bars and holes left from old gates remind Jews that their claim to Venice had its limits. Then, the question remains, For whom do we remember?

This tension about the significance of the Ghetto's memory for local and global audiences can be considered similar to that around the "cosmopolitanization of Holocaust memory." Quoting Daniel Levy and Natan Sznaider, Hirsch and Spitzer emphasize that witness testimonies and the archive accrue their "meanings . . . from the encounter of global interpretations and local sensibilities. The cosmopolitanization of Holocaust memories thus involves the formation of nation-specific and nation-transcending commonalities."[2] This framework for understanding Holocaust memory as situated between national and global is useful for thinking about the claims to the memory spaces and artifacts belonging to the Venice Ghetto and the ethical urgency to cosmopolitanize the archive amid new challenges in the twenty-first century.

The essays in this section offer two rooted perspectives on the history and origins of the archival collections held at the Renato Maestro Library—an institution physically located in the historic Venice Ghetto.[3] The first perspective, offered by Chiara Camarda, librarian and scholar of the early Hebrew book collection of the Jewish Community of Venice, provides an inventory and overview of the key documents in the current collection, with special attention to how they were produced, circulated, and dispersed globally as a result of diasporic movements of the Jewish community. The second perspective, offered by archivist and scholar Federica Ruspio, situates the Renato Maestro archive within the larger framework and methods of preservation for Venetian historical materials and archives that are critical to Italian heritage sites. Both Camarda and Ruspio raise important questions about the ethics of caring for and cultivating the revival of the Ghetto's archive during a time of incredible challenges faced by Venice due to mass tourism, climate change, and dwindling local populations. In search of answers, virtual preservation methods and possibilities point toward new horizons for the archive that promise to strike a balance between the need for safeguarding physically endangered archives and making them accessible beyond the Ghetto's gates.

The Renato Maestro Library and Archive prompts an examination of questions relating to stewardship and care: What ethical considerations are tied to projects of preservation? The preservation of the holdings at the library and archive took on new urgency after the celebration of the five hundredth anniversary of the Ghetto's founding because of a renewed recognition of and attention to its physical precarity; these material objects become symptomatic of other "endangered" archives around the globe. The scholars in this section demonstrate how the history of material culture can help us understand the history of a community and the dynamic tensions that continue to exist around issues of how memories are preserved and made available to the public. The scholars seek to focus on the documents held by Italian Jewish communities, drawing special attention to the collection held in the Venice Ghetto. Camarda, a librarian, and Ruspio, an archivist, demonstrate how they have served as the stewards, guardians, and curators of community memory, housed in these physical traces of the Venetian Jewish community.

Like all Italian ghettos, the Venice Ghetto produced significant documentation that bears witness to the foundation and evolution of the institutions and organizations that characterized internal Jewish life: the *moels'* records, school and financial records, and personal documentation, to give a few examples. The early book collection, especially underutilized, contains volumes that are too old to be used for contemporary religious training or liturgy but that nonetheless hold important value. When a worn prayer book is moved from a synagogue's desk to the "old" book collection, it becomes historical evidence. It no longer serves as an object for prayer, but it can tell us what prayer was like in a recent or remote past and how it has changed across time.[4] It can also tell us who has handled it, when and at what time it was in use and in which synagogue/house/school/brotherhood, and other accidental information recorded in its margins and blank pages. These physical items are irreplaceable primary sources for the study and understanding of Jewish life inside of the Ghetto's walls. There are many challenges, however. The loss of internal documents belonging to the Jewish community of Venice has limited what we can know about the archive and its book collection. It was not until the 1980s, with the founding of the Renato Maestro Library and Archive, that the materials were inventoried, studied, and promoted. The Jewish community of Venice initially commissioned the project of a complete cataloging of its bibliographic and archival collections, and after a preliminary reorganization in the eighties, the inventory in the archive was completed between 2011 and 2013; the early Hebrew books were cataloged between 2013 and 2016.[5] This work paved the way for new studies on the provenance of the volumes and for recovering both individual and collective stories of Venetian Jewry.

The archival materials mirror the historical vicissitudes faced by the Venetian Jewish community: the emancipation and integration of the Jews as citizens of the Austrian empire and then subsequently of Italy; the peak of the Fascist era and a new "ghettoization" in the 1930s; and deportations from 1943 to 1945. This archive thus serves the role of custodian, one that it acquired at the end of the last century; it is a place of memory preservation for the community's members. However, in the twenty-first century, we must also view the archive and library holdings as belonging to a global network of scholars and diasporic bodies and communities whose access to these materials is made possible through efforts at digitizing. The tension between the local specificity of these materials and their importance to a rooted community and their potential to be utilized in global scholarship is one that is central to the holdings.

Together, Camarda and Ruspio prompt us to consider how the footprints left behind by the community are made visible through studying material traces—in this case the archival collections, shedding light on complex pasts. By reanimating the network of exchange that took place between readers and books, we get a fuller picture of the way in which a diasporic people moved to, in, and out of the Ghetto—along with their books and documents—movements that were catalyzed by historic events such as Napoleon's emancipation of the Jews, the hardships of World War II, and the interest in the Ghetto as a tourist destination. This has always been a highly mobile, fluid community with movement in and out of what we might think of as a fixed site with rigid boundaries. This is a diasporic community whose communal record has been left behind, anchored by its books and papers, which enables us to understand the importance of both rooting the archive in physical space and tracing the nodes that branch from the site of the Ghetto in the realm of the virtual. Supplementing the physical and tangible traces of the community's books and records with virtual catalogs and repositories that indicate where a "lost" book ended up can show us a more complete picture of the complex historical and social forces that shaped the collection across space and time.

Memory itself is the past carried into the present, allowing us to infuse history with dynamic energy that points us toward new futures. By thinking through the case study of the Renato Maestro Library and Archive, we examine its role in the Venice Ghetto through the framework of memory studies. What broader lessons or takeaways can we extrapolate from the case study of the Venice Ghetto and its endangered archive?

NOTES

1. Marianne Hirsch and Leo Spitzer, "The Witness in the Archive: Holocaust Studies/Memory Studies," *Memory Studies* 2, no. 2 (2009): 163.
2. Daniel Levy and Natan Sznaider, *Holocaust and Memory in the Golden Age* (Philadelphia: Temple University Press, 2006), 11–12, quoted in Hirsch and Spitzer, "Witness in the Archive," 164–65.
3. By "library" we mean the manuscripts and printed book collections of the Jewish community that once belonged to the Talmud Torah, the synagogues, and the library of the *Convegno di Studi Ebraici* (conference of Jewish studies) or were donated by some of its members in the last two centuries. The community did not produce these books and manuscripts but collected and owned them. Many books arrived from faraway places, and they still bear the *footprints* of their former owners. At the same time, they tell the story of a community that has nourished itself on the continuous arrivals and departures of merchants and scholars from all over Europe. An example of this phenomenon is the manuscript of Piove di Sacco, preserved in the Renato Maestro collection. Its history is still to be reconstructed, but it bears the memory of a Jewish settlement that has disappeared and testifies to the tradition of a manuscript production that characterized this small town in the fifteenth century. Today, this set is composed of fewer than twenty boxes containing records and files from the seventeenth to the end of the eighteenth century that has fortunately survived the mass dispersion that followed the destruction of the Ghetto's gates in 1797.
4. At a certain time, for example, liturgical volumes included prayers for the Italian king.
5. Partial catalogs of both collections existed but were incomplete (and the old book catalog was on a single manuscript copy). See Eurigio Tometti, ed., *Inventario dell'Archivio della Comunità Israelitica di Venezia* (Venice: Comune di Venezia, 1984), and Moshe Rosenfeld, *Katalog hasefarim ha`ivrim kehillat kodesh Venezia* [Catalogo dei libri ebraici della Comunità ebraica di Venezia] (Jerusalem: Merkhaz meda' judaica, 1991). The new inventory of the archive is available online at https://siusa.archivi.beniculturali.it; the new catalog of the Hebrew book collection is online at http://renatomaestro.org/it/ and can be found in Chiara Camarda, ed., *Ha-sefarim shel ha-Geto. I libri del Ghetto: Catalogo dei libri ebraici della Comunità Ebraica di Venezia (secc. XVI–XX)* (Padua: Il Prato, 2016).

CHAPTER ONE

HEBREW BOOKS IN THE VENICE GHETTO

CHIARA CAMARDA

This essay summarizes two years of cataloging and researching the early Hebrew book collection of the Renato Maestro Library and Archive in the Venice Ghetto. Starting from information provided by the catalog, we can trace the history of this library, situating it within its cultural context. Given the impressive historical background of Hebrew printing in Venice, one enters this library with great expectations and curiosity. Many books in the present-day collection have been printed, sold, studied, and kept in Venice across the centuries and are still part of the heritage of this Jewish community. Even a quick visit, however, gives a sense of negligence and isolation: few readers are inside, employees and volunteers are asked to open its doors only on occasion, and no cultural events take place to draw attention to its holdings. This is a frozen memory space that contains early books as well as modern collections, but misses its target.

Located in the Campo del Ghetto Nuovo, next to the Jewish Museum, this library owns 2,373 catalogued volumes printed between the sixteenth and the twentieth centuries.[1] Of these volumes, a total of 226 editions were published in Venice, a surprisingly small number considering the ceaseless activity that characterized Venetian print shops for about three centuries. The earliest book in this collection is the third volume of Isaac ben Jacob Alfasi's *Sefer Rav Alfas* printed by Daniel Bomberg in 1522,

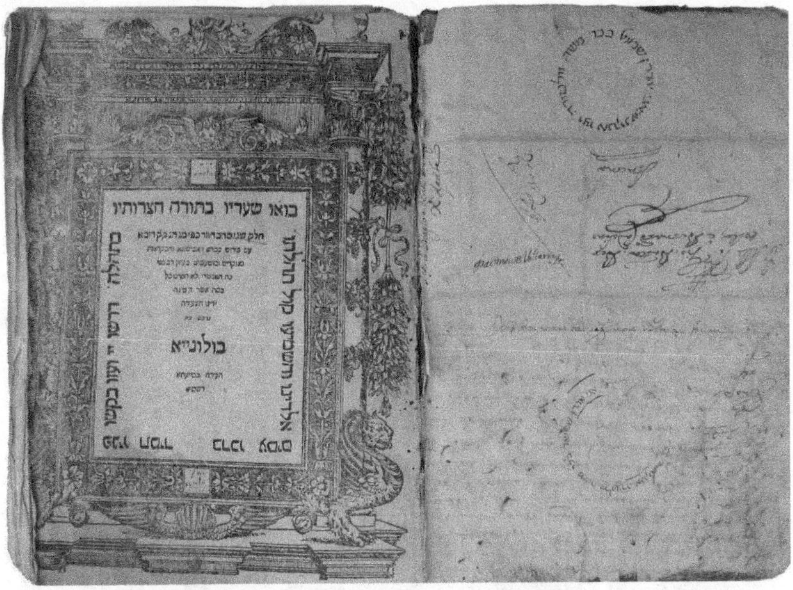

FIGURE 6. Maimonides, Moses, *Mishneh Torah* (Venice: Giustinian, 1550, s. m. C.G2.01), Venice, Renato Maestro Library and Archive. —Photograph by Chiara Camarda.

but according to old inventories, earlier volumes were extant up to the beginning of the twentieth century.

Over the last several years, my research has focused on tracing the history of these volumes, to determine what part of the prolific Venetian production could still be found in situ, to make a list of the missing books, and to identify the provenances of the copies.[2] Therefore, while compiling the catalog, I concentrated on the provenance of books as part of my doctoral thesis, trying to identify former owners and old collections that were donated to this library. It was not easy to locate this information: very little evidence can be found in the community's archive, and in some cases, I had to rely on the memories of witnesses.

Once the cataloging and the research were complete, I asked myself why such an important treasure had been neglected for such a long time, leading to the deterioration of some volumes and the loss of others. Of course, this case is not unique: many Italian (Jewish and non-Jewish) institutions share similar conditions. They all lament the lack of monetary and human resources that would enable them to grant access to the public—and beyond that, to enhance and enrich their collections. Few libraries dedicate any of their budget to collection enhancement, as

FIGURE 7. *Maḥazor* (Bologna: Refa'el Talm i, 1540, s. m. C.M2.15.B), Venice, Renato Maestro Library and Archive. —Photograph by Chiara Camarda.

funds are often barely sufficient to cover the expenses of primary services.

Considering how few people visit the Renato Maestro Library—and that those who do typically consult the archive rather than the Judaica collection—another question emerges: Is this early book collection actually representative of the education and training of the Venetian Jewish community of the past? Some years ago, a rabbi came to the library asking about Talmud editions that could be useful for his students: he found none. All of them were obsolete. The same thing happened with prayer books; when new ones were bought for one of the synagogues, the old ones were donated to the library. What does a library do with many copies of the same edition? As they are early books, they cannot be disregarded as useless duplicates, for their margins and blank pages may serve as archival sources to collect information about the members of the local community in a specific period. The printed catalog of the early books includes a detailed index of the provenances found on the marginalia of the copies, a useful key to quickly find this archival information.

We will now dig deeper into the Hebrew book collection of the Renato Maestro Library, an institution that inherited the collections of the former Talmud Torah Library and keeper of the bibliographic treasures that survived this community's vicissitudes until the present day. Venice is especially relevant for the history of Hebrew books. Hundreds of accurate and beautiful editions were issued by its well-known printers and sold all over Europe and the Mediterranean. One would expect the Venetian Jewish community to own a large and rich collection of such editions, as they were printed not far from the Ghetto (mainly in the Rialto area) and they were in Hebrew, but on the contrary, looking at the shelves containing the 2,373 early Hebrew books, one might think: That's it? That's all that remains? Through my investigation, I try to determine why this collection is so small, the actual impact of Hebrew printing in the Venetian context, where these books come from, and why many items that were part of this collection are now missing.

To explain why Venice was so important in the field of Hebrew book production and trade, we will follow the history of Hebrew printing in the Venetian lagoon from the sixteenth to the eighteenth century, when it faced an irreversible decline. Then, looking at the context of the local Jewish community, we will concentrate on the public and private book collections acquired by the Renato Maestro Library. Finally, we will trace the history of this library with the help of archival and bibliographic sources, oral history, and provenance-related information that can be found in the blank pages and in the margins of the volumes. This kind of information can be very useful in identifying the locations of book collections across time; learning about their readers, owners, or curators; and understanding how the current collection formed and grew.

SIXTEENTH-CENTURY VENICE: THE CRADLE OF HEBREW PRINTING

Many people have written about Venice and its Ghetto from different perspectives: scholars, writers, and journalists; Italian and foreign Jews visiting Venice as part of their collective cultural history; students from all over the world; Venetians who claim ownership of the space because they are writing about their own city; and so forth. From the vantage point of a librarian, historical investigation begins with the books and the archives. I approached the Renato Maestro early Hebrew book collection with trepidation and excitement, knowing that I was holding centuries-old volumes that had survived many generations and aware that I had the responsibility of introducing them to the public through new online and paper catalogs.[3]

Why was this project so important? The reading public of a given collection housed at a library or a particular archive is much broader and geographically scattered today than it once was, when the heritage of small Jewish communities was destined to be used only by its own community. While the birth and death records are still consulted by local Jews and descendants of former community members (mainly to create family trees), few people are interested in studying the bibliographic and archival collections as a whole or in detail, which is now the role of scholars and researchers. For these new audiences to find this material (and for the material to be found by its readers), it is necessary to update the online resources and online public access catalogs (OPACs) of each institution and to divulge as much of the collection's content as possible through the publications of edited catalogs and descriptions of the preserved documents. The second, and more particular, reason that this specific archive is so important is that Venice was the cradle of Hebrew printing, the place where the first stable Hebrew press was opened.[4]

Although a few examples exist of Hebrew books printed elsewhere in Italy before this period, they were rare attempts, with the sole exception of Gershom Soncino's wandering press, which printed many volumes in different towns. Soncino became recognized for the quantity and high quality of his publications; however, economic competition forced him to leave Italy for the Ottoman Empire. Although he wished to, he was never able to bring his business to Venice.[5]

The Serenissima Repubblica, home of Aldo Manuzio, the most famous Greek and Latin printer of the fifteenth and sixteenth centuries, was fertile ground for this new activity. Manuzio himself promised to print Hebrew books and issued some sheets in Hebrew characters as well as a sample page for a Hebrew edition of the Pentateuch, but he was hesitant to invest in Hebrew printing given its lack of popularity among mainstream audiences.

Though Manuzio abandoned the project, Daniel Bomberg seized the chance to have his name forever associated with the greatest Venetian Hebrew printing press. Bomberg originally arrived as a merchant from Antwerp, seeking to expand his trade in the Venice port. His friend Felice da Prato, a converted Jew, convinced him to establish a Hebrew press, and he embraced this visionary project by strategically investing in making Hebrew printing both profitable and functional. As time passed, it became clear that this work was not mere business for Bomberg; what emerges from the reading of his biographies is that Hebrew printing became his life's mission.[6] It is widely speculated that Bomberg studied Hebrew and kept close friendships with some of his workers, especially with Cornelius Adelkind (who even named his son Daniel after his employer).[7]

Bomberg's print shop would go on to issue the major works of the Jewish literary tradition and is remembered particularly for publishing the first complete editions of both the Babylonian and the Palestinian Talmud, making available for the first time on a large scale two cornerstones of Jewish oral law; manuscript copies of the entire works were extremely expensive and rare. Wishing to provide the best possible edition of any work he printed, Bomberg sent one of his workers around Europe and the Mediterranean looking for different manuscripts of the texts that he intended to publish, financing their purchase and collation. In addition, he attended to the aesthetics of his books in terms of paper quality, typeset, and woodcut decorations and reached a formal perfection that could hardly be surpassed.[8]

The Venice Ghetto attracted scholars from different communities, and experts on Hebrew classical literature found themselves gathered in a place where rich manuscript collections, like those of Cardinal Grimani, were available—and where it was easy to find the necessary equipment to establish a printing press. Umberto Fortis, who has reflected on the overlapping historical events that occupy the Venice Ghetto (its simultaneous foundation in 1516 and the issuing of the first Hebrew editions of seminal texts) even goes so far as to affirm that the extraordinary quality of the Venetian *cinquecentine*, the books printed in the sixteenth century, could not have been reached without the cultural atmosphere created by the Ghetto from its inception.[9] (Their quality was due not only to the beautiful paper, typeset, and decoration but also the philological accuracy of the texts.)

When Hebrew printing began, Venice was already an important center of production. The local government included members of the high culture, and new business opportunities were welcomed and encouraged. Besides Manuzio, famed for his beautiful Greek and Latin books, other printers such as Francesco Marcolini, Gabriele Giolito, and Lucantonio Giunta contributed to the glory of the lagoon. For example, Giunta, a noble Florentine, had moved to Venice with the purpose of founding a Latin press: "Egli sceglie Venezia per un evidente calcolo economico: Venezia è il maggiore centro tipografico del mondo, è là che si possono fare gli affari migliori: ed è questo il suo scopo, non altro. E il mezzo più sicuro per ottenere guadagni cospicui è quello di mettersi al servizio del maggior committente possibile, dell'istituzione che per sua natura usa e consuma più libri di ogni altra: la Chiesa. E Lucantonio diviene il maggiore produttore e fornitore di libri religiosi del mondo." (He chooses Venice for a clear economic reason: Venice is the major printing center of the world and there it is possible to make the best deals, and that is his only purpose. The best way to obtain notable earnings is to enter the service of the greatest existing customer: the Church. Therefore Lucantonio Giunta became the major maker and supplier of religious books in the world.)[10]

Sixteenth-century Venetian printers actively participated in the cultural life of the city. They were literate men, interested not only in profit but also in the quality and value of the works that they were publishing, with an eye both on the market trends and on trying to influence them. Their choice to print many works in *volgare* (vulgar idioms, the language spoken by common people) contributed to the diffusion and development of Italian-language literature. Of course, not all printers were intellectually involved in their activity. Hundreds of print shops operated in Venice at that time, and many were only aiming to make a profit.

The existence of specifically Hebrew presses did not seem exceptional in this city, where other printers issued works in many different languages. Some Arabic works, for instance, appeared for the first time in 1499 in Manuzio's *Hypnerotomachia Poliphili*. Greeks and Armenians, under Turkish dominion, were not allowed to print books in their own countries, but they could do so in Venice, spurring the development and diffusion of their respective presses, even if they were sometimes managed by local printers.

An Armenian printing press was established in Venice in 1512, the same year in which the Cyrillic alphabet appeared in print for the first time.

Slavic presses did exist in Russia and Transylvania, but those in Venice could count on a broader commercial network and thus flourished. All of the Oriental churches (Greek, Ukrainian, Russian, Serbian, Bulgarian, Romanian, and Melkite Greek Catholic) had their books printed in Venice, and liturgical books were the most requested. Other significant branches of the Venetian printing industry produced cartographic maps (especially Giunta and Tramezzino) and musical scores (Giolito, Marcolini, Tramezzino, and Scotto).[11]

Venice was a good place for the establishment of new presses because it was easier there than anywhere else to buy paper at a competitive price; to learn the craft at another print shop; to find literate and experienced proofreaders, editors, and commentators; and, above all, to distribute and sell printed books, which were listed in catalogs and advertised in different marketplaces. The city was not free from issues and problems that made printing difficult from time to time, but its printers adapted and rose again even from the worst economic conditions.

In the middle of the sixteenth century, during the last years of Bomberg's activity (he ceased printing in 1549), two other printers entered the scene in a turbulent way: Marco Antonio Giustinian (active 1545–52) and Alvise Bragadin (1550–54 and 1563–75), who both published an edition of Maimonides's *Mishneh Torah* in 1550. First, Giustinian refused Rabbi Meir ben Isaac Katzenellenbogen's request to print this work with the addition of his own glosses. The Paduan rabbi then turned to Bragadin, who accepted the task. Shortly afterward, Giustinian changed his mind and published the work, including some of the rabbi's notes, without notifying him. Both printers tried to discredit their rival's edition and involved Jewish and Christian authorities in their quarrel. In 1553, their dispute resulted in extremely serious consequences, leading to the burning of the Talmud and other *halakhic* works in different Italian cities.[12] The two printers, who unwittingly provoked this unrest, faced financial ruin. Giustinian was forced to close his print shop in 1552, never to reopen; Bragadin's press closed in 1554, marking the temporary end of Hebrew printing in the city. Other towns, such as Mantua, Cremona, Ferrara, and Sabbioneta, benefited from the idleness in Venice, and new printers issued Hebrew books there under the protection of local patrons.

In 1563, Hebrew printing in Venice resumed, and the city soon regained its leading position, with Bragadin (who had reopened his print shop) and other famous printers contributing to the long-lasting fame of the Venetian Hebrew presses. Their printers' marks became symbols of excellence. This was the case for Giovanni Di Gara (active 1564–1609); Giorgio Cavalli (1564–70); Giovanni Griffio, also known as Grifo (1544–76); Cristoforo Zanetti (1546–77); and Meir Parenzo (1546–48), the only Jew publishing books under his own name in spite of laws that prevented him from doing so. Meir's father Jacob had come to Venice from Parenzo on the Dalmatian coast of Italy, hence their last name. Meir probably learned the printing trade at the Bomberg press, where he worked together with Cornelius Adelkind in 1545. He was then employed by Carlo Querini as a typesetter and copy editor. Then, from 1546 to 1548, he worked on his own, publishing five works. Back at Querini's press, he published an edition of the Mishnah with Bertinoro's commentary, but from circa 1550 onward he mainly worked with Alvise Bragadin.[13] David W. Amram highlights that "the Bragadini employed members of the family of Parenzo until far into the seventeenth century. Many of the books published by Meir Parenzo are quite as handsome as those published by Adelkind and show no sign of the approaching decline of the Venetian press."[14]

In northern Europe, print shops were in a different position: public and university libraries were their principal customers, and they issued the works that professors required. As the main center for book production, Venice had many printers and booksellers who imported and exported books. The purchasers here belonged to different social classes, as has been demonstrated by Martin Lowry in his analysis of the sales records of bookseller Francesco De Madiis (1484–88), who sold more than twelve thousand books in about four years. Some of his customers were minor booksellers who purchased many copies of the same works; others were bibliophiles, priests, or friars buying single copies of many different works to enrich their libraries; and many individuals bought just one or two books, especially during the fair seasons when the town was populated by visitors.[15]

With respect to Hebrew books, we know that Christian Hebraists, friars, university libraries, and Jewish communities from Italy and Europe were among their buyers, but private Jewish collectors existed as well. The Jewish community with its schools certainly had at least one library, but we do not have any historical artifacts—other than the books themselves—concerning this book collection prior to the eighteenth century. Looking at the catalog published in 2016, however, we can deduce some useful information. The Hebrew books dating back to the sixteenth century in the Renato Maestro Library and Archive clearly belonged to one library of the Jewish community, namely, that of the Talmud Torah. They contain rabbinical literature, including Talmudic treatises (although the greater part of them have disappeared), Bibles, midrashic works, prayer books, sermons, and a few other works. Among these is the Zohar printed in Mantua in 1558–60 that was acquired through a private donation. Yet considering the impressive scale of local book production, the number of sixteenth-century editions in this library is surprisingly small; many important volumes that once belonged to this collection disappeared during the second half of the twentieth century owing to war and the movement of people.

SEVENTEENTH CENTURY: THE FIRST HINTS OF DECLINE

In the seventeenth century, the Jewish population in the Ghetto grew from about seven hundred people in 1516 to about 4,870 in 1655.[16] During this golden age of Venetian Jewry, the most famous Venetian rabbi, Leone da Modena, also known as Leon Modena (1571–1648); the well-known poet Sarra Copia Sullam (1592–1641); and Rabbi Simone Luzzatto (1580–1663) shaped cross-cultural experiences among the Venetian Christian and Jewish communities. As biographies of these outstanding figures prove, interaction between Jews and non-Jews in Venice was quite frequent. Debates were not unusual, and there were friendly relations among Jews and Christians, although the latter often attempted to convert the former. The Jewish population itself was diverse thanks to several waves of immigration that expanded the Ghetto's population and living quarters. Between 1541 and 1633, Ghetto Vecchio and Ghetto Nuovissimo were added to accommodate the drastic increase of the Jewish immigrant population. These new residents were diverse in their cultural and religious practices. Indeed, five synagogues were created within this concentrated area, an important reminder of the different *minhagim* (mores) of its inhabitants. Other European Jewish communities—like those of Hamburg and Amsterdam—were also dealing with the issue of the immigration of "New Christians," Jewish converts from the Iberian Peninsula who wished to return to Judaism. These communities looked to Venice as an example because of the integration of its citizens, its culture and knowledge, and the fact that the local population remained faithful to Judaism.

Venice became a model for communities attempting to reconcile issues internal to heterogeneous Jewish communities. For example, when Marrano Jews in Amsterdam and Hamburg were contesting the Oral Law, these communities turned for advice to Venetian rabbis, known to be very well educated and experienced. In 1618, Venetian rabbis pronounced a *ḥerem* (excommunication) against those Jews who rejected the Oral Law, including against Baruch Spinoza and Uriel da Costa.[17]

The political and religious conflicts following the Reformation and the Anglican schism brought about strict control of the printing business, as books were considered a dangerous instrument of Protestant propaganda. Venetian presses began to decline, diminishing in number from about one hundred fifty at the beginning of the sixteenth century to thirty-four in 1598.[18] This recession is traditionally attributed to the actions of the Counter-Reformation and in particular to the repression of Hebrew printing by the Congregation of the Index, whose purpose was to regularly update the *Index librorum prohibitorum* and to suggest emendations to those pieces not fully censored. Of course, we cannot ignore more explicit intimidation tactics such as the unexpected fires that were lit from time to time in Venetian squares, burning books that had been suddenly labeled as "prohibited." This banning of books caused many printers to leave the city, as many financiers of Hebrew presses withdrew their support. Today, scholars tend to emphasize economic factors, such as the competition from foreign presses and the protectionist laws of other governments that favored their own local printers, as primary reasons for the decline of Hebrew printing in Venice.[19] These circumstances were exacerbated by a ferocious plague that killed one-third of the Venetian population in 1630, contributing to a rapid halt in book production for two years.

In 1632, when the members of the printers' guild gathered again for the first time, they lamented their enormous problems: only five printing presses were working, many printers had fled the city or died, only inexperienced workers were available, and it was hard to provide paper and typeset because they had been sold to foreign customers. Paper production, too, was limited, as the plague had killed many of the papermakers who had formerly supplied Venetian presses. The situation was, perhaps, better than members of the guild depicted in their accounts, which purposely exaggerated the dire conditions to attract the attention of the government and obtain its support. Indeed, two years later, sixteen printing presses were working in Venice, and their number doubled in less than ten years, when many workers who had fled the city came back.[20]

The presses soon recovered, and Venice regained its leading role among Italian publishers—though not among Europe's. Two well-known presses, the Stamparia Bragadina (founded by Alvise Bragadin) and the Stamparia Vendramina (founded by Giovanni Vendramin in 1630), were actively printing Hebrew books in town but were far from reaching the splendor of the sixteenth-century Venetian printing industry. From the first half of the seventeenth century, trade was concentrated around the Jewish communities of Leghorn and Amsterdam and was later centered in Germany (seventeenth century onward); Poland (some presses opened in Kraków and Lublin as early as the sixteenth century); and Russia, Lithuania, and Ukraine (eighteenth and nineteenth centuries). These new printing centers gained leading positions owing to the flexibility and tolerance of their local governments, which had an interest in supporting this new business. The Hebrew books printed in Amsterdam, in fact, were intended for export rather than for the use of its Jewish population.[21]

Looking at the Renato Maestro book collection, we find seventy-five seventeenth-century editions: half of these were published in Venice, eleven in Amsterdam, and only two in Leghorn. The collections of both the Talmud Torah library and of private individuals—wealthy members of the Jewish community—were growing. Their collections were so valuable that they were usually distributed in last wills and testaments, a phenomenon thoroughly described by Marino Zorzi: "Per gli Ebrei il libro costituiva un fatto centrale nella religione e nella identità storica; i membri della comunità possedevano molti libri, come quel Benedetto Levi cui attorno al 1684 appartenevano seicentotrentanove opere latine, volgari ed ebraiche, o come il rabbino Samuel Aboaff, che nel 1694 lasciava oltre cinquecento opere ebraiche." (For the Jews the book constituted a central aspect of their religion and their historical identity. Members of the community owned many books, like Benedetto Levi to whom—around 1684—belonged six hundred thirty-nine Latin, Vernacular, and Hebrew works, or like rabbi Samuel Aboaff who, in 1694, left behind more than five hundred Hebrew works.)[22]

THE JEWISH COMMUNITY IN THE EIGHTEENTH–TWENTIETH CENTURIES

By the middle of the eighteenth century, while the Latin, Greek, and Italian print shops in Venice were going through a new phase of prosperity, the above-mentioned Hebrew presses had joined under the name "Stamparie Bragadina e Vendramina." Among the workers of both presses were two members of the Foa family who had managed a print shop in Venice since at least 1766: Gad ben Isaac, who started a business of his own in 1792, and Gad ben Samuel, who opened a press in Pisa around 1779.[23]

Despite the reduced activity of Venetian presses, their editions are the best represented in the collection that we are considering. This fact can be explained by the protective laws that made importing books difficult and by the decreasing financial and cultural status of the Jews of the Ghetto, who were satisfied with biblical, liturgical, and halakhic works.[24] The library of the Talmud Torah constitutes the core of the Renato Maestro early book collection, but we have little information about the date it was founded or about its management. As Federica Ruspio points out elsewhere in this volume, this library has been moved several times, along with the administrative offices, associations, and institutions linked to the Jewish community.

These shifts started once the Venetian Republic was defeated by Napoleon and the wooden gates of the Ghetto were torn down and burned on July 11, 1797, in the Campo del Ghetto Nuovo—subsequently renamed the Contrada dell'Unione (Neighborhood of Reunion).[25] In the period that followed, the area went through major changes, and the Jews were no longer responsible for its maintenance. Many buildings were demolished, paralleling what occurred in other parts of the city under French rule.[26] This first emancipation, however, lasted only a short period. The ancient order was restored just three months later with the Treaty of Campo Formio, when Napoleon ceded Venice to Austria: "Considerably less sympathetic to either the Rights of Men in general or the Rights of Jews in particular, the Austrians soon reimposed many of the old restrictions, even if they shied away from actually replacing the big gates. Jews found it extremely difficult to buy property outside the area, take up certain occupations, study for various professions, or serve in local government; in January 1798 even the name of the neighborhood was changed back to Ghetto."[27] The nineteenth century was characterized by several political changes that affected the situation of Venetian Jews. Between 1806 and 1814, Venice was once again under French rule, until the Austrians reconquered the city after Napoleon was defeated. The population rebelled against them only in 1848 under the leadership of Daniele Manin, who became dictator for a short time. During this revolution, widespread throughout the different states of Italy, Jewish equality was proclaimed almost everywhere.[28] The Austrian government, however, continued the assault and, after once more conquering Venice, exiled Manin to Paris and put the Jews under strict control because of their involvement in the uprising. In 1866, Venice was finally annexed by the Italian Kingdom.[29]

By then, although Venetian Jews had established an important role in the economy of the city and its political sphere, the Jewish community was no longer a unified group; segregation had generated a feeling of separateness. Their shared lifestyle slowly disappeared once living in the Ghetto was no longer compulsory. Beginning in the early 1800s, wealthy Jews started to purchase houses and buildings outside the Ghetto, moving to nicer neighborhoods. As time passed, poorer families remained in the Ghetto, and richer Jews entered this space only for religious purposes.[30] As Riccardo Calimani has pointed out, "Ormai, se fino al 1797 prevaleva la storia dei gruppi e dei gruppetti che confluivano nelle tre nazioni principali, la Todesca, la Levantina, la Ponentina, con l'integrazione e il conseguimento della piena emancipazione, la prospettiva si rovescia. Emergono nomi di famiglie, con le loro storie, con i loro destini individuali, mentre la comunità ebraica rimane sullo sfondo." (Although history revolved around the groups and subgroups that made up the German, Levantine, and Ponentine communities until 1797, the perspective changes after integration and emancipation. Family names emerge, with their own stories and destinies, while the Jewish community remains in the background.)[31]

This phenomenon involves books and libraries: wealthy families had their own book collections, some of which were donated to the Jewish community's library when their owners passed away. Therefore, although most of the sixteenth-century volumes belonged to public institutions (Talmud Torah, synagogues, *battey midrash*), many later editions were donated privately. At the beginning of the twentieth century, the Jewish population of Venice was scattered throughout the urban grid. Jewish children attended public schools and were perfectly integrated into society. In an attempt to provide a Jewish education to younger generations, Rabbi Adolfo Ottolenghi promoted, in 1932, the renovation of the Jewish school of the Ghetto (though he had desired a school in a more central location), inviting all

Jewish families—not just those living there—to send their children there.[32] His wish was sadly realized in 1938, when the Fascist regime imposed separate schools on all Jews, who were no longer accepted in the public ones.

At that time, many Jewish families were living in San Marco, while others were scattered in Cannaregio.[33] Jewish cultural and administrative offices were located outside the Ghetto, like the Convegno di Studi Ebraici, located on the Calle del Rimedio (Castello, Venice), where our library was most likely located as well. There, in 1938, a primary school was hurriedly organized as racial laws were enforced. On June 15, 1941, the register of people consulting the library stopped abruptly; it resumed on April 26, 1946, when the library reopened.[34]

Later on, the school and the library were transferred to Campo SS. Filippo e Giacomo, Ponte Storto 4756, and then, from 1959 to 1967, to Calle del Dose 5877. During this period, Cesare Vivante, a young scholar, dedicated his free time to the management of this library. In 1967, when this book collection was brought back to the Ghetto Vecchio, he organized its transfer to the community center, to be stored in a building with the chief rabbi's apartment and rooms for the community's activities. There, the library was organized on shelves; books and periodicals in Latin script were cataloged by two librarians from the Biblioteca Nazionale Marciana (Marciana National Library). The library opened to the public in 1982, officially dedicated to Renato Maestro, a council member and former vice president of the Jewish community who died in 1974 and whose bequest had provided for the library's reorganization.

In 1989, the books were transferred into the building where the Scuola Canton and the Scuola Grande Tedesca are located.[35] The library was moved for the last time in 2006, when the ground floor of its current building was renovated to host the present-day Renato Maestro Library and Archive. Located next to the Jewish Museum in the Campo del Ghetto Nuovo, on the ground floor surrounded by water on two sides, one can hear and see the gondoliers passing in front of its windows. The library and its archive are undetectable from the outside.

The library's location may seem perfectly reasonable, as it is in the center of a space perceived as the Jewish neighborhood due to two large synagogues that are still in use, the Levantine and the Ponentine, and the presence of a Chabad-Lubavitch community that is much more visible than the traditional local community. The majority of those living in the former Ghetto, however, are non-Jews. The Ghetto Nuovissimo has very few traces of its former Jewish character, whereas in the Ghetto Vecchio near the synagogues, there is a public kindergarten and a non-kosher café. All of the city's Jewish institutions and facilities are, however, located here; there are no more Jewish offices or schools scattered across different parts of the city. Kosher bakeries, restaurants, and hotels; the community center, its classrooms, and the mikveh—everything is concentrated in this area. The community is much smaller than it used to be, and it is probably easier both for local Jews and for visitors to have everything in the same place. This area also attracts many non-Jewish visitors who wish to learn about Jewish history and life in Venice. The concentration of Jewish historical artifacts and architecture does not function as it had, as a marker of segregation, but acts as a blueprint of the past that can provide insight into the everyday experiences of the various Jewish communities that inhabited the space over the last five hundred years. And yet, in spite of the Jewish character of these institutions, there are several non-Jews, with training in Jewish studies, working in the information center, the community offices, the museum, and the library.[36]

Robert C. Davis summarizes this by stating that the Ghetto had almost completely lost its Jewish character when it finally started reinventing itself, turning itself into "a Site of Memory and a general tourist attraction, while continuing to serve as the focus of Venice's Jewish community."[37] Today, the ties between Jewish and non-Jewish institutions, and their relationship to local governments, are so tight that it seems almost unnecessary to mention them. The commemoration of the five hundredth anniversary of the founding of the Ghetto, for instance, involved the whole city, and a big exhibit was specially organized in the Ducal Palace.[38]

THE "RENATO MAESTRO" HEBREW BOOK COLLECTION: PROVENANCE INFORMATION AND ARCHIVAL SOURCES

A book's provenance includes different kinds of traces, called *footprints*, that give the reader some hints regarding the history of the specific copy at hand. This is one of the most fruitful research fields in library studies, and research is being conducted all over the world to index and follow the virtual path of these footprints. Columbia University, for instance, hosts Footprints: Jewish Books through Time and Place, a database with virtual maps that will include the list of the Renato Maestro collection's provenances.[39]

Labels, ex libris, stamps, handwritten notes, drawings, calculations, shopping lists, memoranda—they all tell a story immortalized in books' margins, covers, and blank pages. The librarian's task is to unveil it. Gathering all the footprints found in individual books, one can trace the story of an entire book collection.

The Renato Maestro Library and Archive incorporated and enlarged the small library of the Fraterna Generale di Culto e Beneficenza degli Israeliti of Venice, an old name for the Jewish community. The Fraterna Generale was founded in 1929, although the core of its Hebrew book collection, as previously stated, comes from the Talmud Torah library, whose inventories are still kept in the archive. Identifying the copies that were a part of this original collection is not as easy as it may appear. Some labels marking shelf locations are missing or covered with new labels, many title pages are missing, and old inventories include very basic descriptions that may lack imprint information or any useful detail regarding the peculiarities of single copies. Some books are from local synagogues, but only thirty-nine of these have a stamp that proves this provenance. Worn prayer books, replaced by more recent editions, were often sent to the community's library, either to be kept or sent to the *genizah,* where worn Hebrew religious books that may contain the name of God are stored before burial. These volumes, although part of a synagogue's collection, were not necessarily marked with a stamp or a label. A few boxes marked "Genizah" have never left the library, and the books they contained have been put back on the shelves. More volumes have been found in abandoned rooms in the synagogues' buildings. These probably belonged to their public collections, but this cannot be proven, as the only surviving inventory includes a brief list of the books that were donated to the Spanish Synagogue from 1896 to 1926.

The list of provenances that has been published in the printed catalog can be summarized thusly:[40]

- old Talmud Torah collection, 568 editions
- Comunità Israelitica di Venezia, name used from 1930 to 1989 before becoming the Comunità Ebraica di Venezia, 72 copies
- religious schools, 69 copies
- synagogues, 39 copies definitively
- gifts from non-Venetian institutions, 17 copies
- rabbis' private collections, about 15 copies
- associations, 10 copies
- private donors, remaining volumes

Among the copies arriving from religious schools, the majority (thirty-eight) belonged to the Scuola Israelitica di Religiosa Istruzione. From 1818–30, Jewish schools were called Scuole Israelitiche d'Istruzione; later the name became more specific, changing to Scuole Israelitiche di Religiosa e Morale Istruzione. In the Renato Maestro Library, this full name appears only on a single copy in handwritten form; in all other cases, there is a stamp of the Scuole Israelitiche di Religiosa Istruzione, and the full name does not appear in any of the archive's papers. Discrepancies such as these are often resolved by assuming that the two reference the same institution, but the shorter name was more convenient for fitting on a stamp.

Single copies were donated to the library by local Jewish associations: Associazione Donne Ebree d'Italia, or ADEI; ADEI Wizo of Mestre; *Biḳur ḥolim;* Circolo Cuore e Concordia; the youth group of the Circolo Cuore e Concordia; and *Shemesh tsedaḳah* (a burial brotherhood). The Società del Casino Buoni Amici donated four copies that are especially interesting: they all contain the same edition of *Tiḳun lel Shavu'ot ve-lel Hosha'ana Rabbah* (Vienna: Schmid, 1831) and arrived from the same collection, as verified by labels with serial shelf marks. The Società del Casino Buoni Amici of Venice is difficult to track down: it appears only in a cadastral list, which situates it in Cannaregio. Similar cultural circles bearing this name existed throughout Italy; some of them still exist. Originally linked to the ideas of Jacobinism, they do not have a Jewish character, so it is surprising to find prayer books with this stamp, one of many points of entry for contemporary scholars to engage with this valuable material.

Thirteen non-Venetian institutions appear in the provenance list as well, all of which donated single Hebrew volumes to the library, with the exception of the Alliance Israélite Universelle, which donated five books. Only a few rabbis left footprints in the Hebrew books, and only a small portion of these actually prove that the rabbis donated these volumes. Leone Luzzatto (1841–1918) donated four books, while seven belonged to Adolfo Ottolenghi (1885–1944). Moisè Coen Porto (1834–1918) may be the former owner of four copies, but this is uncertain: in two copies he is mentioned in a note as the addressee of the volume; in one, he himself drafted several class rosters (but the book could have belonged to a school and not necessarily to him); on the fourth, only his surname is legible on the back of the volume, not enough to prove its provenance.[41]

The index of footprints in the catalog includes hundreds of names, not all of which correspond to the owners of the books in which they appear.[42] Two outstanding names, for instance, are Giuseppe Bassi and Angelo Sullam. Bassi, called *il maestro* (the teacher), whose Hebrew name was Yosef ben Shelomoh (1864–1916), donated ten books to the library. He was a teacher of Judaica at the Collegio Ravà in Venice and was associated with the monthly magazines on Jewish culture, society, history, and literature *Il Vessillo Israelitico* and *Il Corriere Israelitico.* He was also vice rabbi and ḥazan at the Levantine Synagogue and presided over the Fraterna Vespertina devotional society. Angelo Sullam (1881–1971), the founder of the Venetian Zionist group (1903) and organizer of the fourth Italian Zionist Congress in Venice, was born and raised in the city and graduated in the field of law in Padua. He managed his family paddy fields while working at the Ministry of Foreign Affairs as a mediator between the Italian government and the Zionist representatives in Jerusalem. From 1919 to 1929 he presided over the Fraterna Generale di Culto e Beneficenza degli Israeliti of Venice, and from 1921 to 1964 he was president of the Comitato Italiano di Assistenza agli Emigranti Ebrei, founded to assist Jewish refugees from Eastern Europe passing through Italy on their way to their final destination. After the war, he managed an agricultural firm while teaching economics and law regarding the reclamation of land at the University of Padua.

At the end of the 1970s, Sullam's heirs divided his books according to subject matter and distributed them to different libraries. Volumes and documents on law, politics, and economics were donated to the Consiglio Regionale del Veneto; the historical books are now at the Centro di Documentazione Ebraica Contemporanea (CDEC) in Milan; and religious and Hebrew books, and works of interest to the Jewish community, were donated to the Jewish community of Venice.[43] The donation to the Jewish community seems to be the smallest one; of these books, there were only thirty-three volumes in Hebrew: twenty-eight are liturgical volumes (including several copies of the same works), four contain biblical texts, and only one is a work on ethics.

With the Sullam collection came some books that must have once belonged to the Artom family, thanks to Angelo Sullam's marriage to Enrichetta Artom. Her family hailed from Asti, Piedmont, and because she was the only one who moved to Venice, thirteen books bearing the footprints of the Artoms likely arrived by way of her and her husband. Indeed, names on Enrichetta's family tree correspond exactly with some names found on Renato Maestro books. Another piece of evidence is the stamp of the Foa bookshop in Acqui (not far from Asti) that appears once in association with Angelo Sullam's ex libris, once with Israel Artom's signature, and once with both the stamp and signature. It is probable in this case that the books bearing interrelated footprints were part of the same collection donated to the library by Angelo Sullam's heirs.

Several family names in the index of footprints occur multiple times, meaning that different people with the same surname (possibly members of the same family) held these volumes in their hands. It is not always possible, however, to determine if these books were part of a family collection. To decide whether owners and readers with the same surnames were relatives—the most frequently recurring surnames on the books' white pages and margins are Artom, Calimani, Curiel, Fano, Levi, Polacco, Salvadori, and Vivante—and to form a hypothesis about the common provenance of the library's volumes, I traced the family trees of these names with the help of existing publications and archival sources, especially the birth and death registries of Venice's Jewish community.[44]

As a result of this research it was proven that the members of the Calimani, Salvadori, and Vivante families who left their traces on the books were indeed connected, although this is hardly surprising in a small community. These people belonged to different descending branches of their family trees, meaning that the books may have been scattered among different houses and institutions and did not arrive at the library as a unified collection. This is the case for the Vivante family, merchants from Corfu, whose footprints include those of Leon di Menachem Vivante (ca. 1700–ca. 1780) and his sons, Menachem (Mandolin), Eliezer (Lazzaro), Maimon, and Jacob Vita. Family members who appear in the list of footprints belong to all four branches of the family. Therefore, it is likely that the books were brought to the library by different people.

The case of the Polacco family is distinct: in spite of the many names appearing in the books, only a few of them are associated with ownership notes. The name "Polacco" often appears on the lists of students drafted on the blank pages of books or in inscriptions found on the margins of books belonging to public collections such as schools or synagogues. In this case, therefore, their family tree is not as helpful; their footprints do not constitute proof of ownership. There are, however, two exceptions: a few volumes were actually donated by Pellegrino and Bruno Polacco. Pellegrino di Giuseppe signed five copies belonging to him that were donated by Ambra Dina in 1991. Bruno Pellegrino Polacco (in Hebrew, Geršon ben Avraham

Polacco, Cesenatico 1917–Livorno 1967), who was the former owner of five Hebrew books in this collection, served as ḥazan and vice rabbi in Venice and was later appointed rabbi in Ferrara (1953–63) and Livorno (1963–67).

ARCHIVAL SOURCES

When footprints are lacking, it is possible to trace the history of a book collection and its provenances thanks to old catalogs and archival sources (lists of books, library records of new books, donations, book exchanges, and so on). The archival sources containing relevant information on the early books collection of the Renato Maestro Library are an eighteenth-century handwritten list of 130 titles (Notebook 70); a nineteenth-century inventory of the Talmud Torah Library including 737 editions (Notebook 71); a booklist of the Spanish Synagogue (nineteenth–twentieth century); and a card catalog probably dating back to the 1920s.[45] Useful, if partial, information comes from other sources such as brief articles, the private correspondence of scholars who visited the library in the past, formal letters belonging to the library staff, occasional reports on this collection (especially the one commissioned by the Unione delle Comunità Israelitiche Italiane and compiled in 1937 by Isaiah Sonne), oral histories, and the footprints, evidence found in the books and artifacts themselves.[46]

In examining these sources, it becomes clear that a significant number of books that once formed a part of this collection have disappeared: not hundreds, but the most precious and rare, meaning they must have been taken by someone who knew the library's content, who could read Hebrew, and who could recognize the volumes. No proof has been found yet, but there are rumors that these books were sold to help manage the enormous financial and social problems generated by World War II.

Unfortunately, the most obviously missing volumes were part of a complete Bomberg Talmud which included nine treatises of the first edition, twenty-nine of the second edition, and eleven of the third.[47] The other missing sixteenth-century books include the third volume of the first Rabbinical Bible (Venice: Bomberg, 1517); the fourth volume of Jacob ben Asher's *Arba'a Ṭurim* printed by Bomberg in 1522 and the entire edition of the same book published in Riva di Trento (Madruzzo-Marcaria at Antonio Broën's, 1561); and the second volume of Maimonides's *Mishneh*

Torah printed by Bomberg in 1524, as well as the famous edition of the same work published by Bragadin in 1550, responsible for the trial that resulted in the burning of the Talmud.

All of these volumes were still a part of the collection in 1937, when Isaiah Sonne, director of the Rabbinical College of Rhodes in 1936–38, visited this library and compiled a report that listed its most important editions. Of the thirty-six printed books he described, eighteen of them are now missing. His descriptions are quite detailed; in a few cases, he even noted the presence of marginalia and owners' inscriptions that may be helpful in identifying these volumes today. The books missing from the library, however, number more than eighteen and did not disappear all at once. In analyzing Notebook 71, for instance, I can identify at least eighty missing books; descriptions of these, however, are lacking, and imprint information is not always provided, making it impossible to determine the exact number with certitude.[48]

This phenomenon of missing and absent books is characteristic of many early book collections in Italy, especially Jewish ones. People who fled the country during the war probably thought that it was safer to bring their valuables—including their books—with them. In her essay, Ruspio demonstrates that important documents frequently disappeared from Venice's Jewish archive only to reappear later in the United States or in Israel.[49] The same thing happened to early modern books. During World War II and its immediate aftermath, individuals stole important documents to bring to places that they considered safer (which was probably true, although the action is lamentable). In some cases, bankrupted Jewish institutions, dealing with war survivors and the enormous task of rebuilding their communities, are said to have secretly sold valuable books. Later on, the Israeli government made many idealistic attempts to collect archives and libraries from all over Europe so as to keep the memories of the Jewish diaspora together and safe. Italian institutions have almost always refused to renounce their heritage, seeing it as a part of their national identity. This was especially true in Venice, where leaders went so far as to refuse to release details regarding its collection to the Unione delle Comunità Israelitiche Italiane of Rome when, in 1953, it sent a questionnaire to all the communities inquiring after the state of their libraries and archives.[50]

CONCLUSIONS: THE STATE OF THE LIBRARY TODAY

In the present-day context of the Venice Ghetto, the Renato Maestro Library and Archive represents a silent part of the cultural scene, even more so now that the library's entrance is hidden by the Jewish Museum. Though this library also includes a modern collection of local Jewish history, fiction, and art, it is rarely visited by members of the local Jewish community. Locals who do come inside are mainly interested in the archival papers that may be useful for personal genealogical research. The modern book collection, which offers an exhaustive overview of Venetian Jewry, is instead used mostly by scholars and researchers from other cities and abroad who do not belong to the local Jewish community.

Although part of local Venetian Jewish history, the library's early Hebrew book collection is even more neglected and does not seem to have a share in present-day Jewish cultural life. Indeed, the relationship between this cultural heritage and its contemporary heirs seems weak. Until now, this collection has been preserved, too delicate and fragile for public consultation, and has become even more endangered—until recently—by the absence of labels and a complete catalog. Only a few people had any idea of the content of these books, suggesting that they were appreciated and preserved more for their economic value than their content.

Though precious, books are not preserved to remain closed and stored, unknown and useless. They can survive through generations and constitute a unique testimony of human knowledge and culture at different times in history. These volumes, however, have not yet met their readers and so transgress three of Ranganathan's five laws of library science: books are for use, every reader his/her book, and every book its reader.

The OPAC and printed catalog have been created with the intention of changing this situation. We can now reach scholars who may have an interest in studying this collection but did not know that it existed. If the modern Judaica collection is neglected as well, it is because the library can only be found by people deliberately looking for it—its OPAC is not synchronized to the national one—who must have an appointment to visit.

There are many different ways to enhance and transform this place, as well as other Italian Jewish libraries, into vibrant and dynamic spaces. It could be done through conferences, seminars, workshops, internship programs, activities with local schools, and attracting researchers in Hebrew and Jewish studies from the local university; some of these activities have taken place in the past, but not continuously. A lack of funding has prevented, until now, the library from growing and implementing services such as ensuring regular and fixed hours of operation and hiring long-term employees, leaving it at risk of being a frozen conservation site. There is a sort of contradiction in the community's attitude toward its own heritage: in spite of its protectiveness, it neglects these collections and their preserving institution.

The city of Venice is torn between two tendencies: on the one hand, it resembles a history park where thousands of people pay an entrance fee to crowd its streets daily, running to the Piazza San Marco, too hurried to appreciate other places around them. On the other hand, it hosts prestigious cultural institutions and events and attracts scholars from all over the world, providing wonderful libraries, research services, and different museums, concerts, lectures, and workshops. In a similar way, I have realized that this library is either neglected and forgotten, as a frozen space that preserves collective memories, or appreciated as an important and unique source of information that attracts scholars who come from around the world specifically to consult its archival and documentary sources. Looking at the current impasse in the cultural life of the Venice Ghetto and its library and archive, a question looms: Is this place really meant to be only a memory space? Or could it be more than that?

The COVID-19 pandemic has worsened the situation of all cultural institutions, sometimes jeopardizing their ability to reopen. The hope for a better future for small libraries like the Renato Maestro seems weaker than ever before: the community is facing huge expenses to restore the local Jewish Museum (which has always been a higher priority), and there is no project planned for the library and archive to attract people and promote its holdings. In addition, the library and archive's location in a ground-floor space bordered on two sides by the canal puts books and documents at risk of flooding in the case of an extraordinarily high tide: the building was recently restored and its walls insulated, and although the tide has never yet reached the library's windows, the risk is not unreal. Hopefully the MOSE (Modulo Sperimentale Elettromeccanico) system will prevent such a catastrophe.[51] Difficult as it may be, this is the time to think creatively about the present and future of this site of Jewish memory. As Ruspio points out, the books and papers that disappeared from the Renato Maestro collection have reappeared in well-known institutions abroad—kept there as important, unique treasures, often digitized and made available online.[52] Such an example has great potential for the remainder of the Ghetto archive, the greatest part of this heritage, the part that is still at the core of the Venice Ghetto. The future archive must address the realities of climate change and the post–COVID-19 world by investing in both material and virtual preservation for multiple audiences—both local and global. Such a project, however, requires a coordinated engagement of the main social and cultural players of the local Jewish institutions. This returns to the central motif of the collection of the Venice Ghetto's endurance through its movement and how it has traveled so far to become globally relevant to tourists as well as locals. Pointing out once more the importance of this heritage, there should be a deep investment in fortifying the partnerships between the Jewish Community and Italian preservation societies to make the Renato Maestro Library and Archive more available to the public and to enhance its consultation in scholarly contexts.

NOTES

My work is the result of a process of cataloging and research that I have dedicated to the early book collection of the Renato Maestro Library and Archive for about four years, working at the library as a librarian and, in the meantime, completing my PhD dissertation that was dedicated to the analysis of this collection, its history, and its provenances. I am grateful to many people who crossed my path during this journey and offered their help and advice, starting with my PhD supervisor, Professor Piero Capelli.

I would like to acknowledge the Jewish Community of Venice and especially Dr. Gadi Luzzatto Voghera—former director of the Renato Maestro Library and Archive—for entrusting me with the cataloging of this early Hebrew books collection and for giving me full access to the Renato Maestro bibliographic and archival collections. My gratitude goes to Dr. Umberto Fortis, who shared with me his knowledge of this library's history and vicissitudes that he had personally witnessed.

I wish to thank my colleagues Federica Ruspio and Barbara Del Mercato, who shared with me their office as well as their experience.

I am grateful to the staff of the Central Archives for the History of Jewish People in Jerusalem and of the Archival Department of the National Library of Israel for allowing me to consult all the documents that I requested, including the ones that were not yet ready for consultation. I also wish to thank Giacomo Corazzol, Marcella Ansaldi, Michela Zanon, Andreina Contessa, Carlo Fano, and Manuela Fano for providing me useful information on the former owners of the volumes that I was cataloging.

1. There are about one hundred extra volumes with many missing pages that have not been cataloged. The library owns a collection of twelve thousand modern books as well.
2. I use the word "copy" to mean a specific, unique item (e.g., a book that is different from any other) because it has provenance information such as stamps and handwritten notes.

3. The electronic catalog is available through the library's website: http://renatomaestro.org/en. For a printed catalogue of the Hebrew book collection, see Chiara Camarda, ed., *Ha-sefarim shel ha-Geṭo. I Libri del Ghetto: Catalogo dei Libri Ebraici della Comunità Ebraica di Venezia (Secc. XVI–XX)* (Padua: Il Prato, 2016).
4. I am referring to Bomberg's press, described in the following paragraphs, which opened in 1516.
5. See Giuliano Tamani, ed., *L'attività Editoriale di Gershom Soncino, 1502–1527: Atti del Convegno (Soncino, 17 Settembre 1995)* (Soncino: Edizioni del Soncino, 1997), and Moses Marx, *Gershom Soncino's Wander-Years in Italy, 1498–1527: Exemplar Judaicae Vitae* (Cincinnati, OH: Society of Jewish Bibliophiles, 1969). On Hebrew printing in Italy, see also Daniele Nissim, *I Primordi della Stampa Ebraica nell'Italia Settentrionale: Piove di Sacco-Soncino (1469–1496)* (Soncino: Associazione Pro Loco Soncino, 2004); David W. Amram, *The Makers of Hebrew Books in Italy: Being Chapters in the History of the Hebrew Printing Press* (London: Holland Press, 1963); and Hayyim B. Friedberg, *Toledot ha-defus ha-ivri: Be-medinot Iṭalyah, Espanyah Porṭugalyah ve-Tugarmah mi-reshit hithavuto ve-hitpatḥuto be-'erekh shenat 230 [1470]* [. . .] [History of Hebrew typography in Italy, Spain-Portugal and Turkey from its beginning and formation around the year 1470. Biographies of the first printers, their assistants and successors with bibliography of all existing Hebrew incunabula and fifty facsimiles derived from manuscripts and printed sources. A contribution to the history of the Jews.] (Tel Aviv: Bar-Juda, 1956).
6. See A. M. Habermann, *Ha-Madpiss Daniel Bomberg u-Reshimat Sifre Beth Defusso: The Printer Daniel Bomberg and the List of Books Published by His Press* (Zefat: Museum of Printing Art, 1978), and Bruce Nielsen, "Daniel van Bombergen, a Bookman of Two Worlds," in *The Hebrew Book in Early Modern Italy*, ed. Joseph R. Hacker and Adam Shear (Philadelphia: University of Pennsylvania Press, 2011), 56–75.
7. Adelkind's original name was Israel, but he adopted the name of Daniel Bomberg's father, Cornelius, because of the admiration that he had for the Bomberg family. See Abraham Meir Habermann, "Adelkind, Israel Cornelius," in *Encyclopaedia Judaica*, ed. Fred Sklonik and Michael Berenbaum, 2nd ed. (Detroit: Thomson Gale, 2007), 1:386.
8. Only Soncino's editions can compete with Bomberg's. For more on Bomberg, see Bruce Nielsen, "Daniel van Bombergen, a Bookman of Two Worlds," in *The Hebrew Book in Early Modern Italy*, ed. Joseph R. Hacker and Adam Shear (Philadelphia: University of Pennsylvania Press, 2011), 56–75; Sharon Liberman Mintz and Gabriel M. Goldstein, eds., *Printing the Talmud from Bomberg to Schottenstein* (New York: Yeshiva University Museum, 2005); Abraham Meir Habermann, *Ha-Madpis Daniel Bomberg u-Reshimat Sifre Beth Defusso* [The printer Daniel Bomberg and the list of books published by his press] (Tsefat: Ha-Muze'on le-omanut ha-defus, 1978); and Avraham Rosenthal, "Matay hitḥil Dani'el Bomberg lehadpis," *Sinay* 78 (December–January 1977): 186–91.
9. Umberto Fortis, *Editoria in Ebraico a Venezia* (Venice: Arsenale, 1991), 30–36.
10. Marino Zorzi, "Dal Manoscritto al Libro," in *Storia di Venezia*, vol. 6, *Dal Rinascimento al Barocco*, ed. Gaetano Cozzi and Paolo Prodi (Rome: Istituto della Enciclopedia Italiana, 1994), 911.
11. Zorzi, "Dal Manoscritto al Libro," 924–26.
12. On this topic, see Amram, *Makers of Hebrew Books*, 254–70; Marvin J. Heller, *The Sixteenth-Century Hebrew Book: An Abridged Thesaurus* (Leiden, Netherlands: Brill, 2004), xx; Joshua Bloch, "Venetian Printers of Hebrew Books," in *Hebrew Printing and Bibliography*, ed. Charles Berlin (New York: New York Public Library, 1976), 81–82; and Paul F. Grendler, *The Roman Inquisition and the Venetian Press: 1540–1605* (Princeton, NJ: Princeton University

Press, 1977), 91–92. See also Paul F. Grendler, "La Distruzione di Libri Ebraici a Venezia nel 1568," in *Venezia Ebraica: Atti delle Prime Giornate di Studio sull'Ebraismo Veneziano: Venezia, 1976–1980*, ed. Umberto Fortis (Rome: Carucci, 1982), 99–127.

13. *Encyclopaedia Judaica*, s.v. "Parenzo."
14. Amram, *Makers of Hebrew Books*, 368.
15. Martin Lowry, *Nichola Jenson and the Rise of Venetian Publishing in Renaissance Venice* (Oxford: Blackwell, 1991), 278–320. See also Angela Nuovo, *The Book Trade in the Italian Renaissance* (Leiden, Netherlands: Brill, 2013), 102–5. For more on private libraries, see Marino Zorzi, "La Produzione e la Circolazione del Libro," in *Storia di Venezia*, ed. Gaetano Cozzi and Paolo Prodi, vol. 7, *La Venezia Barocca* (Rome: Istituto della Enciclopedia Italiana, 1994), 973–76. *Zornale di Francesco De Madiis*, manuscript, Ital. XI, 45 (7439), 1484–88, Biblioteca Marciana, Venice.
16. The actual number is uncertain. See Riccardo Calimani, *Storia del Ghetto di Venezia* (Milan: Mondadori, 1995), 169.
17. Calimani, *Storia del Ghetto*, 187.
18. Zorzi, "Dal Manoscritto al Libro," 941.
19. See Zorzi, "La Produzione e la Circolazione," 921, and Mario Infelise, "La Crise de la Librarie Vénitienne, 1620–1650," in *Le Hivre et l'Historien: Études Offertes en l'Honneur du Professeur Henri-Jean Martin*, ed. Frédéric Barbier (Geneva: Librairie Droz, 1997), 343–52.
20. Zorzi, "La Produzione e la Circolazione," 930–31.
21. Herbert I. Bloom, *The Economic Activities of the Jews of Amsterdam in the Seventeenth and Eighteenth Centuries* (Williamsport, PA: Bayard, 1937).
22. Zorzi, "La Produzione e la Circolazione," 976.
23. Amram (*Makers of Hebrew Books*, 368) writes that Gad ben Samuel opened his press in Pisa in 1785, while R. Posner and I. Ta-Shema (The Hebrew Book: An Historical Survey [Jerusalem: Keter, 1975], 154) affirmed that he moved there in 1796, but I have found editions attesting his presence in Pisa at least from 1779.
24. See Lelio Della Torre, "La Cultura Presso gli Ebrei in Italia nel Secolo Decimottavo," *Il Corriere Israelitico*, year 4 (1865–66), 270–72, and Marino Zorzi, "La Stampa, la Circolazione del Libro," in *Storia di Venezia*, vol. 8, *L'ultima fase della Serenissima*, ed. Piero Del Negro and Paolo Preto (Rome: Istituto della Enciclopedia Italiana, 1998), 830–31.
25. Calimani, *Storia del Ghetto*, 292–301.
26. Donatella Calabi, *Venezia e il Ghetto: Cinquecento Anni del "Recinto degli Ebrei"* (Turin: Bollati Boringhieri, 2016), 132–39.
27. Robert C. Davis, introduction to *The Jews of Early Modern Venice*, ed. Robert C. Davis and Benjamin Ravid (Baltimore: Johns Hopkins University Press, 2001), viii.
28. Benzion Dinur (Dinaburg), "Emancipation," in *Encyclopaedia Judaica*, ed. Fred Sklonik and Michael Berenbaum, 2nd ed. (Detroit: Thomson Gale, 2007), 6:379.
29. Calimani, *Storia del Ghetto*, 302–12.
30. Calabi, *Venezia e il Ghetto*, 143–62.
31. Calimani, *Storia del Ghetto*, 312.
32. Calabi, *Venezia e il Ghetto*, 163. For more information, see Adolfo Ottolenghi, *La Scuola Ebraica di Venezia attraverso la Voce del suo Rabbino*, ed. Elisabetta Ottolenghi, Elia Richetti, and Renata Segre (Venice: Filippi, 2012).
33. Two of the six Venetian *sestieri* (six neighborhoods).
34. Sigrid Sohn, "La Circolazione della Cultura Ebraica nella Comunità di Venezia: La Biblioteca Archivio 'Renato Maestro,'" in *E li Insegnerai ai Tuoi Figli: Educazione Ebraica in Italia dale Leggi Razziali ad Oggi*, ed. Anna Maria Piussi (Florence: Giuntina, 1997), 191.
35. Sohn, "La Circolazione della Cultura Ebraica," 192–93; Calabi, *Venezia e il Ghetto*, 164–65.

See also Renata Segre, ed., *Gli Ebrei a Venezia, 1938–1945: Una Comunità tra Persecuzione e Rinascita* (Venice: Il Cardo, 1995).

36. Scholars and professors of Hebrew and Jewish studies in Italy are mostly non-Jews, like myself.
37. Davis, introduction, ix.
38. The exhibit *Venezia, gli Ebrei e l'Europa, 1516–2016*, took place from June 19 to November 13, 2016, at the Doge's apartments.
39. This list has been published in Camarda, *I Libri del Ghetto*, 661–76. For the database, see Michelle Chesner, Marjorie Lehman, Adam Shear, and Joshua Teplitsky, eds., Footprints: Jewish Books through Time and Place, Columbia University Libraries, https://footprints.ctl.columbia.edu.
40. Camarda, *I Libri del Ghetto*, 661–76.
41. These numbers concern the early Hebrew books collection. The library also keeps an early Latin books collection and a modern collection on Jewish history and culture, whose provenances have not been analyzed.
42. Camarda, *I Libri del Ghetto*, 661–76.
43. See Giovanni Sordini and Giovanna Tedeschi, eds., *Catalogo del Fondo Angelo Sullam* (Venice: Consiglio Regionale del Veneto, 2007), and Giovanna Tedeschi and Pierluigi Ciprian, eds., *Fondo Angelo Sullam* (Venice: Biblioteca del Consiglio Regionale del Veneto, 2011).
44. A useful collection of the information included in the registries of births, deaths, and marriages can be found in Edoardo Gesuà sive Salvadori, *L'Albero del Ghetto: Repertorio Ragionato dello Stato Civile nella Comunità Ebraica Veneziana dall'Unità d'Italia alla Grande Guerra* (Florence: Giuntina, 2016).
45. Sohn, "La Circolazione della Cultura Ebraica," 193.
46. The catalog of this collection includes an index of the provenances: ex libris, signatures, inscriptions, stamps, and censor's notes. See Camarda, *I Libri del Ghetto*.
47. Isaiah Sonne, "Relazione sulla Biblioteca della Comunità Israelitica di Venezia," typewritten, ARC. 4* 796, box AC-5098, Archive of Isaiah Sonne, National Library of Israel Archive Department, Jerusalem.
48. Notebook 71, *Catalogo dei libri ebraici della Biblioteca del Talmud Torà*, 19th century, handwritten, box 15, Renato Maestro Archive.
49. See Federica Ruspio's essay, "The Ghetto's Archival Heritage," in chap. 2.
50. The name *Unione Comunità Israelitiche Italiane* was used from 1930 to 1989, when it was changed to the *Unione delle Comunità Ebraiche Italiane* (UCEI). This information is based on "Attività dell'UCII dal 1948," box 97, Archivio Storico, UCEI, Rome.
51. MOSE stands for Experimental Electromechanical Module, a system of mobile dams protecting the city of Venice and its lagoon from the phenomenon of high water.
52. See chap. 2, 61–62 and 70–71.

CHAPTER TWO

THE GHETTO'S ARCHIVAL HERITAGE

FEDERICA RUSPIO

This essay presents the initial results of my investigation of the Venice Ghetto's archival heritage and history. In my role as both a historian studying the new Portuguese Christians in early modern Venice and an archivist with the opportunity to work in the Renato Maestro Library and Archive, I have always been surprised by the scarcity of documents belonging to the Ghetto's history in the early modern period, and even more so when I consider the historical and symbolic role of the Jewish community of Venice through the centuries.

Today, the Venice Ghetto is known as the world's first, and thousands of tourists visit its museum and its synagogues. In 2016, cultural events, conventions, and a sumptuous exhibition at the Palazzo Ducale celebrated the five hundredth anniversary of its establishment, involving some of the most important scholars of Jewish studies. In spite of its reputation, however, the archival legacy of the Ghetto is sparse. In terms of material records, we find that only a few registers and documents from the early modern age still survive in the Renato Maestro archive, as if they were pieces of a mosaic that has been slowly dismantled since the end of the Serenissima Republic of Venice in 1797. On the other hand, browsing through catalogs and inventories online, we realize that most of the documentation has been disseminated, and many of the documentary sources, important roots of the memory of the Ghetto, have spread and are now located in libraries and archives in Italy and abroad. Therefore, not only the memory of but also sources on the Ghetto have traveled in time and space.

My main question concerns the reasons for this dispersion. What do these losses teach us about those who kept and handed down the Ghetto's legacy and the way that they conceived of their past through the ages? How has the memory of the Ghetto in the early modern period been perceived as part of the identity of the Jewish community in Venice?

Talking about historical archives means meditating on the memory of the institutions or communities that produced, organized, and preserved them over the centuries. An archive is not just the mirror image of an organization and its functions but also represents the way in which a certain body organizes its memories. At the same time, we should consider it the result of a dynamic process constantly influenced by its own history and the political, social, and economic context.[1] In accordance with this viewpoint, we can affirm that the entire archive, not just its documents, is an important source that sheds light on the identity of the Jewish community of Venice and on the way in which its perception of itself changed over time.

The site of the Ghetto, its treasures and its cultural heritage, has been rediscovered recently, during the last quarter of the twentieth century. During that period, the decision to gather the historical documentation of the Jewish community in the Renato Maestro Library and Archive and to open it to the public was the result of a process of recovering its roots in the history of the city. After a brief outline of its story and heritage, I will dwell on the early modern archives and the state of the ancient Venetian Ghetto in Jewish studies. As we shall see, despite the rich bibliography on the subject, the dispersion of documentation and primary source material has limited the possibility of acquiring a robust understanding of its history that might otherwise be attained by studying this site through the source material produced by its own institutions.

According to the testimony of scholars who have studied these missing papers, such as Moisè Soave, Leone Luzzatto, Riccardo Pacifici, and Adolfo Ottolenghi, the largest period of loss took place between the beginning of the nineteenth century and the first half of the twentieth. This dispersion of documents was caused by multiple factors. The process of assimilation erased the memory of past segregation for many Venetian Jews. The nineteenth-century Jewish institutions that were in charge of the preservation of the ancient archives of the Jewish nations were burdened by religious and charitable duties and, dealing with widespread poverty, did not have the resources to prevent these losses. Many documents and registers were added to the private collections of former officers and their heirs, who attempted to preserve them in their own homes; the perception of what was public and what was private was different from what it is today. Finally, many documents disappeared into the burgeoning antiques markets, purchased by scholars and collectors abroad and subsequently donated to or purchased by university or state libraries.

The Renato Maestro's collection went through a similar process: we know that rare and precious books went missing, though it is difficult to estimate the losses, and a number of them were found to be preserved in the synagogues, administrative offices, and educational institutions of the community. Over time, the number of books has increased thanks to donations and bequests, as Chiara Camarda explains in detail elsewhere in this volume.[2] The donations to the archive began in the second half of the twentieth century and primarily consisted of modern papers and materials from private collections. Although these materials enrich our understanding of the Ghetto's twentieth-century heritage, the ancient archives were affected by an inexorable centripetal effect. The same phenomenon can be seen in demographic shifts, as many Jews who assimilated into the Venetian society moved away from the religious institutions of the community to which they had once belonged. My last question thus concerns the current situation of the early modern archives. How should the Jewish community of Venice repair these losses and support the memory of the Ghetto?

Thanks to both the internet and digitization projects, the Renato Maestro Library and Archive is still able to recover the early modern memory of its Jewish community in alternative ways. Though its sources are now preserved elsewhere, a virtual reconstruction could restore the original composition of the ancient archives through a shared effort on the part of all the custodians. Since the sources that can keep the memory of the Ghetto alive have traveled in the last centuries, new perspectives could be offered by a virtual reconstruction of the ancient archives to overcome the distances between the countries and the single institutions that preserve this material today.

THE RENATO MAESTRO LIBRARY AND ARCHIVE AND THE REDISCOVERY OF THE GHETTO AND ITS HERITAGE

The first Ghetto, whose name spread throughout the world as a synonym for segregation, was founded in sixteenth-century Venice, when the Serenissima Republic permitted the settlement of a Jewish minority on its mainland and forced it to live in a restricted area, the former site of an ancient foundry. As the 2016 events for its five hundredth anniversary demonstrated, the Venice Ghetto is not just a metaphor: it is an urban and architectural site, a place of high cultural and historical value with a deep symbolic and evocative meaning, "a dynamic site in which, and around which, Jewish identity has been constantly negotiated" depending on the host society.[3]

This awareness has heightened recently: after existing as a poor and neglected neighborhood during the nineteenth and most of the twentieth century, it was only in the 1970s that the Ghetto regained a central role in the life of the Venetian Jewish people and in the artistic and historical context of Venice and Italy.[4] The Israelite community offices returned to the Ghetto in 1967. In 1971 the Comitato per il Centro Storico Ebraico di Venezia (Committee for the Historic Jewish Center of Venice) was established and, supported by Italian and foreign institutions, succeeded in restoring the ancient Jewish cemetery in the Lido and other important buildings such as the Scuola Grande Tedesca and Scuola Italiana (German and Italian synagogues, respectively).[5]

Significantly, in 1976, lectures on Jewish history from the early modern to the contemporary ages were held in the community center.[6] The community and the Committee for the Historic Jewish Center of Venice supported important cultural enterprises, such as the curation of the permanent exhibition of the new Jewish Museum of Venice, inaugurated in 1989.[7]

Of the most important cultural events linked to Venetian Judaism in the 1980s, two deserve to be mentioned in particular. Gli Ebrei e Venezia, an international conference held in 1983 at the Giorgio Cini Foundation in Venice, brought together Italian and foreign scholars, reflecting on the Jewish minority and its place within the Venetian context from the fifteenth to the eighteenth century. The second event took place in 1988, when the documentary exhibition *Gli Ebrei a Venezia, 1938–1945: Una Comunità tra Persecuzione e Rinascita* was set up at the Querini Stampalia Library for the fiftieth anniversary of the promulgation of the Fascist racial laws that gradually but inexorably excluded Jews from Italian civil society from September 1938 until the end of World War II. This exhibit dealt for the first time with the difficult periods that Venetian Jews lived through during the years of persecution until the dramatic epilogue of the deportations.[8]

In 1981, a new library was founded by bequest of Renato Maestro, a former president of the Jewish Community of Venice who died in 1974. The Renato Maestro Library and Archive opened in 1982. As Camarda explains in detail, the library initially housed the ancient and modern collections of books arriving from private donations and the libraries of the Talmud Torah religious school[9] and from the cultural association of Jewish studies called the Convegno di Studi Ebraici (formerly known as the Circolo di Coltura Ebraica).[10] This archival documentation was stored in the Renato Maestro Library and Archive in 1989. The collection primarily contained the nineteenth- and twentieth-century administrative archives of the main religious and charitable institutions: the Comunità Israelitica di Venezia (1930–89), formerly known as the Fraterna Generale di Culto e Beneficenza degli Israeliti di Venezia (1829–1930, henceforth Fraterna Generale); the synagogues; and ancillary organizations like the Fraterna della Misericordia degli Israeliti di Venezia (1832–1930), which was in charge of the medical care of indigent Jews and the Jewish cemetery in the Lido. In addition, small archives of former officers of the community were part of the documentation, and by the 1970s, private archives of families and individual people had been added. These documents, which had been stored in the attic of the Scola Levantina, were put in order and inventoried with the financial support of the Regione Veneto and the Municipality of Venice.[11]

Documentation of the early modern period, originally preserved in the community's administrative office, was also moved and recorded in the inventory taken in the 1980s. These documents were produced by the so-called Università degli Ebrei di Venezia (1516–1797), the main institution that ruled over the Jewish inhabitants of the Ghetto, and by the three nations, named after the respective synagogues: the German Italian; the Levantine (Jews coming from the Ottoman Empire, mainly of Sephardic origin); and the Ponentine (Sephardic Jews coming from the converso communities of the Iberian Peninsula and Western Europe).

In the years that followed, despite inconsistent oversight and further renovations, the Renato Maestro Library and Archive was involved in cultural and publishing projects and enriched its heritage by collecting oral and documentary testimonies of the years between 1938 and 1945. The archive also continued to receive donations from private collections, and in 2014, the Renato Maestro was given the archive of the historian Attilio Milano, one of the most important twentieth-century scholars of Jewish studies, by his heirs. The new acquisitions were organized and described in inventories in 2014 and in 2019, thanks to the financial support of the Ministero dei Beni Culturali, Ambientali e del Turismo. Documentation of the collection of artifacts preserved by the Renato Maestro Library and Archive has been described in the Sistema Unificato delle Soprintendenze Archivistiche (SIUSA), a national Web portal where the inventories and the data sheets on the archives and their "creators" can be consulted.[12]

JEWISH STUDIES AND THE ARCHIVES OF JEWISH VENETIAN INSTITUTIONS OF THE EARLY MODERN AGE

Emblematic of the desire to recover and preserve the memory of the past and bring it back to the Jewish historic center of the Ghetto, the Renato Maestro Library and Archive was created in response to a growing interest in Italian Judaism, especially in the medieval and early modern ages, both in Italy and globally. By the 1970s, scholars were drawing attention to Jewish sources preserved by libraries, public archives, and Italian Jewish communities, and the number of conferences, monographs, essays, and reviews progressively increased.[13]

Many worthy studies have focused on the Venice Ghetto, but two aspects need to be highlighted.[14] The first concerns the bibliography of the period from the end of the fifteenth century to the fall of the Serenissima Republic of Venice. As a result of the dispersion of early modern archival materials, scholars focused instead on documentation produced by Venetian institutions with jurisdiction over the Ghetto. They studied the Jewish settlement from an external point of view, in other words, considering its history only through the lens of its relationship with the host community.[15]

The second aspect concerns the fact that the ancient sources preserved in the Renato Maestro Library and Archive are scarcely known and their worth is underestimated: visitors and scholars usually ask to consult the death and birth records. No one has published materials based on its early modern archival materials; discoveries have yet to be made. For example, recently, writing about the ancient archive of the Jewish communities of Venice, Ariel Viterbo reported the existence of two ancient minute books, the Libro delle parti dell'Università dei Ponentini (1669–91) and the Registro delle parti della Scuola Levantina (1686–1727), neither of which has been studied.[16]

The Renato Maestro ancient archives consist of seventeen boxes with materials spanning from the sixteenth to the eighteenth century. This collection includes mainly copies of the papers of Venetian institutions, such as writings and prints brought to trial (*scritture in causa* and *stampe in causa*).[17] However, besides the minute books just mentioned, it also includes the following documents:

- one register of the general assembly of the Università degli Ebrei of Venice[18]
- one *squarzo* and four volumes—registers and inventories—of the Ponentine synagogue,[19] together with registers of copies of notarial deeds (*instrumenti*), bank accounts, and a letter book of the Brotherhood for the Redemption of Captives, all pertaining to the Ponentine nation[20]
- one register of deliberations, one squarzo, and some records of accounts and donations of the Italian synagogue[21]
- seven registers of births and deaths[22]
- documents on the Ponentine charity Aiutar Fratelli,[23] and two registers of the Sovvengo Tedesco, another charity association of the Ashkenazim[24]

These documents are all that remain of the ancient archive in the Jewish community of Venice, but they are hardly the only known sources produced by local Jewish institutions in the early modern age. Focusing on Venice, the State Archive keeps the collection of the Fraterna della Misericordia degli Ebrei Tedeschi di Venezia ed Altre Fraterne degli Ebrei, which included registers and papers (mainly of German confraternities), dating from the end of sixteenth to the middle of the eighteenth century, donated by the heirs of Abraham Lattes, a former rabbi of the Jewish Community of Venice, around 1883–85.[25] Furthermore, prime sources on the Ghetto's history and inhabitants can be found in the archives of those institutions of the Venetian Republic with jurisdiction over it and in the registers of notarial deeds and testaments. Thanks to the Judaica Europeana project, a selection of these documents was digitized in 2012 and can be consulted on the website of the State Archive of Venice.[26]

The search for similar documentation should not be restricted to Venice or even Italy. A quick perusal of the catalogs of foreign cultural institutions shows that minute and account books and papers, originating from Venice Ghetto institutions, are spread throughout the world. Some are owned, for example, by the Jewish Theological Seminary of New York and the Central Archives for the History of the Jewish People of Jerusalem, but research should be extended to American and English university libraries or even to the National Moscow Library, as Andrea Y. Lattes has recently reported.[27]

The only published studies focusing on the archival material of the early modern period from an internal perspective have used sources originally produced by Venetian Jewish institutions but owned by other institutions. David J. Malkiel studied and edited the so-called Libro Grande dell'Università degli Ebrei, the 1632 Italian translation of the recordings of the main Venetian Jewish Council kept in the Ufficiali al Cattaver archive in the State Archive of Venice. Daniel Carpi studied the holdings of Eretz Israel, focusing on artifacts produced by Italian and German Jews in the period between 1576 and 1733 and the regulations of the Università degli Ebrei of Venice from the end of the sixteenth to the beginning of the seventeenth century. In addition, he transcribed a register of the Italian German nation (1644–1711). The sources that he used, prior to being part of the collections of the Jewish Theological Seminary and the Central Archive for the History of the Jewish People, were owned by the library of the Talmud Torah school in Venice.[28]

THE GHETTO'S ARCHIVAL HERITAGE IN THE PAST TWO CENTURIES

The material items belonging to the archival heritage of the Ghetto mirror the movement of a diasporic people between the nineteenth and the first half of the twentieth century. The losses of these documents and artifacts date back almost to the fall of the Serenissima Republic of Venice in 1797. Regarding this period, only a few testimonies survived; we have almost no information on the archive's original structure and composition, the quantity of registers and documents that it included, or the way in which it was preserved and bequeathed.

The abolition of the Ghetto in 1797 did not cause the immediate end of its institutions. In the following years, the synagogues and the confraternities administration remained almost unchanged. The distinctions between the three nations (the German Italian, the Levantine, and the Ponentine) disappeared over time, however, and gradually merged together, focusing on charitable rather than ritual aims. During the second Austrian rule, in 1829, the Università degli Ebrei was replaced by the Fraterna Generale, the main authority that ruled over rites and charitable activities, financed by donations, legacies, and the so-called *tassa del culto*, a tax paid by the Jews registered in the community based on declared income.[29]

The process of emancipation and integration of Jews into Venetian society varied, depending on one's socio-professional status. In the first half of the nineteenth century, just a handful of wealthy families took advantage of the political changes. They were followed by a newly forming middle class of professionals and officials, which gradually integrated into Venetian society at large. The Jewish population, however, was mainly composed of the lower class, a situation that persisted until the middle of the twentieth century. In 1834, the Austrian authorities knew that 180 out of an estimated 380 families (1,950 people overall) were destitute. This proportion remained almost unchanged throughout the century and increased at the beginning of the next one.[30]

These social and economic characteristics influenced the housing choices of Venetian Jews: many families chose to live far away from or in any case outside the Ghetto, while the ancient Jewish site became a neglected area inhabited only by the poor. The office of the Fraterna Generale was moved from the Ghetto to San Canciano, still in the *sestiere* (district) of Cannaregio, and then to the Castello sestiere, near Piazza San Marco. The rabbi's house and some minor charities were the only institutions left in the Ghetto, next to the synagogues.

No information exists on the existence of earlier historical archives in the documents dating back to the first half of the nineteenth century. The registers of the Fraterna Generale dealt mainly with the heavy burden of caring for the large number of needy families. Since the Jewish institution suffered from both financial problems and dwindling membership, the Fraterna Generale could not care for its archives or undertake their conservation. Understanding the value of ancient sources was destined to be a prerogative of the elites.

This is the case of the Lattes donation, received by the State Archives of Venice in the mid-1880s. Rabbi Abramo Lattes, the son of Elia Aron Lattes and his successor at the head of the Jewish congregation, was an extraordinary figure in the history of Venetian Jewry.[31] He promoted important charitable organizations, such as the establishment in the Ghetto of a branch of the municipal *casa di industria* (workhouse) in 1844, giving unemployed Jews the same right to learn a job as other Venetian citizens. He is also known to have taken part in the revolution against Austrian domination in 1848–49. Upon his death in 1875, Lattes left his precious library to his son Moisè, a scholar who studied at the Rabbinical College of Padua and worked with Moisè Coen Porto, the new head rabbi of the Venetian community.[32] Moisè Lattes regularly visited the State Archive of Venice, wrote about Jewish literature and history, and made use of his collections and the library of the Talmud Torah. He died prematurely in 1883, and his heirs—brothers Elia, a philologist and archaeologist, and Alessandro, a legal historian—entrusted his bibliographic and archival estate to Italian public cultural institutions. Archival documents and registers were donated to the State Archive of Venice; the manuscripts were given to the Ambrosiana Library in Milan; and almost three thousand volumes, books on Jewish history and literature and catalogs of Jewish libraries and ancient rule books, formed the Jewish Lattes collection in the Braidense National Library in Milan.[33] The heirs, however, did not give away the entire estate: at the beginning of the twentieth century, Elia Lattes still held his father's manuscripts.[34]

During the second half of the nineteenth century, some scholars investigated the history of the Venetian Jews in the early modern period. They had studied at the Rabbinical College of Padua (or had followed a similar path) and were all disciples of Samuel David Luzzatto, known as "Shadal." Joining Moisè Lattes was the chief rabbi Moisè Coen Porto, his deputy Leone Luzzatto and, notably, the "master," Moisè Soave, a teacher of humble origins who became one of the most important figures of the Jewish erudite world in his time in Venice.[35]

Their essays appeared in publications such as *Vessillo Israelitico, Corriere Israelitico,* and *Mosè Antologia Israelitica* and contained testimonies on archival and library material, which at that time were still preserved by the Fraterna Generale.[36] As with the Lattes collection, most of the registers produced by early modern institutions became part of private libraries. Few were still owned by the Fraterna Generale, as Moisè Soave reported in his essays on the Brotherhood for the Redemption of Captives established in Malta. Writing about his search on this topic, the "master" said that in 1875 he had the opportunity to consult the Archive of the Spanish Synagogue of Venice, finding thousands of ancient letters in Portuguese, Spanish, Italian, and Hebrew.[37] Manuscripts were also preserved by the rabbi in the Talmud Torah library, as Moisè Lattes reported, a statement that can be verified by the two incomplete catalogs written by Rabbi Moisè Coen Porto and Rabbi Sabato Ancona.[38]

The first report on the historical archive of the Jewish community dates back to the late 1870s, when, during a general recognition of the archives in Veneto, Bartolomeo Cecchetti, director of the State Archive of Venice, wrote a summary of its contents, including the names of the relevant institutions and their chronological span and range.[39] The same information was reported by Edgardo Morpurgo during his inquiry into Jewish monumental and documentary heritage in Veneto, a study that appeared in *Corriere Israelitico* between 1911 and 1913.[40] In the preface of the list of ancient archives, Morpurgo says that for many reasons, over the centuries, much of this tangible heritage was lost. Some documents, however, had been preserved by Rabbi Moisè Coen Porto in his office; others had been entrusted to the State Archive of Venice by Rabbi Lattes; and still others were kept in various repositories. The headquarters of the Fraterna Generale in San Canciano had only recent documentation, and Morpurgo strongly recommended that the ancient documentation be put in order as soon as possible, as it was fundamental for understanding the role of the Università degli Ebrei of Venice. Without an inventory of ancient documents, he declared, no one could guarantee the accuracy of his list or the summary produced by Cecchetti.[41]

Unfortunately, since the description is brief, it is impossible to give an accurate estimate of the composition of the archive. No doubt, however, the number of documents owned by the Jewish community at that time was greater than it is today. Morpurgo refers to a register of deaths from the last part of the sixteenth century that today is untraceable. Even the documentation of the Brotherhood for the Redemption of Captives was reported to cover a longer period of time than is represented by the only book of letters extant today in the Renato Maestro. There were once three *libri* (books) belonging to the brotherhood in which were recorded the dowries assigned to indigent girls from 1576 to 1840. In addition to some references to volumes that cannot be identified, we may also be missing a record of births and deaths between 1566 and 1815.

It is likely that this loss of material dates back to the last quarter of the nineteenth century: the list of Edgardo Morpurgo cannot be considered as a source, as it was a transcription of Cecchetti's report. This hypothesis is supported by reflections composed in 1931 and 1932 by Rabbi Adolfo Ottolenghi, who studied the documents that he managed to find stored in old cupboards as he organized the rabbinic archive. Comparing his findings to the information provided by the aforementioned publications, in 1931 Ottolenghi pointed out that most of the ancient documents, once preserved by many families, had ended up abroad owing to the negligence and the ignorance of his people.[42] In 1932, taking up this subject in an essay for the four hundredth anniversary of the Ashkenazi synagogue Scola Canton, Ottolenghi again complained that while he had been able to recover the historical documents of the Spanish and Italian synagogues, he did not succeed in recovering the German ones, despite the evidence of their existence found in the essays of his predecessors. Even without proof of their exportation abroad, he was sure they had ended up in foreign archives and libraries due to community negligence.[43]

Ottolenghi notes the disappearance of the two Scuola Grande Tedesca registers mentioned by Cecchetti and quoted in the essays of Leone Luzzatto: a regulation (*regolazione*) of 1611 and an inventory of holy assets, dated 1649. When Luzzatto wrote about them in his 1878 essay "Di alcuni Luzzatto di Venezia," he affirmed he was the owner.[44] Moreover, Adolfo Ottolenghi drew attention to the disappearance of some manuscripts by Leone da Modena, such as the original of his autobiography, once held by the Treves de' Bonfili family, then donated to Abraham Lattes, and finally, Ottolenghi says, entrusted to the Braidense National Library (his information was incorrect because the manuscript was actually donated to the Ambrosiana Library in Milan). Ottolenghi also recounts that an epistolary of the famous rabbi, once studied by Moisè Soave, had been acquired by the British Museum in London (now the British Library) at the beginning of the twentieth century.[45] Finally, the rabbi complains about the loss of the manuscripts of Jacob Emanuele Cracovia and Abramo Jonà that concerned the internal debates of the community during the period between the last days of the Serenissima and the arrival of the Napoleonic troops. Ottolenghi had found references to them in correspondence between Moisè Soave and the bibliographer and collector Moritz Steinschneider, published in the *Vessillo Israelitico*,[46] and had wondered about the location of the ancient documents consulted by Soave; they could no longer be found either in the community archive or with his heirs.[47]

It is possible that Ottolenghi mentioned Steinschneider in his speech as he probably suspected that these documents had disappeared in the antiques market. As a matter of fact, between the 1850s and the 1880s, Moisè Soave and Steinschneider were more than close correspondents: the Venetian teacher sought and bought many manuscripts on behalf of Steinschneider, whose titles and quantities remain unknown. In the same years, Steinschneider was also in contact with Leone Luzzatto and with Rabbi Moisè Coen Porto.[48] This involvement in the world of antiques and collectibles highlights how only a small elite group of scholars were aware of the value of the community's archival heritage—and how weak and marginal the community itself had become in its role as a conservational institution responsible for watching over the memory of the past.

In the last quarter of the nineteenth century, the migration of collections of manuscripts, printed books, and ancient documents was a widespread phenomenon not limited to the Jewish community of Venice. The contents of Shadal's library, for instance, were scattered among the Berlin National Library, the British Library, and other cultural institutions in Paris and Oxford. A similar fate was met by the manuscripts of Marco Mortara, a disciple of Shadal and rabbi of the community of Mantua. These became part of the Kaufmann Collection, purchased by the Budapest Academy of Sciences in 1906. Many leading figures of those years took part in the cultural movement called Wissenschaft des Judentums (Science of Judaism), of which Steinschneider and Shadal were distinguished members, and were linked to the rabbis who emigrated to the United States. Among them was Sabato Morais, who in 1886 founded the Jewish Theological Seminary in New York.[49]

When Ottolenghi wrote about the fate of the ancient archives at the beginning of the twentieth century, the attitude of Italian Jews toward their own past and cultural heritage was radically changing. A renewed interest arose as a result of a broader reflection on the urgent need for a history of Jews in Italy, promoted by Umberto Cassuto in 1911 during the first conference of young Jews held in Florence.[50] Ottolenghi's words on the dispersion of the Jewish archival heritage echoed those of Cassuto, who in 1929 had reported that most of the Hebrew manuscripts preserved in foreign libraries were of Italian origin.[51]

In 1935, the Unione delle Comunità Israelitiche Italiane (Union of the Italian Jewish Communities) appointed the palaeographer Isaiah Sonne to carry out an inquiry on the bibliographic and archival heritage kept by the Jewish communities in Italy. Unfortunately, with regard to the Jewish community of Venice, Sonne could report only on ancient books and manuscripts and provided no information on the ancient archive.[52] He declared himself bitterly disappointed by what remained of the once-illustrious tradition of the early modern typography and book trade in Venice. At the time, in fact, the community owned only two collections: the Talmud Torah library, organized by Rabbi Riccardo Pacifici, and that of the former rabbi Moisè Coen Porto, which had so little value in Sonne's opinion that he reported extensively only on the Talmud Torah's collection. He believed that some of the manuscript losses dated back perhaps even to the eighteenth century, and despite a lack of collaboration on the part of the community, he verified the disappearance of some precious manuscripts once preserved in some unattended bookcase, described by Moisè Lattes in his essays published in the *Mosè Antologia Israelitica* in 1879.

This is the only information we have on the state of Venetian Jewish heritage at that time. It is known that, at the end of the 1920s, the English historian Cecil Roth came into contact with Ottolenghi and probably studied the documents kept by the Jewish community so as to write his monograph on the Jews in Venice and, later, his essay on the Jews of Malta.[53] In his essay, in fact, he relies on two epistolary books of the Brotherhood for the Redemption of Captives, dating back to 1654–70 and 1671–1711.[54] Today, only one of them is still in the Renato Maestro archive; the other is owned by the Wellcome Library in London, purchased at auction in 1932.

The archive suffered no losses during the Second World War.[55] According to a report written in 1945 by Luigi Torchio, the former officer in charge of confiscated Jewish assets by Fascists during the deportation, thirteen registers of birth and death records were to be handed over to police headquarters. In fact, during the Italian Social Republic, in October 1944, the Ministry of Interior gave the order to confiscate all archives of the Jewish communities and to send them to the Ispettorato generale della Razza e Demografia, the Fascist institution that had jurisdiction over the Jews, but Torchio was able to postpone the execution of this order until the end of the war, keeping the documentation safe.[56]

In August 1963, after a partial reorganization of the Jewish Community archive, a brief list of registers, files, and papers was compiled, but it does not enable us to understand the structure of the historical archive at that time.[57] From the 1960s until establishment of the Renato Maestro Library and Archive, no other information on the dispersal of or on surviving documentation has been found. A thorough investigation should be made as to what happened after the end of World War II, when many

Jewish cultural assets were transferred from Italian Jewish communities to the new State of Israel.[58]

TOWARD A RECOVERY OF THE ARCHIVAL HERITAGE OF THE GHETTO?

Although much of the archival heritage connected to the history of the Ghetto has disappeared, the Renato Maestro Library and Archive still has the opportunity to reclaim its own memory, fulfilling the reason why it was founded in the 1980s: it can become a real center for Venetian Jewish studies.

As a first step, the center should encourage the donation of any private archives belonging to families who were or still are a part of the community. In the past, many documents, even institutional ones, were kept by private individuals: the history of the Lattes donation is hardly the only case, as in the past it was a widespread practice for officers to keep documents in their homes; over time, these precious sources have become part of family archives. The Renato Maestro could hold these important testimonies of the past and could inherit other types of sources, such as accounting books and private inventories, letters, and family memories, as a real house of memory for the community.

Another important step concerns digitization. For years, cultural institutions have been promoting and supporting cultural heritage digitization campaigns to preserve, enhance, and share their resources worldwide. This need is now felt even more strongly given the increasingly evident effects of climate change and the pandemic that broke out in Europe at the beginning of 2020. Due to the measures taken to contain the spread of COVID-19, the free movement of people had suddenly slowed and was often dramatically suspended, imposing severe restrictions on access to museums, libraries, and archives—and therefore on the active presentation of cultural heritage as we knew beforehand. These changes have further accelerated and increased digitization and the need to make cultural resources available online, also fostering the expansion and widening of an audience that has discovered cultural treasures through virtual expositions, tours, and webinars.

In this scenario, the case of Venice has become emblematic. The flood on November 12, 2019, caused enormous damage to the city and its inhabitants and put its cultural heritage at serious risk. The Renato

Maestro Library and Archive was not damaged, but the question of preserving and keeping the archive safe has to be addressed—along with making it accessible and enhancing its assets. By digitizing its heritage, it could recover its symbolic cultural role.

Today, thanks to the internet, the virtual catalogs of many cultural institutions are accessible, allowing us to trace and locate some of the missing documents that were once part of the Venetian Jewish archives. The Lattes Collection, preserved in the State Archive of Venice, and the documents of the Venetian institutions that had jurisdiction over the Ghetto have been digitized and are available online thanks to the Judaica Europeana project. The catalog of the Jewish Theological Seminary in New York includes almost twenty-five descriptions of documents from the Jewish institutions of Venice, also partially digitized. The Central Archive for the History of the Jewish People keeps similar documentation, and further investigations should be conducted at the National Library of Israel in Jerusalem. We have recently discovered that the epistolary book of the Brotherhood for the Redemption of Captives is at the Wellcome Library in London; a thorough investigation should also be conducted of the collections of the British Library and the Bodleian Library. In 2014, with the financial support of the Gladys Krieble Delmas Foundation, Brandeis University in Massachusetts digitized and made available an accounting book of the Italian nation dating to the eighteenth century. Finally, in the fall of 2017, the National Library of Moscow and the National Library of Israel in Jerusalem signed an agreement to digitize the Guenzburg Collection with funding from the Peri Foundation.

From the point of view of an archivist, what I have mentioned in this essay are catalogs of bibliographic collections that describe documents with bibliographic, nonarchival standards. Catalogs and inventories are different genres of documents based on different working methods. Only an analytic inventory can restore the original archival bonds between the documents—and consider them as parts of organic structures, webs of connection structured by and through the knowledge of the historical and institutional context they inhabit. These are the essential prerequisites for studying the Venetian Jewish settlement from an internal perspective.

It is critical to create a virtual inventory of all of the documents kept in Italian and foreign institutions: putting the Renato Maestro at the center of such a collective project would make it possible to carry out its

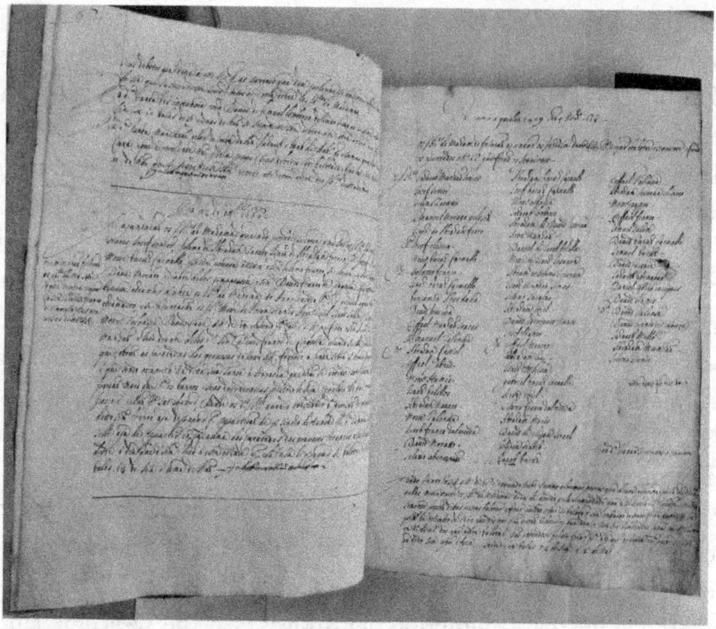

FIGURE 8. Libro delle parti dell 'Università dei ponentini, register, 1669–1691, Scuola Kahal Kadosh Talmud Torah degli ebrei ponentini, Jewish Community of Venice, Renato Maestro Library and Archive, Venice. —Photograph by Federica Ruspio.

FIGURE 9. Left: Maestro do escrinho do Kahal Kadosh Talmud Torah, register, 1700–1735, Scuola Kahal Kadosh Talmud Torah, fond, last quarter sixteenth to eighteenth century, Jewish Community of Venice, Renato Maestro Library and Archive, Venice. Photograph by Federica Ruspio. Right: Inventario dos sefarim da pratta e mobeis do Kahal Kadosh Talmud Torah, register, 1703–1757, Scuola Kahal Kadosh Talmud Torah, fond, last quarter sixteenth to eighteenth century, Jewish Community of Venice, Renato Maestro Library and Archive, Venice. —Photograph by Federica Ruspio.

original historical mission.[59] Since the entire cultural heritage is interconnected, such a project should also involve the Renato Maestro Library and Archive and the Jewish Museum of Venice so as to create a worldwide network of study, research, and sharing that would enable us not only to reconstruct its original composition but also to see the changes that occurred through the centuries and to trace the events that accompanied the journeys of books, documents, and artifacts toward and out of the Ghetto.

This initiative would ensure that the Renato Maestro Library and Archive serves as one of the central actors in representing and shaping Jewish historical identity from the site of the Venice Ghetto itself. It could make it possible to virtually re-create the Ghetto at the time of its establishment and to counterbalance the recent trends toward "museumification" that have affected the entire city of the lagoon, reducing the Ghetto to a mere metaphor, an empty stage rather than one of the main expressions of Jewish historical identity.[60]

APPENDIX

Archives and Collections Preserved in the Renato Museum Library and Archive

ABBREVIATIONS

b./bb.	box/boxes
doc.	document
fasc./fascc.	file/files
reg./regg.	register/registers

Archives of Institutions and Associations

Comunità ebraica di Venezia. Università o Nazioni e altre istituzioni israelitiche precedenti l'unificazione in Fraterna generale

16th, last quarter–18th
bb. 10

The archive includes documentation of *Kahal Kadosh Talmud Torah* in Venice (Ponentine/Sephardic nation) and of *Università degli ebrei levantini viandanti di Venezia* (Levantine/Ottoman Jews)

Comunità ebraica di Venezia. Scuole, fraterne e sovvegni

17th, second half–20th, first half
bb. 29

The archive includes administrative and accounting documentation of the synagogues (Scuole or Scole) and the ritual and charitable institutions: *Scuola Canton di Venezia; Scuola italiana di Venezia; Scuola levantina di Venezia; Scuola spagnola di Venezia; Sovvegni riuniti spagnolo e tedesco di Venezia; Sovvegno aiutar fratelli della nazione ponentina di Venezia; Sovvegno tedesco di Venezia; Fraterna maritar donzelle della Nazion tedesca di Venezia; Fraterna mattutina di Venezia; Fraterna vespertina di Venezia; Fraterna vestir poveri di Venezia; Istituzione israelitica per le circoncisioni e le puerpere di Venezia. Fraterna israelitica di misericordia e pietà di Venezia*

18th, last quarter–20th second quarter
bb. 33

Comunità ebraica di Venezia, formerly *Comunità israelitica di Venezia*, formerly *Fraterna Generale degli Israeliti di Venezia*

19th, beginning–1930
bb. 551

Gruppo sionistico veneziano

1920–68
fascc. 2

Comitato italiano assistenza emigranti ebrei. Ufficio di Napoli

1921–22
b. 1, fascc. 2

Associazione cuore e concordia di Venezia

1922–37
reg. 1, doc. 1

Associazione donne ebree d'Italia. Sezione di Venezia

1928–sec. 20th, last quarter
bb. 6

Comitato per il centro storico ebraico di Venezia. Presidenza Alberto Mortara

1971–89
bb. 12

Biblioteca archivio Renato Maestro di Venezia

20th, second half
regg. 7, fascc. 83, catalog 17

Archives of Family or Persons

Levi Polacco Daniel

1846–84
fasc. 1

Sullam Luigi

1876–91
fasc. 2

Sullam Costante e Luigi

1887–1911
fasc. 1

Nunes Vais Arbib Bianca

19th, end–20th, third quarter
bb. 4

Lattes Luzzatto, famiglia

19th, end–20th, last quarter
bb. 2

Milano Attilio
1891–1993
bb. 10

Ravenna Felice
1913–14
fasc. 1

Lattes Dante
1916–1966
bb. 15

Sullam Guido
20th, first quarter–20th middle
b. 1

Voghera Giorgio
20th, second quarter–20th, third quarter
bb. 2

Sereni Paolo
20th, second quarter–20th, last quarter
bb. 6

Geschmay Giovanni
1959–64
fasc. 1

Fano Luciano
1963–65
b. 1

Levi Raffaello
1964–68
bb. 2

This archive also includes two boxes of papers of the *Ufficio ricerche deportati* (1945–50), the bureau in charge of collecting information on the survivors of the extermination camps.

Miscellaneous/Collections

Comunità ebraica di Venezia. Documenti di dubbia attribuzione
17th, beginning–20th, beginning
bb. 5

Sinagoga spagnola di Venezia. Partiture
1894–1942
docc. 531

Comunità ebraica di Venezia. Archivio fotografico
20th, beginning–20th, last quarter
bb. 2

Comunità ebraica di Venezia. Provenienze diverse
20th
b. 1

NOTES

1. In this essay, the word "archive" will be used with three different meanings. First, the archive is synonymous with "fonds" (*fondo*), the documents produced or acquired by a creator (bench, central, and noncentral state offices; public authorities; private institutions, families, and persons) during its activities. Second, "archive" indicates the building or the repository in which a creator preserves its archive. Finally, "archive" is used for the custodian institution that preserves archives and fonds. See the glossary in Paola Carucci, *Le fonti archivistiche: Ordinamento e conservazione* (Rome: La Nuova Italia Scientifica, 1983). Regarding the nature and the concept of the archive, see Claudio Pavone, "Ma è tanto pacifico che l'archivio rispecchi l'istituto?," in *Intorno agli archivi e alle istituzioni: Scritti di Claudio Pavone*, ed. Isabella Zanni Rosiello (Rome: Ministero per i Beni e le Attività Culturali, 2004), 71–75.
2. See chap. 1.
3. Donatella Calabi, "Venezia, Gli Ebrei e l'Europa: Cinquecento anni dall'istituzione del Ghetto di Venezia," in *Venezia, Gli Ebrei e l'Europa, 1516–2016*, ed. Donatella Calabi (Venice: Marsilio, 2016), 18–35; Shaul Bassi, "From All Their Habitations: The Venetian Ghetto and Modern Jewish Identity," *Judaism: A Quarterly Journal of Jewish Life and Thought* 51, no. 4 (Fall 2002): 469.
4. Simon Levis Sullam, "Reinventing Jewish Venice: The Scene of the Ghetto between Monument and Metaphor," in *Cultural Representations of Jewishness at the Turn of the 21st Century*, ed. Magdalena Waligórska and Sophie Wagenhofer, European University Institute Working Papers (Florence: EUI, 2010), 13–25.
5. The Committee for the Jewish Historical Centre in Venice was established in Milan in 1971. From 1972 to 1990, it was managed by the economist Alberto Mortara and then by Cesare Vivante. For more, see Comitato per il Centro Storico Ebraico: Presidenza Alberto Mortara, fond, Jewish Community of Venice, 1971–1989, Renato Maestro Library and Archive, Venice; Luisella Mortara Ottolenghi, "Salvare Venezia: Verso la fine del vecchio quartiere ebraico," *Shalom* 5, no. 4 (1971): 13; and Cesare Vivante, "Comitato per il Centro Storico Ebraico," *Quaderni di Insula: Documenti sulla Manutenzione Urbana di Venezia* 13 (2002): 48–49.
6. Umberto Fortis, ed., *Venezia Ebraica: Atti delle prime giornate di studio sull'Ebraismo veneziano (Venezia, 1976–1980)* (Rome: Carucci, 1982).
7. The Israelite Museum's "Vittorio Fano" was opened as a temporary exhibition in 1954; a permanent exhibition was started in the 1970s and finished in 1989. Documents related to "Vittorio Fano" from 1954 to 1984 are available at the Renato Maestro Library and Archive; see also related correspondence in 1951 and 1964, Jewish Community of Venice, 1818–1975, Renato Maestro Library and Archive, Venice, and Micaela Procaccia, "Documentazione, esposizione, musealizzazione: Mostre e musei dell'Ebraismo italiano," *Rassegna Mensile di Israel* 76, no. 1/2 (2010): 323–50.
8. Gaetano Cozzi, ed., *Gli Ebrei e Venezia, Secoli XIV–XVIII: Atti del Convegno Internazionale organizzato dall'Istituto di Storia della Società e dello Stato Veneziano della Fondazione Giorgio Cini [. . .]* (Milan: Edizioni Comunità, 1987), and Renata Segre, ed., *Gli Ebrei a Venezia, 1938–1945: Una comunità tra persecuzione e rinascita* (Venice: Comunità ebraica di Venezia, 2001).
9. Documentation on the Talmud Torah school is preserved in *Scuola Religioso Morale Maschile*, subseries, Scuole d'istruzione, Comunità Ebraica di Venezia, 1873–1935, Renato Maestro Library and Archive, Venice. See also Simon Levis Sullam, *Una Comunità Immaginata: Gli Ebrei a Venezia (1900–1938)* (Milan: Unicopli, 2001), 103–4, 108–9; and Gadi Luzzatto Voghera, "Gli Ebrei," in *Storia di Venezia: L'Ottocento e il Novecento*, ed. Mario Isnenghi and Stuart Woolf (Rome: Istituto della Enciclopedia Treccani, 2002), 619–47.

10. See Chiara Camarda, ed., *I libri del ghetto: Catalogo dei libri ebraici della Comunità Ebraica di Venezia (Secc. XVI–XX)* (Padova, Italy: Il Prato, 2016), and Levis Sullam, *Una Comunità Immaginata*, 138–53.
11. Eurigio Tonetti, ed., *Inventario dell'Archivio della Comunità Israelitica di Venezia* (Venice: Comune di Venezia, 1984), and Sigrid Sohn, "La Circolazione della cultura ebraica nella Comunità di Venezia: La Biblioteca-Archivio 'Renato Maestro,'" in *E li insegnerai ai tuoi figli: Educazione ebraica in Italia dalle Leggi razziali ad oggi*, ed. Anna Maria Piussi (Florence: Giuntina, 1997), 194.
12. For a list of the archives preserved in the Renato Maestro Library and Archive, see the appendix below.
13. Daniel J. Cohen, "Sources for the History of the Jewish People in Archives in Europe and in Israel," *Newsletter (World Union of Jewish Studies)*, nos. 17–18 (1981): 5–22; Mauro Perani, "Jewish Studies in the Italian Academic World," in *Jewish Studies and the European Academic World: Plenary Lectures at the Viith Congress of the European Association for Jewish Studies (EAJS), Amsterdam, July 2002*, ed. Albert Van der Heide and Irene E. Zwiep (Paris-Louvain: Peeters, 2005), 67–116; Micaela Procaccia, "Gli archivi delle istituzioni ebraiche," in *Storia dell'Italia nel secolo ventunesimo: Strumenti e fonti*, ed. Claudio Pavone, vol. 3, *Le fonti documentarie* (Rome: Ministero per i Beni e le Attività Culturali, 2006), 377–99; and Shlomo Simonsohn, "Lo stato attuale della ricerca storica sugli ebrei in Italia," in *Italia Judaica: Atti del I Convegno Internazionale, Bari 18–22 Maggio 1981* (Rome: Ministero per i Beni Culturali e Ambientali, 1983), 30–31.
14. An exhaustive bibliographic survey of the subject cannot be provided here; for a starting point, see Cozzi, *Gli Ebrei e Venezia*; Robert C. Davis and Benjamin Ravid, eds., *The Jews of Early Modern Venice* (Baltimore: Johns Hopkins University Press, 2001); Uwe Israel, Robert Jütte, and Reinhold C. Mueller, eds., *"Interstizi": Culture Ebraico-Cristiane a Venezia e nei suoi Domini dal Medioevo all'Età Moderna* (Rome: Edizioni di Storia e Letteratura, 2010); and Donatella Calabi, ed., *Venezia, gli Ebrei e l'Europa, 1516–2016* (Venice: Marsilio, 2016).
15. This is a common tendency influenced by the fact that documentation in the public archives is abundant and more accessible, whereas the historical archives of the communities are often incomplete. For recent historiography on Jews and Jewish sources, see Gadi Luzzatto Voghera, "A proposito della storiografia sugli Ebrei di Venezia nel cinquecentenario della fondazione del Ghetto," *Quellen und Forschungen aus italienischen Archiven und Bibliotheken*, no. 96 (2016): 488–97; Procaccia, "Gli archivi delle istituzioni ebraiche," 377–99; Fausto Pusceddu, "Archivi italiani e fonti documentarie relative alla storia degli Ebrei in Italia," in *Italia Judaica*, 229–38; Renata Segre, "La società ebraica nelle fonti archivistiche italiane," in *Italia Judaica*, 239–50; and Ariel Viterbo, "The Conservation of History: The Archives of the Jewish Communities in the Veneto," in *The Italia Judaica Jubilee Conference*, ed. Shlomo Simonsohn and Joseph Shatzmiller (Leiden: Brill, 2013), 240–41.
16. *Libro delle parti dell'Università dei ponentini*, register, Scuola Kahal Kadosh Talmud Torah degli Ebrei Ponentini, Jewish Community of Venice, 1669–91, Renato Maestro Library and Archive, Venice, and *Registro delle parti della Scuola Levantina*, Jewish Community of Venice, 1686–1727, Renato Maestro Library and Archive, Venice. See also Viterbo, "Conservation of History," 239–46.
17. This type of document consists of collections of testimonies, handwritten or printed, by the counterparts in a lawsuit. See Maria Francesca Tiepolo, ed., "Venezia," in *Guida generale degli archivi di Stato italiani*, ed. Claudio Pavone (Rome: Ministero per i Beni culturali e Ambientali, 1994), 4:1131.
18. Registro dei Verbali del Capitolo Generale, Documenti di Dubbia Attribuzione, collection, Jewish Community of Venice, 1793–1804, Renato Maestro Library and Archive, Venice.

19. The *squarzo* or *squarcio* is an abstract or a rough copy of a register. See Giuseppe Boerio, *Dizionario del Dialetto Veneziano* (Venice, 1856), 698. These kind of registers, produced by the Ponentine institutions, were Registro squarzo parti della Scuola (1726–75); Maestro do escrinho do Kahal Kadosh Talmud Torah (1700–1735); Scontro del Banco Kahal KadoshTalmud Torah (1722–25). Inventario dos sefarim da pratta e mobeis do Kahal Kadosh Talmud Torah (1703–57). Inventari: Descrizione di "mobeis, seffarim, pratta e recebeidas" (1765–1846). All are preserved in Scuola Kahal Kadosh Talmud Torah, fond, Jewish Community of Venice, sixteenth–eighteenth century, Renato Maestro Library and Archive, Venice.
20. These registers consist of copies of recordings from other Venetian institutions and notaries: registro di decreti pubblici relativi al commercio dei gioielli (1629–73); Registro copie di scritture pubbliche (1654–1718); Registro copie partite di Zecca (1656–1718); Registro di instrumenti diversi de danari presi a censo vitalizio dalla nation delli Hebrei ponentini (1675–96); and Registro instrumenti pubblici (1718–21). The letter book Deputati della nazione ponentina al riscatto degli schiavi (1654–70) is the only surviving item from the Brotherhood for the Redemption of Captives. All are preserved in Scuola Kahal Kadosh Talmud Torah, fond, Jewish Community of Venice, sixteenth–eighteenth century, Renato Maestro Library and Archive, Venice. Finally, another account book of the Ponentine nation, Noua imposta sendo deputados os segnores Iacob Franco de Almeida, Ioseph Iesurum, Raffael Gabai (1684), is part of Documenti di Dubbia Attribuzione, miscellaneous, Jewish Community of Venice, sixteenth–twentieth century, Renato Maestro Library and Archive, Venice.
21. These documents consist of account books and recordings of resolutions. Registro deliberazioni, ricevute, inventari, depositi (1712–1803); Registro squarzo deliberazioni (1792–1807); Registri contabili e giornali delle offerte (1791–1832); and Registri contabili e giornali delle offerte (eighteenth–twentieth century). Preserved in Scuola Italiana, fond, Jewish Community of Venice, eighteenth–twentieth century, Renato Maestro Library and Archive, Venice.
22. The seven registers date from the seventeenth to the end of the eighteenth century with a gap in the second half of the seventeenth. See Documenti di Dubbia Attribuzione, miscellaneous, Jewish Community of Venice, sixteenth–twentieth century, Renato Maestro Library and Archive, Venice.
23. Regolazione del Sovegno sive Fraterna di aiutar fratelli della nazione degli ebrei ponentini di Venezia, register, Sovvengo Aiutar Fratelli della Nazion Ponentina, Jewish Community of Venice, 1771–88, Renato Maestro Library and Archive, Venice.
24. Registro deliberazioni, register, Sovvengo Tedesco, Jewish Community of Venice, 1700–1712, Renato Maestro Library and Archive, Venice; Registro dei fratelli iscritti a ruolo, register, Sovvengo Tedesco, Jewish Community of Venice, 1756–1840, Renato Maestro Library and Archive, Venice.
25. When donated, the Lattes' materials became part of the Miscellanea codici, but in the 1860s they were moved to Scuole Piccole e Suffragi, an archive that gathers all the fonds of the small Venetian confraternities, preserved in the State Archive of Venice. A brief description of the collection is given in the manuscript of the inventory of this archive, written in the nineteenth century and updated in the twentieth. See Scuole Piccole e Suffragi, manuscript, nineteenth–twentieth century, Archivio di Stato di Venezia, Venice, 130–31, and Tiepolo, "Venezia," 4:1029–30, 1088–89, 1095.
26. The Judaica Europeana Project at the State Archive of Venice has been coordinated by the Istituto Centrale per il Catalogo Unico (ICCU); the results are available at http://www.judaica.archiviodistatovenezia.beniculturali.it. For an overview of the project,

see https://pro.europeana.eu/project/judaica-europeana. Today, the Judaica Europeana Project is carried out by the Jewish Heritage Network (https://jhn.ngo).

27. Andrea Y. Lattes, "Le confraternite ebraiche di Venezia nel XVII secolo ed i loro documenti: Una prima analisi," in *Materia Giudaica XXIII: Rivista dell'Associazione Italiana per lo Studio del Giudaismo* (Rome: Giuntina, 2018).

28. Libro grande dell'Università degli Ebrei, Ufficiali al Cattaver, 1632, Archivio di Stato di Venezia, Venice, and David J. Malkiel, *A Separate Republic: The Mechanics and Dynamics of Venetian Jewish Self-Government, 1607–1624* (Jerusalem: Magnes Press, 1991). Daniel Carpi, "Ordinances of the Community of Venice, 1591–1607," in *Exile and Diaspora: Studies in the History of the Jewish People Presented to Professor Haim Beinart*, ed. Aaron Mirsky, Avraham Grossman, and Yosef Kaplan (Jerusalem: Ben-Zvi Institute, 1988), 443–69; Daniel Carpi, "Le 'Convenzioni' degli anni 1624 e 1645 tra le tre 'nazioni' della comunità di Venezia," in *Shlomo Simonsohn Jubilee Volume* (Tel Aviv: Tel Aviv University, Faculty of Humanities, Chaim Rosenberg School of Jewish Studies, 1993), 25–70; Daniel Carpi, "The Activity of the 'Italian Congregation' of Venice on Behalf of the Jewish Communities of Eretz Israel during the Years 1576–1733," *Henoch* 21 (1999): 331–60; and Daniel Carpi, ed., *Minutes Book of the Council of the "Italian" Jewish Community of Venice, 1644–1711* [Hebrew] (Jerusalem: Ben-Zvi Institute for the Study of Jewish Communities in the East, 2003). When they were still owned by the Jewish Community of Venice, the sources were described by Rabbi Riccardo Pacifici in "I Regolamenti della Scuola Italiana a Venezia nel secolo XVII," *Rassegna Mensile di Israel* 5, no. 7/8 (1930): 392–402.

29. Fraterna Generale di Culto e Beneficenza degli Israeliti di Venezia, *Regolamento per la Fraterna Generale di Culto e Beneficenza degl'Israeliti di Venezia* (Venice, 1828), and Luzzatto Voghera, "Gli Ebrei," 629–31.

30. Untitled manuscript, b. 503, Miscellanea, Jewish Community of Venice, 1834, Renato Maestro Library and Archive, Venice. On the poverty of Jewish people in Venice between the second half of the nineteenth and the first half of the twentieth century, see Levis Sullam, *Una Comunità Immaginata*, 49–50, 78–81.

31. Abraam Lattes, "Cenni sulla Comunità Israelitica di Venezia," in *Venezia e le sue lagune*, ed. Giovanni Correr (Venice, 1847), 103–7; Adolfo Ottolenghi, "Abraham Lattes nei suoi rapporti colla Repubblica di Daniele Manin," *Rassegna Mensile di Israel* 5, no. 1 (1930): 25–35; and Angelo M. Piattelli, *Repertorio biografico dei rabbini italiani dal 1861 al 2015* (Jerusalem, 2017), 31.

32. Leone Luzzatto, "Rabbino Mosé Dr. Lattes: Necrologio," *Corriere Israelitico* 22 (1883): 119–20, and Piattelli, *Repertorio*, 35. The testament of Abramo Lattes was written in 1862. See Liquidazione come esecutore testamentario dell'onorevole eccellente rabbino maggiore Abramo Lattes de 6 novembre 1875, Sullam Luigi, b. 551, Renato Maestro Library and Archive, Venice.

33. Aldo Luzzatto and Luisella Mortara Ottolenghi, eds., *Hebraica Ambrosiana, Fontes Ambrosiani* (Milan: Il Polifilo, 1972), 11; Biblioteca Nazionale Braidense, *La Biblioteca Nazionale Braidense di Milano* (Milan: self-pub., 1976), 7.

34. Adolfo Ottolenghi, "Il governo democratico di Venezia e l'abolizione del Ghetto," *Rassegna Mensile di Israel* 5, no. 2 (1930): 25.

35. Moisè Coen Porto, "Moisè Soave," *Corriere Israelitico* 21 (1882): 203–4; Marino Berengo, "Luigi Luzzatti e la tradizione ebraica," in *Luigi Luzzatti e il suo tempo: Atti del Convegno Internazionale di Studio (Venezia, 7–9 Novembre 1991)*, ed. Pier Luigi Ballini and Paolo Pecorari (Venice: Istituto Veneto di Scienze Lettere ed Arti, 1994), 527–41; Aldo Luzzatto, ed., *La Comunità Ebraica di Venezia e il suo Antico Cimitero* (Milan: Il Polifilo, 2000), 864–65; Cesare Musatti, "Il Maestro Moisè Soave," pts. 1 and 2, *Archivio Veneto* 36 (1888): 383–97; 37 (1889): 381–419.

36. On these authors, see Attilio Milano, *Bibliotheca Historica Italo-Judaica* (Florence: Sansoni, 1954); Gadi Luzzatto Voghera, "Riflessioni sulla storiografia ebraica dell'Ottocento in Italia," *Materia Giudaica* 15/16 (2010/2011): 121–28; and Attilio Milano, "Un Secolo di stampa periodica ebraica," *Rassegna Mensile di Israel* 12, no. 7/8/9 (1938): 96–133.
37. Moisè Soave, "Malta e gli schiavi ebrei," *Corriere Israelitico* 17 (1878/1879): 54.
38. Moisè Lattes, "Notizie e documenti di letteratura e storia giudaica," *Mosé Antologia Israelitica* 2 (1879): 177–80; N. 71. Elenco libri de ragion del Talmud Torah in custodia del rettore Moisè Coen Porto, quindi del rettor Sabato Ancona, Scuole d'Istruzione, Jewish Community of Venice, [post 1879]–1892, Renato Maestro Library and Archive, Venice.
39. Bartolomeo Cecchetti, ed., *Statistica degli Archivi della Regione Veneta* (Venice, 1881), 2:167.
40. Edgardo Morpurgo, "Inchiesta sui monumenti e documenti del Veneto interessanti la storia religiosa, civile e letteraria degli Ebrei," pts. 1, 2, and 3, *Corriere Israelitico* 49 (1910/1911): 167, 201–3; 50 (1911/1912): 1–4, 41–43, 61–62, 145–47, 165–68, 205–7; 51 (1912/1913): 5–7, 53–56.
41. Morpurgo, "Inchiesta sui monumenti," 49:167.
42. Adolfo Ottolenghi, "Spigolature storiche di vita ebraica veneziana," *Rassegna Mensile di Israel* 6, no. 5/6 (1931): 211–18.
43. The so-called Scola Canton was one of the Venetian Ashkenazi synagogues, built around 1531–32, at the corner (*canton* in the Venetian dialect) of the Ghetto Nuovo square. Adolfo Ottolenghi, *Per il IV Centenario della Scuola Canton: Notizie storiche sui Templi veneziani di rito tedesco e su alcuni templi privati con cenni della vita ebraica nei secoli XVI–XIX* [. . .] (Venice: Tipografia del "Gazzettino illustrato," 1932), 12–13.
44. Leone Luzzatto, "Di alcuni Luzzatto di Venezia," *Mosé Antologia Israelitica* 1 (1878): 302–3.
45. Adolfo Ottolenghi, "Leon Da Modena e la vita ebraica del Ghetto di Venezia nel secolo XVII," *Rassegna Mensile di Israel* 37, no. 12 (1971): 739–63.
46. From 1877 to 1881, in the form of letters to Moritz (Moshe) Steinschneider, Moisè Soave published seventeen brief essays on Jewish history and literature based on the information he had found in his own books and manuscripts or in sources he could consult at that time. See Moisè Soave, "All'illustre Mosè Dr. Steinschneider di Berlino," pts. 1, 2, 3, and 4, *Vessillo Israelitico* 25 (1877): 378–82; 26 (1878): 54–58, 79–84, 111–19, 149–53, 187–90, 217–21, 251–53, 281–83; 27 (1879): 104–8; 28 (1880): 16–18, 45–48, 80–86, 117–20, 174–78, 211–14. See also Attilio Milano, *Bibliotheca Historica Italo-Judaica: Supplemento, 1954–1963* (Florence: Sansoni, 1964), 62.
47. Ottolenghi, "Il governo democratico," 88–104.
48. On Moritz (Moshe) Steinschneider, see Reimund Leicht and Gad Freudenthal, "Introduction: Studying Moritz Steinschneider," in *Studies on Steinschneider: Moritz Steinschneider and the Emergence of the Science of Judaism in Nineteenth-Century Germany*, ed. Reimund Leicht and Gad Freudenthal (Leiden: Brill, 2012), xv–xxxii. On the epistolary of Steinschneider with Venetian scholars preserved by the Jewish Theological Seminary, see Asher Salah, "Steinschneider and Italy," in Leicht and Freudenthal, *Studies on Steinschneider*, 422–26.
49. Mauro Perani, "Italia 'Paniere' dei manoscritti ebraici e la loro Diaspora nel contesto del collezionismo in Europa tra Otto e Novecento," in "Il collezionismo di libri ebraici tra XVII e XIX secolo. Atti del convegno, Torino, 27 Marzo 2015," ed. Chiara Pilocane and Amedeo Spagnoletto, special issue, *Rassegna Mensile di Israel* 82, no. 2/3 (May/December 2016): 81–84; Asher Salah, "La Biblioteca di Marco Mortara," in *Nuovi studi in onore di Marco Mortara* (Florence: Giuntina, 2016), 149–68.
50. Umberto Cassuto, "Per una storia degli Ebrei in Italia," *Rassegna Mensile di Israel* 82, no. 2/3 (2016): 349–53; Bruno di Porto, "Umberto Cassuto, Lo Storico," *Rassegna Mensile di Israel* 82, no. 2/3 (2016): 209–37; and Mario Toscano, "Tra ricerca scientifica e costruzione dell'identità: Il progetto della Società per la storia degli Ebrei in Italia (1911–1939)," *Rassegna Mensile di Israel* 82, no. 2/3 (2016): 193–208.

51. Perani, "Italia 'Paniere' dei manoscritti ebraici," 64.
52. Isaiah Sonne, "Relazione sulla Biblioteca della Comunità Israelitica di Venezia," in *Relazione sui tesori bibliografici delle Comunità Israelitiche d'Italia, anni 1935–1937*, typewritten, 1 and 3, Centro Bibliografico dell'Unione delle Comunità Ebraiche Italiane "Tullia Zevi," Rome.
53. Cecil Roth, "The Jews of Malta," *Transactions of the Jewish Historical Society of England* 12 (1928–31): 218–42, and Cecil Roth, *History of the Jews in Venice* (New York: Schocken Books, 1975). Regarding the research of Cecil Roth on the Jewish community of Venice, see the 1922–29 correspondence of Rabbi Ottolenghi, Ufficio Rabbinico, Comunità Ebraica di Venezia, series, Jewish Community of Venice, 1852–1966, Renato Maestro Library and Archive, Venice. Regarding Ottolenghi's focus on the importance of the Jewish past and Roth's studies, see also Levis Sullam, *Una Comunità Immaginata*, 147, 232–33.
54. Roth, "Jews of Malta," and Cecil Roth, "Lettere della Compagnia del riscatto degli schiavi in Venezia," *Rassegna Mensile di Israel* 15, no. 1 (1949): 31–36.
55. Michele Sarfatti, "Contro i libri e i documenti delle Comunità israelitiche italiane, 1938–1945," *Rassegna Mensile di Israel* 69, no. 2 (2003): 362–85.
56. Luigi Torchio, "Cenni sulla gestione della Comunità israelitica di Venezia dal gennaio 1944 all'agosto 1945," Testimonianze, b. 6, typescript, Giorgio Rossi, August 13, 1945, Renato Maestro Library and Archive, Venice; "Corrispondenza varia del sequestratario," b. 51, Jewish Community of Venice, 1944–45, Renato Maestro Library and Archive, Venice.
57. "Elenco sommario del contenuto delle buste d'archivio," b. 502G, typescript, Jewish Community of Venice, 1963, Renato Maestro Library and Archive, Venice.
58. Procaccia, "Documentazione," 335–36.
59. Bassi, "From All Their Habitations," 478.
60. Levis Sullam, "Reinventing Jewish Venice," 21–22.

PART II

THE BLUEPRINT

GLOBAL ARCHETYPES (1516–2016)

AMANDA K. SHARICK AND KATHARINE G. TROSTEL

In this grouping of essays, the Ghetto, Shylock, and the five hundredth anniversary act as a set of blueprints that together allow us to unpack the relationship between Venice and its Ghetto and between the Venice Ghetto and the world. A blueprint is a tool for encoding memory, for representing the interrelation of part to whole. It depicts and orients a specific spatial relationship for the purpose of making this configuration transportable. But, by its very nature, it elides the complexity of a lived network of experience. It never fully corresponds to reality; it is a simplification, an abstraction. It articulates a plan rooted in the values of the present that is, by design, intended to be reconstructed elsewhere. A blueprint requires interpretation by the architect. It carries within it both the limitations of the present and the potential to be implemented or utilized in unintended and unimagined ways in new times and spaces.

Shylock, for Shaul Bassi, an associate professor of English at Ca' Foscari University of Venice with deep family ties to the Venice Ghetto, exemplifies a different kind of blueprint. In the lead-up to the five hundredth anniversary of the Venice Ghetto in 2016, Bassi spoke to a crowded lecture hall on January 26, 2016, at the University of California, Santa Barbara. Central to the talk's focus was the complex and intertwined history of the Venice Ghetto and its relationship to its most famous literary figure: Shylock, from Shakespeare's *The Merchant of Venice* (1600). Religious studies scholar Richard Hecht's introduction to the evening cited Bassi as a veritable link between "the past . . . present, and most importantly the future of the Venetian Ghetto."[1] This future included a decade of work to mobilize key stakeholders and partners, including the National Endowment for the Humanities, to take on the project of revitalizing the Ghetto for its five hundredth anniversary. At the center of this revitalization effort was the idea to stage *The Merchant of Venice* in the Ghetto. Bassi explains that his desire to produce the play in the Ghetto is rooted in their entangled histories: "I consider both the Ghetto and Shakespeare's play as fundamentally ambivalent documents of Western civilization, having been both instruments of intolerance and catalysts for cross-cultural understanding, vehicles of antisemitism and portals of knowledge of and sympathy for the Jews. . . . We intend to take the full onus of this ambivalence, rejecting any univocal interpretation of the place or the play, attempting instead to work into a major theatrical event the multiple historical implications of a unique site, one that has seen its distinctly local name—*Ghetto*—become a global metaphor—Ghetto. . . . By unpacking the most famous myth linked to the Ghetto, Shylock, we hope to demystify the stereotypes that have accrued around this exemplary site. Can *The Merchant* in the Ghetto add a new critical layer?"[2]

For literary scholars like Harold Bloom and Stephen Greenblatt, the figure of Shylock and the bias and anti-Jewish hatred that drives Shakespeare's play continue to pose critical challenges as well as opportunities for each new performance.[3] The essays contained in this section consider this phenomenon from multiple perspectives and through multiple iterations of Shylock. The impact of this character—while fictional—is not to be underestimated. Bassi anticipated that there could be no celebration of the quincentennial of the Jewish Ghetto in Venice without acknowledging the Bard's creation: "We're trying to bring Shylock back by organizing the *first ever* performance of *The Merchant of Venice* in the Ghetto next year. Shylock is the most notorious Venetian Jew. But he never existed. He is a kind of ghost that haunts the place. So we're trying to explore the myth of Shylock and the reality of the Ghetto. The relationship between Shylock and the other characters is clearly based on a very intimate understanding of the new social configurations created by the Ghetto."[4] For Bassi, any path to reclaiming the history of the Venice Ghetto must go through the Jewish character of Shylock, who—in the Western imagination—remains a sort of decontextualized blueprint of Jewish experience in sixteenth-century Europe. An imperial ghost not easily exorcised—and one that has endured across the centuries—Shakespeare's Shylock is carefully examined, deconstructed, recontextualized, and reimagined in the essays included in this part as a way to shed new light on the absence of the Venice Ghetto in *The Merchant of Venice*.

In the first essay, "Social and Economic Dimensions of Italian Jewish Public Life in the Age of the Ghetto," Andrea Lattes expands on the historical conditions that transformed Jewish-Christian relationships, creating the social configurations for the first ghetto in the world, and contextualizes Shakespeare's representation of Shylock as moneylender. While scholars like Bassi have noted that the Ghetto is absent from *The Merchant of Venice*, Lattes's examination of the environmental, political, and historical conditions of Italian ghettos demonstrates how they dramatically restructured Jewish life and community formations around the financial needs of Christian institutions—revealing the mechanisms that first gave rise to the stereotype of the Italian Jewish banker. Although the essay makes no mention of Shylock, by foregrounding the history of Italian Jews shaped by the Ghetto, the reader may glimpse the historical blueprint for the character of Shylock. Bassi calls for such historical recontextualizations:

> It is finally time to bring in William Shakespeare, as a reader. For centuries, European Jews have had to serve as money lenders in Christian lands. Since the end of the thirteenth century, the Jew as usurer becomes the figure of any illicit economic activity, the obverse of the positive activity of the Christian merchant-banker. . . . Shakespeare does not mention the Ghetto himself, but the Ghetto is presupposed in *The Merchant of Venice*. We may argue that this specific site originates the Shakespearean text as an indispensable, non-literary *source* since the social and cultural dynamics of the play are enabled by that new space legally constituted by the Republic of Venice in 1516. The social interaction between Shylock and the Christian merchants, his ambivalent relationship with conviviality (the much-discussed contradiction between "I will not eat with you, drink with you," of Act 1, Scene 3, and the invitation to dinner he accepts in Act 2, Scene 5), . . . all the romance between Jessica and Lorenzo are all the result of the creation of a defined and sanctioned space where Jews were simultaneously included in and excluded from the city.[5]

Shakespeare's Shylock, then, is not only a myth of the Christian West's imagination but also a discursive political tool that emerged alongside the development and expansion of the Italian ghetto system. The policies and politics of the Ghetto were then mobilized by Shakespeare's portrayal of Shylock, which carried forward an embedded blueprint for Jewish-Christian relations across centuries and geographies.

In the second essay, "Disruptive Strategies in Post-Shoah Versions of *The Merchant of Venice*," Michael Shapiro considers how Shylock, like the Ghetto, traveled across global stages from Shakespeare's time to the present moment. The essay's sweeping focus on the wide-ranging characterizations of Shylock across these productions—which, due to the sheer volume, benefit from a bird's-eye view—is complemented by Shapiro's robust analysis of the representational strategies used to account for Shylock's Jewishness following World War II. His analysis reveals how this traveling blueprint at once conjures forth the memory of the Venice Ghetto and reconstructs its outline in a new configuration of space and time. To borrow from Diana Taylor's framing of "performance": "Performances travel, challenging and influencing other performances. Yet they are, in a sense, always in situ: intelligible in the framework of the immediate environment and issues surrounding them. . . . [This is an] understanding of performance as simultaneously 'real' and 'constructed,' as practices that bring together what have historically been kept separate and discrete, supposedly free-standing, ontological, and epistemological discourses."[6] In this way, Shapiro shows that each post-Shoah performance of *The Merchant* must grapple with the ways Shakespeare's Shylock is both discursively connected to the collective traumas endured by Jewish communities across history and rooted to the site of the Venice Ghetto.

In their 2017 coedited collection *Wrestling with Shylock: Jewish Responses to "The Merchant of Venice,"* Shapiro and theater scholar Edna Nahshon explain: "*The Merchant of Venice*, which is inextricable from its extensive baggage of literary and theatrical interpretations, has been a flashpoint that activates the sensitivities, fears, memories, and hopes encompassed in the Jewish experience as a minority group within a larger, primarily Christian society. The Jewish wrestling with Shylock is therefore always reflective of a specific time and place."[7] Shapiro's essay extends this claim in a new direction by examining the novel adaptation techniques that bring post-Shoah contexts into contemporary performances of the play to address issues of social prejudice or racism. Whether it is the recentering of Shylock's story line or the substitution of his Jewishness for another ethnic identity, the recombinations of the plot of *The Merchant* become a blueprint for representing—and at times highlighting—enduring social and political conditions that have yet to be recognized or reconciled. They leave the audience asking, Who is Shylock today?

In the third essay, the late Clive Sinclair reflects on viewing Karin Coonrod's adaptation of *The Merchant in Venice* in the Ghetto for the five hundredth anniversary celebrations in 2016. As noted in the opening of this introduction, this staging of the play reconnects the two narratives that had previously been severed—*The Merchant* and that of the Ghetto—into a "creative collision" by examining the possibilities for Shylock's representation.[8] At the invitation of Bassi and Beit Venezia, Coonrod, director of the American company Compagnia de' Colombari, set out to workshop "The Shylock Project" on Isola San Giorgio in the summer of 2015, where the idea for the five-Shylock adaptation Sinclair describes was born.[9] Bassi's vision was to ensure that Coonrod did "not come to Venice to learn the right colour of Shylock's hat." He hoped instead that the staging would bring together the deep historical roots of the play in the Ghetto with the idea that cultural production in the contemporary space of the Ghetto is important to its future: "This international collective of performing artists has come to provoke a creative collision, one that addresses the ambivalence of the play and the place, one that unsettles its audience with Shylock's own words: 'I am not bound to please thee with my answers' (4.1.64). We hope that *The Merchant of Venice* could contribute to a renewed civic dimension of the Ghetto, based on a cross-cultural conversation that uses Shakespeare as a shared language."[10] As Shapiro notes in his essay, how Shylock is represented can and does change the meaning of any performance of *The Merchant of Venice*. In the article "Shylock, Remade in the Venice Ghetto," Coonrod explains this dilemma for the Compagnia de' Colombari to remake the play in the Ghetto: "Certainly, there have been many memorable performances of Shylock across the boards and on the screen. Was there a 21st-century wavelength that would allow this ancient man, this cantor of humanity, to tell us something? . . . The point was not to ignore Shylock's Jewishness, nor to divide his complex character, but to unlock and unveil the common humanity of his being. Shylock the Jew is also Shylock the immigrant, the Other, the stranger. True, a five-actor Shylock would demand more of its audience; but my hope was that the audience would find itself in Shylock. Of course, Shylock cannot be painted with a single brushstroke: The play takes us through his keen mind, his belief, his love, his sorrow, and his murderous rage."[11]

It is no coincidence, then, that these are the sentiments highlighted in Sinclair's review of the play in this collection, which first appeared in the *Times Literary Supplement* in October 2016. As he travels through Venice and the Ghetto to see five separate Shylock performances, Sinclair recalls the summary statements from the play's participants—Stephen Greenblatt and James Shapiro—that "any given production of *The Merchant* causes disquiet, especially when it takes place in the Ghetto."[12] The juxtaposition of the iconic play and the Jewish heritage site throw contrasting light on the scope of Jewish experiences in dialogue for the first time. The setting of the historic Ghetto cannot easily separate itself from the history of the Holocaust (especially given the seven-panel bronze monument to the victims added to the piazza in 1980) or the current conditions of global antisemitism, requiring the actual staging of *The Merchant in Venice* to include security guards stationed at the Ghetto's gates once more.

Through the play's tangled history, rooted in the Ghetto and mobilized by the adaptability of Shakespeare's work, we come to recognize the power of the literary blueprint. From the vantage point of memory studies, a blueprint encodes the social memory necessary for the reproduction of social relations and configurations that created the figure of Shylock. With Bassi's endeavor to take the literary blueprint back to the Ghetto and to reconstruct Shylock once again within this original space, he highlights the reciprocal relationship between the character and his environment. Returning to Bassi's question—"Can *The Merchant* in the Ghetto add a new critical layer?"—we present the reader with this grouping of essays to encourage engagement with the many layers that have come to mark both the iconic and imaginary figure of Shylock and the simultaneously concrete and symbolic space of the Ghetto. We ask that the reader discover what the blueprint of Shylock can offer in the contemporary context: What new readings are possible in the twenty-first century through the lens of "reading-in-place" and site-based memory work? Although a blueprint represents (abstractly) both a specific place and a moment in time, it also allows for the possibility of infinite reproduction of that site in other times and spaces. It is by nature portable and adaptable. In the context of the edited collection's concern with place-based memory, what does it mean to produce this particular work within the space of the Ghetto, recontextualizing the many layers of its history and the play's many productions? Does this symbolic or creative work have tangible effects on the future of the heritage site? In other words, does this type of artistic production encourage long-term investment in the form of recentering the Ghetto as "thinking machine,"[13] or does it simply create an experiential moment, another layer to be added to the collective memories that orbit the site?

NOTES

1. Hecht, introduction to Shaul Bassi, "Shylock in Venice: Staging Shakespeare in the Ghetto," lecture, University of California, Santa Barbara, June 6, 2016, https://www.uctv.tv/public-policy/search-details.aspx?showID=30593.
2. Bassi, "Shylock in Venice."
3. Harold Bloom, *Shylock* (New York: Chelsea House Publishers, 1991); Stephen Greenblatt, "Shakespeare's Cure for Xenophobia," *New Yorker*, July 3, 2017, https://www.newyorker.com/magazine/2017/07/10/shakespeares-cure-for-xenophobia.
4. Bassi quoted in Simon Worrall, "The Centuries-Old History of Venice's Jewish Ghetto," *Smithsonian Magazine*, November 6, 2015, https:/www.smithsonianmag.com/travel/venice-ghetto-jews-italy-anniversary-shaul-bassi-180956867.
5. Bassi, "Shylock in Venice."
6. Diana Taylor, *Archive and the Repertoire* (Durham, NC: Duke University Press, 2003), 3.
7. Edna Nahshon and Michael Shapiro, eds., *Wrestling with Shylock: Jewish Responses to "The Merchant of Venice"* (Cambridge: Cambridge University Press, 2017), xxii.
8. Bassi, "Shylock in Venice."
9. Karin Coonrod, "Shylock, Remade in the Venice Ghetto," *American Theatre*, September 12, 2017, https://www.americantheatre.org/2017/09/12/shylock-remade-in-the-venice-ghetto.
10. Bassi, "Shylock in Venice."
11. Coonrod, "Shylock, Remade."
12. Clive Sinclair, "The Ghetto of Venice," *TLS*, October 21, 2016, https://www.the-tls.co.uk/articles/freelance-766.
13. Shaul Bassi, "Shylock in the Thinking Machine: Civic Shakespeare and the Future of Venice," in *New Places: Shakespeare and Civic Creativity*, ed. Paul Edmondson and Ewan Fernie (London: Bloomsbury Arden Shakespeare, 2018), 161–78.

CHAPTER THREE

SOCIAL AND ECONOMIC DIMENSIONS OF ITALIAN JEWISH PUBLIC LIFE IN THE AGE OF THE GHETTO

ANDREA YAAKOV LATTES

The first section of this essay explores the fluctuating communal formations of the Jews in Italy during key moments of transition from the sixteenth to the eighteenth century. These moments pivot on the changing social contracts between Jews and Christians, most clearly codified in the creation and transformation of the Italian ghetto. Elsewhere in this volume, Chiara Camarda and Federica Ruspio trace the history of print culture as a way to show the evolving relationship between Venice and its Jewish community,[1] but here I focus on how the establishment of the world's first ghetto set the precedent for social contracts between Jews and Christians based on economic needs that were later exploited and expanded on by the Catholic Reformation and the Papal State. One of the more profound effects of the changing social contracts mapped in this essay is the evolution of economic stereotypes of Jews in Italy from bankers and moneylenders to merchants. The archetype of the Jewish banker becomes the prism through which we trace the reshaping of the map of the Jewish community.

In his classic book, Attilio Milano, a historian of Italian Jews, divides their history from the Renaissance to the French Revolution into two periods: he calls the first, 1500–1600, "the Age of Upheavals" (*l'età dei capovolgimenti*), and the second, 1600–1789, "the Age of Oppression" (*l'età dell'oppressione*).[2] This division not only accurately describes historical reality but also serves as a necessary prism through which to look at Jewish life in Italy during the period of discussion. Such a division has the advantage of providing a long-term vision, which enables us to determine the central lines of development that took place within Jewish society, to identify events that caused a change in the lifestyles of the Jews between the sixteenth and eighteenth centuries, and to indicate the permanent structures on which individual and social life were based. At the same time, it is clear that by focusing on the big picture and long-term patterns, we willfully neglect the individual events and unique details that belong to this history.[3]

The years between the late fifteenth and the sixteenth centuries are famous for the flourishing of Renaissance culture in Italy and the outbreak of the Christian Counter-Reformation. Parallel with these phenomena, however, were the upheavals that took place within Jewish society—changes that not only affected the lives of Jews but also shook the systemic relationship between them and the surrounding society. These events touched all aspects of life and radically changed the previously established routine so dramatically that the stereotypes established in the sixteenth century would not change until the French Revolution.

As a result, the period of the Renaissance and the Counter-Reformation became a turning point in the history of the Jews in Italy; they were times of uncertainty, leading historians to refer to them as "the Age of Upheavals." In contrast, the period from the seventeenth to the end of the eighteenth century—known in Italian history for the baroque and the Arcadian movements—did not present significant changes in Jewish social life, and the challenges faced by Jews seemed to be situated more in the cultural and intellectual spheres. Therefore, from this perspective, these days were the quiet that followed the storm. Nonetheless, we have to be accurate: by "quiet" we mean a sense of stability and a lack of substantial changes in Jewish social lifestyles, but certainly not in the souls of those people who were forced to spend their days within the locked walls of the ghetto.

THE NEED FOR JEWISH BANKERS: DEMOGRAPHIC TRENDS

Looking at the map of Jewish settlements and the dispersal of Jewish communities throughout the territory of the Italian peninsula and its adjacent islands, we notice that toward the end of the fifteenth century, most of the Jews were in the central and southern parts of the boot, on the islands of Sicily and Sardinia. Particularly in the regions of Puglia and Sicily, there were very old communities with a magnificent past and tradition of rabbinic yeshivot and cultural production.[4] In Sicily, there were five thousand Jews in both the cities of Palermo and Syracuse, more than in any other city in Italy. In other Sicilian cities, there were many Jews, in the order of thousands, so that on the entire island there were more than thirty-five thousand Jews.[5] In southern Italy too—in what was the kingdom of Naples—there were other ancient and rooted communities, with well-developed cultures, even if the number of inhabitants was smaller than in Sicily.

In contrast to southern Italy, in the center and north there were no large groups of Jews during this period. Some territories did not even allow Jews to settle. Where it was permitted, Jewish settlement in this part of the Italian peninsula was usually characterized by family units formed around a central figure of the banker—a Jew who gave out loans at interest—who received special permission from the authorities to live there. The result was that the Jews were scattered in different cities, often in small towns or even in villages, where banking services were needed. At this stage, they were not yet organized into communities. In any case, the number of Jews living in this part of Italy must have been small, and even in Rome, the Pope's capital, the Jewish population was no more than one thousand people in the early sixteenth century.[6]

During the first half of the sixteenth century, however, this pattern reversed itself completely. The first noticeable change that occurred in Jewish life in Italy dealt with demography and places of settlement. This phenomenon is reflected in the (forced) displacement of Jewish populations from the south to the center of Italy and from the center to the north; in the movement of other Jewish groups that came to Italy crossing the sea or the mountains; and in the relocation of settlements from one place to another. Over the course of several decades, old Jewish settlements with glorious pasts, like those in the southern part of the peninsula and on the islands, were completely dissolved, at the same time as new settlements were established, stabilized, and organized. The result of this process was a reshaping of the map of the Jewish presence in Italy. It is well known that this process had at least two main causes: the first is the above-mentioned demographic flow of moneylenders who started moving from the center to the north of Italy, a movement that began in the Middle Ages and established settlements in various places. These people settled wherever the authorities wanted their services as bankers and allowed their residence, and the Jewish community grew around the figure of the banker and on the basis of his rights defined in a special agreement between him and the ruler: the *condotta* or, in English, charter.[7] The second factor was a series of expulsions of Jews who lived in southern Italy and on the islands that completely eradicated the Jewish presence in those territories; throughout the period in question, from the mid-sixteenth century until the twentieth century, no Jews could be found there. At the end of the fifteenth century, the islands of Sicily and Sardinia were part of the Aragonese Spanish Crown, and as a result, when in 1492 King Ferdinand ordered the expulsion of all Jews from his country, this decree also applied to the inhabitants of the islands. Sicilian Jews in part migrated to Rome or to Thessaloniki, establishing special synagogues according to their custom, as well as to other places. A few years after this expulsion from the islands, a slow process of removing all Jews from the southern part of the peninsula began as well. Between 1510 and 1541, Jews were expelled from all of the lands of the kingdom of Naples, which sprawled across the southern region. By 1541, there were no remaining Jews in southern Italy.

Parallel with these movements, a demographic flow of Jews forced from other countries—Germany, Provence and France, North Africa, Spain, and Portugal—entered the peninsula. The movement of Spanish Jews, sometimes as conversos who sought to return to Judaism, began in the late fifteenth century and continued and intensified over the centuries that followed to the point that in many places, as time passed, they became the dominant ethnic group, such as in the communities of Livorno and Ferrara. In Rome, every Jew who came from outside Italy was nicknamed "ultramontani," that is, "those who came across the mountains," with no recognition of the difference between Sephardi and Ashkenazi. The only distinction was between local Italian Jews and everyone else. Differences based on origin existed elsewhere, too, as in Ferrara and Venice, but in these cases, the authorities distinguished between the more ancient, local nucleus—which usually included the Jews of Italian descent along with those of Ashkenazi origin—and the "nation" of the Sephardim.

These phenomena caused a number of interesting processes. The first and most noticeable was the transformation of Jewish settlements into heterogeneous groups, in which different sounds and languages could be heard: Yiddish, Italian, Spanish, and Portuguese. The homogeneous groups of local Jews, usually made up of a small number of close families, suddenly had to cope with the arrival of foreign Jews. Locals' responses ranged from fear of competition and loss of control, because of political and economic concerns, to anxiety about a potential decline in living conditions. The newcomers also subverted the preexisting demographic, psychological, and political balance in the places they arrived. The almost immediate result of this new situation was increased tensions and quarrels within the communities, first and foremost in large communities such as Rome and Venice, which brought political and public unrest. Initially, the new immigrants tried to build an independent public framework for themselves, which in several cases led to the establishment of special communities that existed parallel to those of the Italians.[8] A different process took place in Rome, as the "ultramontani" eventually united with the Italian community.[9] In this community, toward the end of the sixteenth century, the distribution of ethnic groups was 71.6 percent Italians, compared with 28.4 percent ultramontani, which in turn was divided into approximately 70 percent of the population claiming Sephardi origin and the rest identifying as Ashkenazi or French.[10]

In the end, the picture of the distribution of Italian Jewish communities in the late sixteenth century is absolutely different and completely opposite from the map of Jewish existence a century before. The sixteenth-century distribution, however, would remain stable for centuries to come, even to this day. Jews could not be found at all in the southern peninsula or on the islands, and those living in Italy were now concentrated in the most important cities and in the capitals of the states and duchies in the north and the center. In this period, the end of the Age of Upheavals, after the most famous ghetto had been established, the Jewish settlement in Rome had already doubled four times, reaching a population of almost four thousand people, similar to that in Venice. This level of Jewish population in the papal city remained stable over the next centuries, during the so-called Age of Oppression. Even the plague that broke out in the city in 1656 failed to undermine the demographic balance of the community, and until the end of what I will term the "Ghetto Age" (1555–1870), its population would not exceed a total of five thousand people.[11] Even at their peak, the communities in central and northern Italy failed to reach the size of the Sicilian communities.

Therefore, the total Jewish population in the various Italian communities around the year 1600 was between twenty-one and twenty-five thousand people.[12] Throughout the "Age of Oppression" until Napoleon's conquest at the end of the eighteenth century, the entire Jewish population of Italy would not exceed twenty-five thousand people. In the city of Venice itself, the Jewish population never exceeded five thousand, which it achieved in its heyday in the first half of the seventeenth century.[13] In the city of Florence, however, there were around five hundred Jews at the end of the sixteenth century, a number that remained unchanged until the beginning of the eighteenth century when the population gradually reached one thousand people by the century's end. In Mantua, another famous Jewish community, the Jewish population never exceeded 2,400. In sum, in 1700 only five communities in all of Italy had more than one thousand Jewish inhabitants: Rome, Venice, Ferrara, Mantua, and Reggio Emilia. The Jewish populations of four other communities numbered between five hundred and one thousand members: Turin, Verona, Padua, and Florence. Other communities were even smaller, the Jewish population numbering only in the hundreds or dozens of residents.[14]

The demographic and social processes described so far have been among the key factors that ultimately led to the consolidation of Jewish communities in northern Italy. However, it took a long time for the groups of Jews that gathered around the figure of the moneylender to form communities that were able to create regulations, organizational rules, and their own institutions. Only in the first half of the sixteenth century did the process of designing public life and internal governmental institutions begin within these communities, including an internal process of enacting special and interesting legislation known as "the Banker's Laws."

THE BANKER'S LAWS: THE CONSOLIDATION OF COMMUNITIES

In terms of Italian Jewish public life, the sixteenth century represents a turning point. The many changes that took place in the period between the late fifteenth and early seventeenth centuries led to the development of interesting political and social processes. Here, however, we must distinguish between two different dimensions of social and political processes: one dimension is the internal political process developed within the framework of Jewish society, whereas the other includes the systemic relationship between the Jewish community and the general public. The political processes that took place within the framework of Jewish public life in Italy were enacted through the legislation of regulations in each of the Jewish communities—legislation meant to regulate activities and to determine the nature of administrative institutions, as well as the nature of holding public roles. This phenomenon of outlining internal regulations, one of the most important processes in Jewish political thinking, has been defined by Daniel Elazar as the "constitutionalization" of the Jewish community, a process of "constitutional making," and we should therefore consider this moment as a turning point in the history of the Jewish community.[15] These documents were produced only when the inhabitants of the Jewish settlement in a given place began to develop their political consciousness and had the ability to create an organized Jewish community.[16] This process reflects the evolution of political thinking that took place in this period not only within Jewish society but also more widely in Italian society. In addition, these laws sometimes led to the consolidation of Jewish societal structure with various layers and different groupings, a structure that has remained intact for centuries. Moreover, community regulations were compiled by Jews for Jews with almost no interference on the part of the authorities, an important point in the history of Jewish community organizations.[17]

The most important example illustrating the evolution of these processes occurred in Rome, where the arrival of new Jewish immigrants, a process previously described, caused friction between the existing Jewish population and the new arrivals. These quarrels arose mainly because of attempts by original residents to maintain hegemony and control over the community's activities and economy; they opposed the efforts of the new inhabitants to take part in leadership roles or to obtain appropriate representation in its institutions and economic life. These conflicts resulted in the urgent need to find a solution to satisfy both parties' wishes. The answer was found in the drafting of a community constitution, with the purpose of establishing from the start the rules of the political game within the Jewish community, the composition of their administrative institutions, and the process of electing various positions, thus opening opportunities for the integration of Jews of non-Italian origin. This constitution, more commonly known as "Daniele da Pisa's regulations"—named after the banker who was appointed to compose them—was introduced in 1524 and remained the basis of the political life of the community for nearly three hundred years.[18] Even the enclosure of the Jews within the ghetto walls thirty years later did not change the structure of the Jewish community that was shaped by these regulations.[19] In this way, the drafting of a constitution was a powerful political instrument capable of solving, if only partially, various conflicts within Jewish society.

Daniele da Pisa's regulations were probably the first constitutional document enacted by any Jewish community in Italy. They paved the way for a wave of such documents enacted during the Age of Upheavals in most of the communities in the peninsula's north and center. Here, the process was usually slightly different from what we saw in Rome, the oldest community in Italy. The groups of Jews who settled in these places, following the figure of the banker who lent money and signed the *Condotta* documents, did not initially create real communities. These were the nuclei for future settlements, usually administered by the banker himself or by the heads of households, and there was no need to establish representative institutions.[20] However, over time, as the Jewish community grew and could no longer be managed at the family level, the need arose to enact laws to establish governmental institutions, both from legal and organizational perspectives.[21] The purpose of establishing community institutions in these cases was to achieve favorable conditions and to identify common interests for Jewish residents, such as centralized payment of taxes to the authorities. As a result, the figure of the Jewish banker, who had previously held in his hands the very right to Jewish settlement, lost his formal control over Jewish institutions; the responsibility passed, at least officially, to the community, who from then on elected representatives to manage community institutions.[22] This phenomenon was also reflected in a change on the part of the authorities' attitude toward Jewish groups, who from then on no longer needed to appeal to the banker but rather to the community's leaders. For instance, in the Duchy of Modena as early as the beginning of the seventeenth century, when the last condotta between authorities and Jewish bankers had been signed, the demand for tax payments, which until then had always been directed toward the bankers, was instead addressed to the elected community leaders.[23] New documents were created to reflect these changes, shaping the structure of internal government institutions and the nature of other activities in each community, just as they had been in Rome; in most cases, these documents remained in effect until the early nineteenth century. Consequently, as regulations were introduced into a community, Jewish community institutions were founded and organized.[24] Following Rome, a constitution was promulgated in Verona in 1539, in Mantua in 1539 and again in 1587, in Florence in 1572, and in Ferrara in 1573.[25] In Venice, regulations were proclaimed in 1603 and were subsequently renewed in 1624, and in the city of Pisa they were issued in 1636 and finally in Livorno in 1655.[26]

An entirely different dimension of Jewish public and political life in Italy during this period is that of contact between the Jewish and the Christian societies. Within this context, the system of relationships between the community and government institutions progressed. Thus a major turning point occurred during the sixteenth century that undermined and changed the preexisting situation while simultaneously consolidating new lifestyles that remained in effect over the course of the following centuries. Beginning in the sixteenth century, these relationships were influenced by the changes in the Catholic Church's policy toward Jews, which followed the religious movement of the Counter-Reformation. Although this policy was formulated by church authorities and therefore primarily implemented in the territory of the Papal State, it had a profound influence on the other Christian rulers in Italy and was eventually implemented in their territories. In effect, this strategy included a number of steps to be taken by church leaders and civilian heads and eventually became an expression of both the aggravation and hostility toward the Jewish community and the detachment and separation from it. The adoption of these steps was accelerated by the establishment of the House of the Converts throughout Italy, the burning of the Talmud in Rome in 1553, and the issuance in 1555 of the famous papal seal *Cum Nimis Absurdum*, which led to the establishment of a new type of enforced ghetto, in Rome and then throughout Italy.

Unlike the Venetian Ghetto, established in 1516, the formation of the House of Converts, or Domus Conversorum, was the result of the Catholic Counter-Reformation movement, an initiative of the Spanish priest Ignatius of Loyola, founder of the Jesuit Order. Its purpose was to educate and convince unbelievers to convert to Catholicism and was primarily aimed at Jews. The institution's damage to Jewish communities, however, proved to be not only religious and social but also—and especially—economic: it was up to the synagogues to fund and maintain, and they were obliged to pay a yearly special tax.[27] The idea generated great interest, and the first initiative was implemented in Rome. Afterward, Houses of the Converts were founded throughout Italy. In Rome, the institution was established in 1543; in Bologna, in 1568; in Mantua in 1574; and in Ferrara in 1584.[28] The appearance of this new institution was the forerunner of the establishment of ghettos for all Jews a few years later, and like the ghettos, it remained active and functioning until the nineteenth century.

The most significant change in Church policy, however, was taken by Pope Paul IV when, after being elected pope in 1555, he issued a papal bull that began with the words *Cum Nimis Absurdum*, "because it is absurd," in which he defined the boundaries and definitions of Jewish life within Christian society.[29] The document established fourteen bans, some new and some old, which from then on would apply to Jews. Among these rules was that all Jews must have their residence in only one street of the city, where only one synagogue was allowed, and must wear a yellow identifying mark on their clothes. The Jewish population received news of this constitution with total disbelief and hoped that it would not last long; when they actually had to face this new reality, they were thrown into crisis.[30] In fact, all the decrees that the church tried to impose on the Jews—not always successfully—starting with the Councils of the Lateran issued in the late twelfth and early thirteenth centuries, were now considered compulsory. The guiding principle of the decrees was to create a physical and spiritual separation between Jewish and Christian citizens and to curtail any attempt at social contact or conversation between the two populations.[31] It appears that contact between the two social groups had become quite frequent by then: there were Christians who used to attend Jewish receptions, eat kosher food, and even participate in prayers in the synagogues.[32] The regulations therefore translated to the removal of Jews from civilized society, defined as those belonging to the Catholic faith. This distinction was certainly not a new one. Christians saw themselves as "enlightened," in the sense that they succeeded in seeing the "true light" of Jesus, as opposed to the Jews, who were considered "blind." Therefore, it is not surprising that the most famous decree was the prohibition of Jews from living next door to Christians and their obligation to live on a separate street, enclosed by walls—an arrangement that would later be dubbed a "ghetto."[33]

Following the issuance of this papal bull, the church not only changed its method of interaction with Jews but also significantly modified its way of thinking and theology. Pope Paul IV changed the language that Church leaders in previous centuries had used to try to influence and persuade Jews to accept Christianity, declaring that henceforth Jews must be treated strictly and with degrading discipline. According to the same bull, as long as the Jews remained "blind in their error," they must bend as inferior beings to the Christians; when Jews violated these rules, they committed a criminal offense of a political nature, an act of rebellion, and must be punished by the secular arm of any Christian ruler.[34] These decrees had legal significance and an immediate effect on the territories of the Papal State; they subsequently served as guidelines for other Christian princes and rulers. The establishment of the ghetto in Rome, and then in other cities, was one of the key factors that shaped the relationships between Jews and Christians from the end of the sixteenth to the beginning of the nineteenth century. Indeed, by the beginning of the seventeenth century, eleven ghettos had been founded in Italy, located either in the center of the peninsula, in the Papal States and other small duchies, or in the Veneto area around the city of Venice. A century later, there were already twenty-nine ghettos in the northern and central regions of Italy.[35] By the end of the Age of Oppression in 1797, there were forty-one ghettos in the country. Many did not contain more than five hundred Jews, and some did not reach even one hundred people; the general Jewish population was nearly twenty-five thousand.[36] The policy and its restrictions formulated during the sixteenth century would remain unchanged for centuries to come.

POWERFUL BANKERS AND MARGINALIZED JEWS: SHIFTING SOCIAL STRUCTURES WITHIN THE GHETTOS

Similar to the demographic and political picture we examined before, the blueprint for social formations largely designed during the sixteenth century did not change significantly until the end of the eighteenth century. The same political and social community structure built on stratification and social hierarchy in which community governance was in the hands of taxpaying male family members led to the formation of large groups standing at the margins of social and political life. Here, we include mainly two groups of people: the poor and women. It should be noted, though, that such a social model was not unique to Jewish society but was widespread in European society in general during the Ancien Régime. Nonetheless, we can ask these questions: What groups composed Jewish society, and what types of hierarchy existed? What was the place of the women, the poor, and the marginalized in this society? What did they do in their free time for entertainment? Historians have raised these questions only in recent years. Within these social structures, defined by the consolidation of the constitutional documents of the Jewish communities, there was no social mobility. This meant that the main functions of the community, both political and social, and sometimes even religious, were undertaken by wealthy men. One should not think, however, that the poor and women had no role or place within Jewish society.

In contrast to the structures existing in European society as a whole, where social status was determined at birth, social stratification within the Jewish community was already built on wealth owing to constraints imposed on Jews by authorities. In other words, the leadership of the community was neither in the hands of nobles nor determined by family ties but controlled by wealthy lenders. A number of registers belonging to the various communities that have been published so far demonstrate that in most Jewish communities, the poor did not have the right to vote. As a result, the communities were oligarchic. In Rome, for example, Daniele da Pisa's constitution outlined a social structure—probably one that had already existed—that included four levels: the bankers, the wealthy, the middle class, and the poor. According to the regulations, only the bankers, the wealthy, and the middle class could participate in the political life of the community, but in practice, the control was almost exclusively in the hands of the bankers.

If the poor did not have the opportunity to participate in public life or to play key roles in community affairs, this group's size gave it a special weight in community life. The poorer class was actually the largest in the community, totaling nearly three-fourths of the Jewish population. Moreover, community leaders were concerned with issues pertaining to the poor, as expressed in the documents of the Roman community. "Poor" was defined as a married man who owned property that was worth less than fifty *scudi* and was consequently exempt from declaring his income and paying taxes to the community.[37] However, even this social group was not uniform but divided into two parts: those who had at least something to eat and those who depended on supplies from the community or one of the organizations that operated within it. These supplies usually included not only basic food products but also matzah for Passover, clothing and lessons for children, and dowries for brides about to be married.

As many scholars point out, a number of factors led to the formation of such a large group of poor people, one of them being the will of the authorities and popes to oppress the Jews through taxation. But there were also other objective causes, such as the striking population increase following the movement of Jews who joined the community preceding the ghetto's foundation and did not contribute to its wealth. After them, another wave of Jews arrived in Rome following their expulsion from the Papal State in 1569.

If women held a marginal position in political life and in the management of community affairs in Rome, this was not always the case elsewhere. Women were certainly not restricted to staying at home; on the contrary, some of them had their own property and were skilled in financial investment, crafts, and commerce.[38] The most famous example of such an active woman in the mid-sixteenth century, with business initiative and even international connections, was Dona Gracia Mendes, who was of Iberian origin but, like many other conversos, lived in the cities of Venice and Ferrara for many years.[39] In Rome, too, women were active in various kinds of trade, invested and borrowed money, and even filed lawsuits against one another, and widows had to pay taxes on behalf of the entire family.[40] However, these examples should not be considered exceptional cases, since at the end of the sixteenth century, one-fourth of the debenture holders of the papal treasury, the *Luoghi di Monte,* were women who did not inherit but purchased them.[41]

Even within the rigid social context of the Jewish community, some women held public positions. Occasionally, brotherhoods, which operated within the community specifically to help poor girls and especially to provide them with a dowry, were led by women themselves. In Rome, there were four different foundations that gave dowries to poor girls; the women who ran these organizations were called *parnasesse,* or "managers." Their task was to go around the community collecting donations for their cause and then distribute the money to the girls who needed a dowry. In addition to deciding how to collect donations, the parnasesse had the power to take steps to prevent competition from other women and even to punish them to the point of expelling them from the community.[42] They could choose as well the manner of distributing the money for the dowry, although a male treasurer held it. One of the most interesting results of such a system was that details such as the size of the dowry that each girl would receive were subject to the consideration of the various treasurers, and even the date of the bride's marriage was determined according to the budgetary constraints of those foundations. The community leaders elected the parnasesse for this role, and their nomination was apparently not limited to a fixed term; new parnasesse were appointed as veterans passed away or grew too old.[43]

Within the social life of the community, women also, upon payment, accompanied the dead to the cemetery; they eulogized and grieved the deceased and then even participated in the seven days of mourning, the thirty days, and the rituals for the first anniversary of the death. There were also women who, in a professional way, would mourn the destruction of the Temple on Tishà Be'Av. These practices were quite common and continued to exist despite the attempt of community leaders to abolish them, fearing that the Gentiles would ridicule them: at the time, there was a perception that women should not attract too much attention, especially not from Gentiles. The efforts of community leaders to prevent women from walking the streets alone or simply from emerging excessively from the home are well known. They also tried to limit women's movement in the streets to specific and predetermined purposes, proof of which can be found in the ordinance of the Roman community leaders that forbade brides about to marry from traveling in a carriage as a part of the wedding ceremony under threat of excommunication.[44] Indeed, the authorities supported such efforts, too, as they issued a decree prohibiting women from wandering the streets of the city half an hour after sunset.[45]

The most characteristic social institution of the period between the Renaissance and the Modern Age was the brotherhood in its various forms and evolutions. This institution, which remained in existence for centuries, occasionally served as an organization for helping the needy and providing for the poor as well as a place for social gatherings, religious cults, performances of plays, and readings of literature. The idea of founding this kind of association was not of Jewish invention, as similar institutions flourished in Italian society in an earlier period: "Since the end of the eleventh century, we can find urban artists uniting in fraternities (*Caritates, fraternitates*) on the basis of their profession.

It seems that the associations relating to commerce or religion formed around churches and monasteries that served as a model. Indeed, the first craftsmen associations excelled in religious acts of kindness and charity. At the same time, however, they undoubtedly fulfilled a need for economic protection."[46] Thus, organizations in the form of brotherhoods, literary academies, and sometimes even synagogues constituted social frameworks that provided entertainment and opportunities for gatherings for the entire population.[47] These organizations did not merely copy an institution from the surrounding culture but also added an original Jewish dimension. Following the proliferation in the study of Kabbalah renewed in Safed, in the Land of Israel (located in present-day Israel), brotherly societies were formed throughout Italy to pray and read Kabbalah-based poems together or to read excerpts from the Jewish mystical literature contained in the Zohar and the Kabbalah. These societies, which went by various names such as Hadashim la-Bekarim (News Every Morning) and Shomerim la-boker (Morning Watchers), allowed for the blossoming of special prayer books, the Tiqqunim, which were intended for designated periods of the year and were based on Kabbalistic concepts.

This phenomenon of establishing new associations within Italian society gained momentum during the sixteenth century, due perhaps to epidemics and droughts leading to the mass movement of peasants from villages to towns and to the formation of groups of poor immigrants in need of assistance.[48] Indeed, one of the main motives for the founding of mutual aid societies was linked to the fact that there was no institution or organization to support the needy, and as a result, a strong need existed to establish institutions focused on social and educational aid.[49] Thus the public authority, that is, all government institutions, including the Jewish community, did not consider it their task to provide social services to members. For example, Daniele da Pisa's regulations, which accurately defined the various obligations of the Jewish community of Rome, were not at all concerned with providing for the social needs of its inhabitants. Such services included, in particular, providing assistance and aid for the needy; food to the poor; medical help for those who could not afford it; assistance for girls to get married; and support for an educational system intended primarily for the lower classes. The failure to define the functions required of the public organization (in this case the Jewish community, but that could also be the state or city authorities) stems from a way of thinking at the time, a kind of zeitgeist, according to which government institutions not only refrained from providing these services but also did not see this as their task at all.[50] For example, a fierce debate occurred in the Senate Republic of Venice regarding the throngs of poor in the city. It was then decided that the parishes (i.e., the neighborhood churches), not state institutions, would be tasked with collecting donations for the poor and taking care of their needs.[51] Clearly, aid to the poor was perceived as a religious commandment, not a social need. Therefore, the Jewish community of Rome, even when facing an urgent need to assist the poor, did not take on this responsibility; however, its leaders gathered to establish a specific organization to resolve these issues.[52]

At the same time, other factors also contributed to the foundation of the associations, and many scholars have addressed this interesting aspect. The great Belgian historian Henri Pirenne hypothesized that the economic factor was dominant and decisive in this development.[53] Other historians emphasize that the founding of fraternities within Jewish society stems from religious tradition, the imperative to uphold the precept of charity (*Gemilut Hasadim*), and consequently from the people's desire to give alms as a religious commandment.[54] However, there was a catch: precisely to fulfill its desire to uphold the religious commandment of charity, the ruling elite needed the existence of the poor, so the concern arose that, because of this need, leadership had an interest in preserving the existing social structure.[55] In spite of the reasons outlined above, other historians view the establishment of the ghetto and the need for the existence of social life as the main factors in the founding of the associations.[56]

Either way, even in the Jewish society, as in the Italian society, during this period there was a special momentum behind the formation of various social brotherhoods and associations. In Mantua, for instance, there were five operating associations at the end of the sixteenth century; about 150 years later, more than twenty existed.[57] Similarly, in Rome, nine associations were active in 1617, whereas in the mid-nineteenth century, there were close to forty.[58]

In addition to organizations focused on helping those in need, others organized for the social purposes of learning together, reading poetry and plays, and even acting and singing. In some of these groups, learning was only one of their activities—and not the main one—and they unofficially focused on social entertainment and even eating and drinking together.[59] The most famous of such organizations operated in the ghettos of Venice and Mantua. For example, in 1628 within the Venice Ghetto, a special music academy was founded whose initiators were Jewish musicians and singers, and it organized concerts twice a week, where the heads of the community and its wealthy members gathered.[60] Even in the Roman ghetto, the Italian ghetto with the worst economic and cultural conditions, literary academies were established and theatrical plays were put on the stage for public enjoyment.[61]

BANKERS, MONEYLENDERS, AND MERCHANTS: TRANSFORMING THE IMAGE OF THE ITALIAN JEWS

In the economic sphere, we can point out two major developments that occurred in Italian Jewish life during the period under consideration. The first development, during the Age of Upheavals, uniquely concerns the place of Jews within Italian society: the decline of the historical profession of moneylending and the slow disappearance of moneylenders. The second development was not unique to the Jewish population but a general phenomenon affecting all inhabitants of the peninsula: the continual deterioration of the economic situation and living conditions. This situation, however—which cannot be isolated to a specific century but was gradual and continued throughout this period—had a significant impact on Jews given their social and legal status and the unique system of taxation that applied only to them.

As previously described, moneylending was one of the most important occupations for Jews for centuries, beginning in the Middle Ages. Thanks to moneylenders, many Jewish settlements and communities were founded in northern Italy. It is no coincidence that the character of the Jewish moneylender became an antisemitic stereotype, a figure that characterized and identified all Jews. However, in the transitional period leading to the late fifteenth and early sixteenth centuries, this profession was already under threat. The main causes may have been the anti-Jewish propaganda of the Franciscan monks and the foundation of the Monti di pietà, pawnbrokers who operated a charity.[62] Indeed, the profession of the moneylender had slowly faded away, and Jews moved into different commercial activities, a transition that occurred under different circumstances and at different times. Here too, however, it is possible to highlight a few turning points. The distinct stages of this passage are reflected in the many changes in the attitude of the authorities toward Jewish bankers, which began with the emergence of a new trend: Jews were invited to come and settle in a territory not as bankers but as merchants. At the same time, there was a decline in the renewals of the *Condotte* for bankers until the authorities imposed decrees to reduce or ban the profession. There are many examples: in all of the Tuscan state, which included the cities of Florence and Pisa, moneylending was totally banned as early as 1570.[63] In Padua, Jewish banks closed in 1547, and in Verona, in 1548.[64] During this period, even in the Duchy of Mantua, authorities for the first time prohibited Jews from working in this field. Ten years later, however, they allowed the reopening of a limited number of banks, and the profession was completely eliminated only during Austrian rule in 1770.[65] In the city of Modena, which was an independent duchy belonging to the Este family, the last agreement—the Condotta signed by the authorities and a Jewish banker—was made in 1631, but moneylending was completely prohibited by the duke's order only in June 1767.[66] Even in the Piedmont region, after 1624, no other Condotta with the Jewish bankers was renewed.[67] This process, however, would reach a turning point on October 30, 1682, when Pope Innocent XI issued an injunction prohibiting Jews living in the Papal States from earning a living from this profession, thereby eliminating it.[68] This ended the theological discussion about the nature of lending with interest, which had lasted for centuries within the Catholic Church. More than that, through this prohibition, one of the unique professions of the Jews formally came to an end, against their will. It had sustained them for five hundred years, almost becoming a component of their identity.

After Jewish banking was eliminated and they were barred from all other professions except medicine, the main occupation available for Jews was commerce, sometimes on a large scale but more often on a small scale, even peddling.[69] During the sixteenth century, Jewish businesses not related to banking expanded, at the expense of the moneylenders, and began to replace them, gaining status within Jewish society. One example, serving as a hallmark of the social importance of merchants, is that in 1511, Duchy of Mantua authorities recognized the "Università of the Jews" as a confederated Jewish body, and gave a position to the "merchants" in the tax assessors' committee.[70] However, the central document that directed Jews toward engaging in commerce is the famous bull of Pope Paul IV *Cum Nimis Absurdum,* which states that Jews should not trade food or products consumed for sustenance but only deal with used clothing.[71] Thus Jews in Rome were forced for centuries to engage in trade and crafts related to the textile industry, such as trading in fabrics and clothing, sewing, wool processing, mattress making, and linen rentals.[72] This policy, which was generated by members of the church, also affected the course of rulers throughout Italy. However, in the other ghettos, the situation of the Jews was somewhat better: at times they were allowed to engage in a wider variety of crafts in the context of the ghetto and to register as professional guilds. For example, for the Jews of Modena, it was possible to engage in any kind of trade or craft inside the ghetto's walls.[73] In Florence, the majority of Jews in the early seventeenth century dealt with commerce or crafts related to tailoring or wool processing, but some people were able to enroll in professional urban guilds for wool workers, silk workers, and doctors.[74]

As was previously mentioned, the basis for the issuance of invitations to Jews to settle in a given city slowly changed. The authorities no longer invited moneylenders but rather merchants, mostly Portuguese conversos. The special rights and exemptions from taxation and persecution were now granted "to the Levantines, the Greeks, the Turks, and the Jews," as stated, for example, in an invitation issued by the Duke of Tuscany, Cosimo I, in 1551. In this regard, Cosimo was not the first; he relied on precedents provided in similar documents that had been published elsewhere, like in Venice, whereby foreign merchants were invited to settle and conduct their business.[75] The most famous example is the constitution issued by the Duke of Tuscany, Ferdinando I, on June 10, 1593, meant to invite merchants to settle within the city and establish Livorno's free port, the "Livornina."[76] Two years later, the duke issued another letter, addressed to all "the Jews, Ashkenazi and Italian, who previously lived in the Duchy of Milan, and other French, Polish, Levantines of Thessaloniki, Greeks . . . because we want to encourage foreigners to come and do business and trade in our city of Pisa and in the port of Livorno."[77] However, the business of trading in the Duchy of Tuscany was not the exclusive activity of the ex-conversos but also of the Italian Jewish families, most of them former bankers, who switched to commercial activities and, for that reason, were invited by the ruler to settle in the city of Pisa.[78] Of course, this new tendency, too, to invite merchants rather than moneylenders, spread throughout Italy, and there are many examples. The Piedmont dukes tried, more than once, to invite Jewish merchants to settle in the port of Nice, starting first with an attempt by the ruler Emanuele Filiberto in 1572 and then again in 1648 with King Carlo Emanuele.[79] When, in 1652, the Duke of Modena Francesco I d'Este invited merchants to inhabit his territory, he could rely on the precedent set by other Italian rulers who had issued similar regulations.[80]

The second trend that developed in this period was increased poverty in most Jewish communities in Italy. This process, however, was the result of a more general phenomenon of the deterioration of the entire Italian economy and the loss of its commercial centrality. Consequently, there was a heavier and more pressing taxation of Jews on the part of the authorities. Italy's economic deterioration has been widely studied by various scholars, such as Gino Luzzatto and Carlo Cipolla.[81]

Tracing the historical evolution of the Jewish experience in Italy through the lens of the Jewish banker exposes the nuances of a period often characterized as the "calm," which is more accurately a time of several important shifts within Jewish communities that had lasting influence on how Jews were perceived globally—from Italy to Shakespeare's London. Furthermore, these stereotypes became the embedded archetype informing much of the Western imagination about Jewish-Christian relationships to this day.

NOTES

1. See chaps. 1 and 2, respectively.
2. Attilio Milano, *Storia degli Ebrei in Italia* (Turin: Einaudi, 1963), index.
3. The historian who conceived and wrote about the need for a historical view from a long-term perspective was Fernand Braudel. This view complements rather than replaces the need for archival research on individual documents, a division similar to the one economists make between microeconomics and macroeconomics, between household and business activity as opposed to the state's dealings with large financial systems, national products, and banking. See Braudel, "Histoire et Sciences sociales: La longue durée," *Annales: Economies, Societes, Civilisations* 13 (1958): 725–53.
4. See Milano, *Storia degli Ebrei*, 167–79.
5. Milano, 179. See also Attilio Milano, "La Consistenza Numerica degli Ebrei di Sicilia al Momento della Cacciata," *La Rassegna Mensile di Israel* 20 (1954): 16–24.
6. Ariel Toaff, *Ghetto Roma ba-me'ah ha-16* (Ramat Gan, Israel: Universitat Bar-Ilan, 1984), 40.
7. There is a wide literature on this topic. See, among others, Attilio Milano, "I Primordi del Prestito Ebraico in Italia," *La Rassegna Mensile di Israel* 19 (1953): 275–80; Vittore Colorni,

"Prestito Ebraico e Comunità Ebraiche nell'Italia Centrale e Settentrionale," *Rivista di Storia del Diritto Italiano* 8 (1935): 1–55; and Ariel Toaff, "Banchieri Cristiani e Prestatori Ebrei?," in *Storia d'Italia*, ed. Corrado Vivanti, vol. 11, *Gli Ebrei in Italia* (Turin: Giulio Einaudi, 1996): 267–87.

8. Aron di Leone Leoni, *La Nazione Ebraica Spagnola e Portoghese negli Stati Estensi* (Rimini, Italy: Luisè, 1992), 149.
9. See Ariel Toaff, "The Jewish Communities of Catalonia, Aragon, and Castile in 16th-Century Rome," in *The Mediterranean and the Jews: Banking, Finance, and International Trade (16th–18th Centuries)*, ed. Ariel Toaff and Simon Schwarzfuchs (Ramat Gan, Israel: Bar-Ilan University Press, 1989), 249–70.
10. A. Toaff, *Ghetto Roma*, 36–39.
11. A. Toaff, 39–40; Eugenio Sonnino, "Di qui Cominciò Qualche Terrore Considerabile nella Città di Roma: Popolazione e Sanità nel Secolo XVII," in *Scienza e Miracoli nell'arte del '600: Alle Origini della Medicina Moderna*, ed. Sergio Rossi (Milan: Electa, 1988), 60–69.
12. Alan Charles Harris, "La Demografia del Ghetto in Italia (1516–1797 circa)," supplement, *La Rassegna Mensile di Israel* 33, no. 1 (1967): 1–68.
13. Harris, "Demografia del Ghetto," 9, 10.
14. See the maps in Harris, 62–64.
15. On this topic, see Daniel J. Elazar, ed., *Constitutionalism: The Israeli and American Experiences* (Lanham, MD: University Press of America, 1990), 3–47, and Daniel J. Elazar and Stuart A. Cohen, *The Jewish Polity: Jewish Political Organization from Biblical Times to the Present* (Bloomington: Indiana University Press, 1985).
16. On the origin and development of the Mantua community, see Vittore Colorni, "Le Magistrature Maggiori della Comunità Ebraica di Mantova," in *Judaica Minora*, ed. Vittore Colorni (Milan: A. Giuffrè, 1983), 257–327. See also Shlomo Simonsohn, "La Condizione Giuridica degli Ebrei nell'Italia Centrale e Settentrionale," in Vivanti, *Storia d'Italia*, 11:116–20.
17. Andrea Yaakov Lattes, "Aspetti Politici ed Istituzionali delle Comunità Ebraiche in Italia nel Cinque-Seicento," *Zakhor* 2 (1998): 21–37.
18. Attilio Milano, "I 'Capitoli' di Daniel da Pisa e la Comunità di Roma," *La Rassegna Mensile di Israel* 10 (1935): 410–26.
19. Compare this to what Simonson writes about the city of Mantua, which during the seventeenth and eighteenth centuries indicated a lack of social struggle within the community. On the other hand, the social order that developed in the late sixteenth century maintained its power in the following centuries as well. See Shlomo Simonsohn, *History of the Jews in the Duchy of Mantua*, 2 vols. (Jerusalem: Kiriath Sefer, 1963), 2:380–81.
20. Robert Bonfil, *Gli ebrei in Italia nell'Epoca del Rinascimento* (Florence: Sansoni, 1991), 160–67. For the Florence case, see Stefanie B. Siegmund, "From Tuscan Households to Urban Ghetto" (PhD diss., Jewish Theological Seminary of America, 1995), 57–63; for Mantua, see Simonsohn, *History of the Jews*, 1:223.
21. The growth of the population as a major factor in restructuring and building institutions of the Jewish community is Salo Baron's claim in his classic book *The Jewish Community* (Philadelphia: Jewish Publication Society of America, 1942), 2:23 and the following.
22. See Simonsohn, *History of the Jews*, 1:233–34, and Lattes, *Aspetti Politici*, 25.
23. Leoni, *La Nazione Ebraica*, 157.
24. On this topic, see Lattes, *Aspetti Politici*, 24.
25. For Verona, see Isaiah Sonne, "Avne` binyan le-toledoth ha-yehudim be-Verona," *Kovetz 'Al Yad* 3, no. 13 (1940): 151; regarding Mantua, see Colorni, *Le Magistrature Maggiori*, 273, 293–94, and also Simonsohn, *History of the Jews*, 1:236–55; for Florence, see Umberto Cassuto, "I Più Antichi Capitoli del Ghetto di Firenze," pts. 1 and 2, *Rivista Israelitica* 9 (1912): 203–11 and

10 (1912): 32–40, 71–80, and also Siegmund, *From Tuscan Households*, 57–63; and for Ferrara, see Abramo Pesaro, *Memorie Storiche sulla Comunità Israelitica Ferrarese* (Bologna: Forni Editore, 1967), 30–31.

26. For regulations in Venice, see Daniel Carpi, "Taqqanoneha shel Qehillat Venetsi'ah, 1591–1607," in *Galut ahar Gola, Mehqarim be-toledoth 'am Israel muggashim le-Professor Hayyim Beinhart* (Jerusalem: Ben-Zvi Institute, 1988), 451–60, and Daniel Carpi, "Le 'Convenzioni' degli Anni 1624 e 1645 tra le Tre 'Nazioni' della Comunità di Venezia," in *Shlomo Simonsohn Jubilee Volume: Studies on the History of the Jews in the Middle Ages and Renaissance Period* (Tel Aviv: Tel Aviv University, 1993), 30–40; for Pisa, see Renzo Toaff, *La Nazione Ebrea a Livorno e a Pisa: 1591–1700* (Firenze: Olschki, 1990), 500–515, and 555–68 for Livorno.
27. On this topic, see Andrea Yaakov Lattes, "Gli Ebrei di Ferrara e le Imposte per i Catecumeni," *La Rassegna Mensile di Israel* 65 (1999): 41–54; Luciano Allegra, *Identità in Bilico: Il Ghetto Ebraico di Torino nel Settecento* (Turin: S. Zamorani, 1996); and Giuseppe Sermoneta, *Ratto della Signora Anna del Monte Trattenuta ai Catecumeni Tredici Giorni dalli 6 fino alli 19 Maggio Anno 1749* (Rome: Carucci, 1989).
28. Regarding the Houses of the Converts, see Allegra, *Identità in Bilico*. On the specific case of Bologna, see Antonella Campanini, "L'identità Coatta: La Casa dei Catecumeni a Bologna," in *Verso l'Epilogo di una Convivenza*, ed. Maria G. Muzzarelli (Florence: Giuntina, 1996), 155–76.
29. On this subject see Kenneth R. Stow, *Catholic Thought and Papal Jewry Policy, 1555–1593* (New York: Jewish Theological Seminary of America, 1977), and Renata Segre, "La Controriforma: Espulsioni, Conversioni, Isolamento," in Vivanti, *Storia d'Italia*, 11:707–78.
30. "Namely that they had finally understood that there was to be no going back: The ghetto was to be a permanent institution and fact of life; and the Jews themselves had been given a bill of divorce, at once physical and emotional, relegating them to the margins of Roman Christian society." See Kenneth R. Stow, "The Consciousness of Closure: Roman Jewry and Its Ghet," in *Essential Papers on Jewish Culture in Renaissance and Baroque Italy*, ed. David B. Ruderman (New York: New York University Press, 1992), 387.
31. Segre, "La Controriforma," 716.
32. The famous cardinal of Milan, Carlo Borromeo, lamented this fact, as cited in Segre, 717–18. See also Leone da Modena's autobiographical book, in which he tells us that even monks and priests would come to hear his sermons. See Modena, *Sefer Hayye Yehudah*, ed. Daniel Carpi (Tel Aviv: Universitat Tel-Aviv, 1985), 50.
33. See Milano, *Storia degli Ebrei*, 247.
34. Segre, "La Controriforma," 716.
35. Harris, "Demografia del Ghetto," 9.
36. Harris, 9.
37. Aid for those in need during the seventeenth century was about eight thousand scudi per year, approximately a third of the whole community budget. Therefore, poor people not only did not contribute to the budget but also absorbed it. See Attilio Milano, *Il Ghetto di Roma* (Rome: Staderini, 1964), 151. The registry is published in *The Register of the Jewish Community of Rome, 1615–1695*, ed. Andrea Yaakov Lattes (Jerusalem: Yad Ben Zvi, 2012), 61.
38. Kenneth R. Stow, *The Jews in Rome*, vol. 1, *1536–1551* (Leiden: E. J. Brill, 1995), xi–xiii. See also Ariel Toaff, review of *The Jews in Rome (1536–1557)*, by Kenneth Stow, *Zion* 63 (1998): 132–33.
39. Cecil Roth wrote two interesting books on Donna Grazia Mendes's character and actions in those years, albeit in the style of novels. See Roth, *The House of Nasi: The Duke of Naxos* (Philadelphia: Jewish Publication Society of America, 1948), and Roth, *The House of Nasi: Doña Gracia* (New York: Greenwood Press, 1948).
40. Many examples of this can be seen in Kenneth R. Stow and Sandra D. Stow, "Donne Ebree

a Roma nel'Età del Ghetto: Affetto, Dipendenza, Autonomia," *La Rassegna Mensile di Israel* 52, no. 1 (1986): 63–116.

41. Fausto Piola Caselli, "La Diffusione dei Luoghi di Monte della Camera Apostolica alla Fine del XVI Secolo," in *Credito e Sviluppo Economico in Italia dal Medio Evo all'Età Contemporanea: Atti del Primo Convegno Nazionale, 4–6 Giugno 1987* [La Società Italiana degli Storici dell'Economia] (Verona: Grafiche Fiorini, 1988), 206.
42. Lattes, *Register of the Roman Community*, 50.
43. Lattes, 50, 44.
44. Lattes, 51. Apparently it was common practice for the bride to travel by carriage to the groom's home, where the wedding ceremony would usually be held. For the carriage ride in general as a status symbol at the time, see Almo Paita, *La Vita Quotidiana a Roma ai Tempi di Gian Lorenzo Bernini* (Milan: Biblioteca Universale Rizzoli, 1988), 29.
45. Paita, *Vita Quotidiana*, 290–91.
46. Henri Pirenne, *Economic and Social History of Medieval Europe* (Ramat Gan, Israel: Masada, 1975), 133. See also Viktor I. Rutenburg, "Arti e Corporazioni," in *Storia d'Italia*, ed. Corrado Vivanti, vol. 5, *I Documenti* (Turin: Giulio Einaudi, 1973), 613–42. Ronald F. Weissman emphasizes the religious element of the penitence, which is related to the founding of the wandering monks, the *mendicanti*, who would gather in churches, and founded charitable organizations (*gruppi penitenziali*). See Weissman, *Ritual Brotherhood in Renaissance Florence* (New York: Academic Press, 1982), 44.
47. See Attilio Milano, "La Riposta Attività di un'Opera Pia nel Ghetto di Roma," *La Rassegna Mensile di Israel* 23 (1957): 271–79, 317–25; Simonsohn, *History of the Jews*, 2:399; H. J. Shirman, "Theater and Music in Jewish Neighborhoods in Italy," in *The History of Drama and Hebrew Poetry*, ed. Mosad Bialik (Jerusalem: Mossad Bialik, 1979), 2:70; and Elliott S. Horowitz, "Jewish Confraternal Piety in the Veneto in the Sixteenth and Seventeenth Centuries," in *Gli Ebrei e Venezia: Secoli XIV–XVIII* [Atti del Convegno Internazionale Organizzato dall'Istituto di Storia della Società e dello Stato Veneziano della Fondazione Giorgio Cini], ed. Gaetano Cozzi (Milan: Edizioni Comunità, 1987), 301–13.
48. See Bronislaw Geremek, "Il Pauperismo nell'Età Preindustriale (Secoli XIV–XVIII)," in Vivanti, *Storia d'Italia*, 5:688. Here, he cites from the regulations of a charitable society founded in Rome in 1519, indicating the duties of its members. In the Jewish sector, too, the arrival in the city of Spanish refugees encouraged the process of founding companies. See A. Toaff, *Ghetto Roma*, 18.
49. About the assistance to the needy in non-Jewish Italian society and the various organizations that took care of it, see Geremek, "Pauperismo," 673. In many places, the "societies" were founded many years before the establishment of the ghetto. In Ferrara, for instance, the Gemilut Hasadim Society was founded in 1515, while the ghetto appeared only in 1624. See David B. Ruderman, "The Founding of a *Gemilut Hasadim* Society in Ferrara in 1515," *AJS Review* 1 (1976), and Pesaro, *Memorie Storiche*, 37. On the unclear beginning of the Society of Roman Gemilut Hasadim, see A. Toaff, *Ghetto Roma*, 16.
50. The concept of a welfare state is a modern idea that began to emerge only after the industrial revolution of the last century and was realized during the twentieth century when the necessity that the state care for the health and education of its citizens emerged. See David L. Sills, ed., *International Encyclopedia of the Social Sciences* (New York: Macmillan, 1968), s.v. "welfare state." Compare also with the opinion of Attilio Milano, who writes that it's not true that the community did not want to help the needy, but rather, it simply could not, as all the money that it received was directly taken by the Pope's treasury. Milano, "Le Confraternite Pie del Ghetto di Roma," *Rassegna Mensile di Israel* 24 (1958): 118–19.
51. See Geremek, "Pauperismo," 686–87.

52. Lattes, *Register of the Jewish Community*, 185.
53. Indeed, Pirenne writes: "While these unions and organizations were called by different names: hanses, guilds, societies, charities, brotherhoods (hanses, gildes, compagnies, charités, fraries), there was no difference between them. In this matter, as in other matters, the economic organization was determined by a social need and not by any national spirit." Pirenne, *Economic and Social History of Medieval Europe*, 75. See also the corresponding footnote on page 185, from which we learn that fraternal societies already existed in Carolingian France and that professional associations were established in Germany before the fourteenth century.
54. See, for instance, Bracha Rivlin, *'Arevim zeh le-zeh ba-geto ha-italqi: Hevrot Gemah, 1516–1789* [Mutual responsibility in the Italian ghetto, 1516–1789] (Jerusalem: Magnes, 1991), 15–18.
55. As stated by Geremek, "Pauperismo," 669. Elliot S. Horowitz also follows in Geremek's footsteps with "Jewish Confraternities in Seventeenth-Century Verona: A Study in the Social History of Piety" (PhD diss., Yale University, 1982), 12. See also Weissman, *Ritual Brotherhood*, 204.
56. Simonsohn, *History of the Jews*, 2:399.
57. Simonsohn, 402–6.
58. See Lattes, *Register of the Jewish Community*, 16–17; Hermann Vogelstein and Paul Rieger, *Geschichte der Juden in Rom.* (Berlin, 1895), 2:316; and Milano, *Ghetto di Roma*, 237–40.
59. See Elliott Horowitz, "Coffee, Coffeehouses, and the Nocturnal Rituals of Early Modern Jewry," *AJS Review* 14, no. 1 (1989): 17–46.
60. See Shirman, "Theater and Music," esp. 2:68–80.
61. Shirman, 2:74–75.
62. Segre, "La Controriforma," 714.
63. Umberto Cassuto, *Gli Ebrei a Firenze nell'Età del Rinascimento* (Florence, 1918), 98–117; Michele Luzzatti, *La Casa dell'Ebreo: Saggi sugli Ebrei a Pisa e in Toscana nel Medioevo e nel Rinascimento* (Pisa: Nistri-Lischi, 1985), 82; and Siegmund, *From Tuscan Households*, 1–56, esp. 11–13.
64. Milano, *Storia degli Ebrei*, 284.
65. Simonsohn, *History of the Jews*, 1: 159–60, 179.
66. Leoni, *La Nazione Ebraica*, 157, and Andrea Balletti, *Gli Ebrei e gli Estensi* (Reggio Emilia, Italy: Anonima Poligrafica Emiliana, 1930), 71.
67. Salvatore Foa, "Banchi e Banchieri Ebrei nel Piemonte dei Secoli Scorsi," *La Rassegna Mensile di Israel* 21 (1955): 92–93.
68. Milano, *Ghetto di Roma*, 94, and Attilio Milano, *Ricerche sulle Condizioni Economiche degli Ebrei a Roma Durante la Clausura del Ghetto (1555–1848)* (Città di Castello, Italy: Tipografia dell 'Unione Arti Grafiche,' 1931), 547.
69. Compare, for example, Segre, "La Controriforma," 732.
70. Simonsohn, *History of the Jews*, 1:186.
71. This is determined by section 9 of the papal bull, which states: "Additionally, these Jews may carry on no business as purveyors of grain, barley or other items necessary for human sustenance, but must be limited [in this sphere] to dealing only in secondhand clothing, the arte cenciariae (as it is common called)." English translation from Stow, *Catholic Thought*, 294–98.
72. For the severe deterioration of the economic situation of Rome's Jews in the ghetto, see Milano, *Ricerche sulle Condizioni*, and Milano, *Ghetto di Roma*, 85–109.
73. Leoni, *La Nazione Ebraica*, 162.
74. Siegmund, *From Tuscan Households*, 271–305; see also 445–50.
75. This document was published in Cassuto, *Gli Ebrei a Firenze*, 409–13; see also, in Cassuto, 173–79; and R. Toaff, *La Nazione Ebrea*, 36.

76. See the version in R. Toaff, *La Nazione Ebrea*, 419–36. See also Alfredo Toaff, "Cenni Storici sulla Comunità Ebraica e sulla Sinagoga di Livorno," *La Rassegna Mensile di Israel* 21 (1955): 358–59.
77. Alfredo Toaff, "Cenni Storici," 358–59.
78. See Luzzatti, *La Casa dell'Ebreo*, 143.
79. On this topic, see Foa, "Banchi e Banchieri," 92–93, and Salvatore Foa, "La Politica Economica della Casa Savoia verso gli Ebrei dal sec. XVI fino alla Rivoluzione Francese," supplement, *La Rassegna Mensile di Israel* 27 (1961): 15–42.
80. Leoni, *La Nazione Ebraica*, 37–42, 193.
81. The essays that Gino Luzzatto wrote in economic history were many and impressive. He also dealt extensively with the economic deterioration of the Italian peninsula, although he focused on the decline of the Republic of Venice. See, for example, Luzzatto, *Storia Economica dell'Età Moderna e Contemporanea* (Padua: Milani, 1955), and Luzzatto, *Storia Economica di Venezia dall'XI al XVI Secolo* (Venice: Centro Internazionale delle Arti e del Costume, 1961). See Carlo Cipolla's beautiful descriptions in *Before the Industrial Revolution: European Society and Economy, 1000–1700*, 3rd ed. (London: Routledge, 1993), 241–49; "The Economic Decline of Italy," in *The Economic Decline of Empires*, ed. Carlo Cipolla (London: Methuen, 1970), 196–214; and *Storia dell'Economia Italiana* (Turin: Edizioni Scientifiche Einaudi, 1959), 605. The bibliography on the impoverishment that occurred in Italy from a general point of view is very rich, as seen in the works by Luzzatto cited above. However, on the process of impoverishment that particularly concerned Jews, most studies seem to focus on one specific area, and there is no overall monograph on the subject. See also Alberto Tenenti, *L'Età Moderna, XVI–XVIII Secolo* (Bologna: Il Mulino, 1997), 221–44. On the economic deterioration in Italy in general, see 323–30 especially.

CHAPTER FOUR

DISRUPTIVE STRATEGIES IN POST-SHOAH VERSIONS OF THE MERCHANT OF VENICE

MICHAEL SHAPIRO

WHY VENICE?

Venice occupied a distinctive place in the imaginations of Shakespeare and his contemporaries. Thomas Coryat's travel journal, *Coryate's Crudities* (1611), reported on such wonders to be seen in Venice as actresses performing onstage and Jewish circumcision ceremonies. Ben Jonson's play *Volpone* (1605) presented a city rife with venality and corruption and contrasted its vices with the folly of a pair of English tourists who were merely gullible and pretentious. In Shakespeare's *Othello, the Moor of Venice* (ca. 1603), the city is the site of an interracial marriage that ends in murder, what Shakespeare elsewhere called "a savage jealousy / That sometime savours nobly."[1] In his other Venetian play, *The Merchant of Venice*, the comic villain, Shylock, a Jewish moneylender who is not the merchant of the title, seeks to collect a pound of flesh as forfeited collateral from the title character so as to avenge his daughter's elopement with her Christian lover. And while Shylock is spat on and mocked by Venetian Christians and later fleeced of his wealth and forced to convert on pain of death, never once does the play refer to one of the city's most prominent features—the Jewish Ghetto, established in 1516 as the only area in which Jews were permitted to reside, with its curfew and locked gates. Shakespeare has Shylock refer to "my Jewish gabardine" (1.3.108) but makes no mention of the distinctive hats and badges that Venetian Jews were compelled to wear. As both avenger and victim, Shylock is one of the most famous Jewish characters in world literature. His name remains a pejorative byword for "Jew," and the play, widely taught and performed, has become a barometer for Jewish-Christian relations, past and present. The figure of Shylock embodies the unnamed Ghetto, whose image has modulated as the play was produced and adapted across various historical and cultural contexts. Indeed, the portrayal of the Jewish ghetto-dweller himself and the morality of his actions have also shifted, just as the term *ghetto* has gained new significance in the post-Shoah era.

POST-SHOAH STRATEGIES FOR STAGING *THE MERCHANT*

Despite some reluctance to produce *The Merchant of Venice* immediately after the Shoah, in 1947, New York City, teeming with survivors, hosted three versions of the play—two productions and an adaptation.[2] (The distinction between productions and adaptations is blurry. I see them both as part of what Margaret Kidnie calls "The Work" and what one might call "the Shylock *midrash*."[3]) The first of these 1947 versions was a traditional British touring production starring and directed by Donald Wolfit, part of a U.S. tour which also included *King Lear, Hamlet, As You Like It,* and *Volpone.* Lee Shubert, owner of the Broadway theater Wolfit had contracted to use, tried in vain to get Wolfit to drop *The Merchant* from the bill in New York City, fearing "it may prove offensive to the Jews of the city."[4] The second, *Shylock '47*, was a modestly produced metatheatrical adaptation created by Peter Frye and some Israeli actors, in which performers explicitly addressed the question of whether to do the play at all. The third was a Yiddish adaptation, *Shylock und sein Tochter (Shylock and His Daughter)*, starring Maurice Schwartz, who adapted it for the Yiddish Art Theater from a Hebrew novel by Ari Ibn-Zahav entitled *Shylock, the Jew of Venice,* which had been serialized in Yiddish in the Yiddish Daily, *Morgn Zournal,* in 1947, and translated into English by Julian Melzer under a slightly different title, *Jessica, My Daughter* (1948).[5]

The profusion of post-Shoah versions encourages one to divide them into subcategories to understand them better. Edna Nahshon suggests that the rubrics of "denial, destabilization, and displacement" describe most post-Holocaust productions, whereas Arthur Horowitz proposes the terms "conversion, confrontation, and provocation."[6] I offer the following categories, with the proviso that some productions can be classified under more than one rubric.

Denial means continuing the sympathetic Shylock developed in the nineteenth century. This approach emerged at a time of mass immigration of Jews to English-speaking countries, but now, after decades of assimilation, seems somewhat dated, a bit like "your grandfather's Shylock." The stage production starring Laurence Olivier and directed by Jonathan Miller (1970) and its subsequent television version (1973) made no gesture toward the Holocaust. This approach places *The Merchant* and the Shoah in different mental compartments and ignores any possible connections between them.

Some directors have tried to universalize the play by remapping Jewish-Christian strife onto other ethnic conflicts, such as the antagonism between Muslims and Hindus transplanted from the Indian subcontinent to contemporary Los Angeles as in Shishir Kurup's *Merchant on Venice*. This adaptation was first produced in Chicago in 2017 and revived there in 2018 and in London in 2018 (with minor changes) under the title *Merchant of Vembley*.[7] Bill Alexander's 1987 RSC production cast Antony Sher as "an Eastern Jew closer to his own Semitic roots," who wore a yellow star during the trial scene to evoke Jewish Holocaust suffering but who more often seemed to evoke the historical experience of "Arabs, Palestinians, Iranians, people who are associated in the Western mind with . . . acts of political terrorism.[8]

Other directors have chosen a strategy of decentering Shylock by focusing as much or more on Jessica. Some have even given her equal billing, as in Schwartz's 1947 *Shylock und Sein Tochter*, mentioned above, whereas others have made her the protagonist of the story.[9] Still other directors have sought to historicize the play by situating productions within Jewish historical experience. Schwartz's 1947 version not only decenters Shylock but resets the play in Italy in 1559, the year Pope Paul IV promulgated antisemitic edicts not unlike Hitler's 1935 Nuremberg laws. In 1993, a bilingual Chicago troupe in Albuquerque produced *The Merchant of Sante Fe*, with Shylock as a crypto-Jew in colonial New Mexico.[10] Other directors, like George Tabori and Hanan Snir have staged the play as metadrama by setting it as if it were being performed, respectively, in the Theresienstadt and Buchenwald concentration camps, while elsewhere in this collection Clive Sinclair writes about a recent version in the Venetian Ghetto, staged as if it were a rehearsal.[11]

DISRUPTION

I would propose a fifth strategy: disruption of Shakespeare's romantic comedy: disrupting the play's main plot, Bassanio's wooing of Portia, with intrusive moments designed to force readers or spectators to see the play from a Jewish perspective, that is, in the light or, better, in the shadow of the Shoah.

Disruption was employed at a key moment in Barbara Gaines's production for the Chicago Shakespeare Theater of 2005 with Mike Nussbaum, a beloved Chicago actor then in his eighties, as Shylock.[12] In many ways, this Shylock perpetuated the Victorian tradition—a vulnerable outsider, marked by a foreign accent, physically bullied and even beaten by the Venetians. But Gaines added a powerfully disruptive moment to the end of the trial scene: after Shylock was compelled to agree to convert to Christianity and recited what is in the text his penultimate line—"I am content" (4.1.389)—he then retrieved his skull cap, which had been knocked to the floor, replaced it on his head, walked slowly downstage toward steps leading to the center aisle, paused, looked upward, and recited, in Hebrew, the *Sh'ma*, the affirmation of monotheistic faith recited several times in any Jewish worship service.[13] The inserted prayer, which seemed to nullify his agreement to become a Christian as well as to reassert his Jewish identity, subverted Shakespeare's treatment of his comic villain's final moment.

In his 1999 production for the National Theatre (also available on videotape), Trevor Nunn had added even more intrusive Jewish elements.[14] Shylock (Henry Goodman) and Jessica (Gabrielle Jourdan) converse briefly in an inserted Yiddish dialogue not present in the English text, and they later celebrate Shabbat by lighting candles and singing "Woman of Valor" together in Hebrew. As in the previous example, such disruptions link Shylock and Jessica to the Jewish people and hence to the Nazis' prolonged assault against them. Finally, when Joshua Sobol, an Israeli playwright, directed the play at the Illinois Shakespeare Festival in Normal, Illinois, in 2002, he set it in Fascist Italy but used cross-gender casting, among other things, to thoroughly subvert the romantic comedy. He added no words to the text but made major nonverbal interventions. For instance, Antonio was revealed to be Antonia, Bassanio's inamorata, when she bared her breast to Shylock's knife, just as Portia, married to Bassanio earlier in the play, turned out in the end to be male, so that the play ended with the celebration of a ménage à trois. The backstory Sobol told to his actors, as he later explained to me, was that both Bassanio and Portia's father had arranged for Antonia and Portia, respectively, to adopt cross-gender disguises to save them from arrest and deportation. Shylock, too, was determined to save his child. Sobol again remained faithful to the text, but his staging made it clear that Shylock was facilitating Jessica's "elopement" by preparing a casket of money and jewels for his daughter to "steal" for use as bribes or means of support. Clearly, Sobol was willing to undercut the romantic plot so as to highlight the subtext of Shylock's successful scheme to send Jessica to safety. As he did in his own *Vilna Trilogy*, Sobol also staged vignettes of Jews suffering under Fascist rule, replicating iconic photographs such as the tossing of Shylock's books into a simulated fiery furnace below stage, or Tubal on his knees overseen by a Fascist guard as he scrubbed the sidewalk with a toothbrush. The actor playing Shylock in Sobol's version did not have to work very hard to evoke sympathy: as with any production set in the Holocaust, even a miserly, vengeful Shylock will appear sympathetic in contrast to his Nazi tormentors, the perpetrators of medical experiments, enslavement, mass murder, and other atrocities.

The strategy of disruption was used in productions of *The Merchant* long before the Holocaust. In the latter half of the nineteenth century, Edwin Booth, who played Shylock costumed as an Oriental patriarch, cut the entire fifth act, as Henry Irving, dressed as a Victorian gentleman, sometimes did. By ending the play after the trial scene, Booth, Irving, and others were willing to forgo the moonlight and music of the lovers' return to Belmont, along with their mock quarrels and bawdy jokes, thereby reshaping the play into the *Tragedy of Shylock*, as it was sometimes retitled.[15] Most modern directors have found subtler ways to evoke sympathy for Shylock than amputating the fifth act, sometimes following Shakespeare's lead by adding details of Jewish significance.

THE *MERCHANT OF VENICE* IN SHAKESPEARE'S DAY

Just as Shakespeare later added exotic "Moorish" details to his portrait of the Moor in *Othello*, he thickened the Jewish texture of the Italian novella he used as his primary source for *The Merchant*—a tale in Ser Giovanni Fiorentino's fourteenth-century collection *Il Pecorone*, published in Italian in 1558.[16] He added Shylock's long account from Genesis 25 of how Jacob outwitted Laban, plus biblical oaths and allusions and details of Jewish dietary laws, and provided Fiorentino's anonymous, isolated Jewish moneylender with a name, a family, a synagogue, and two fellow male Jews—Tubal, who appears, and Chus, who is merely mentioned by Jessica when she arrives in Belmont in 3.2. Later productions have stressed Shylock's religious identity by introducing Jewish ritual objects—prayer shawls, skull caps, mezuzot—or, as has been mentioned, by staging such Jewish rituals as the lighting of Shabbat candles and inserting bits of Hebrew or Yiddish.

It is hard to gauge Shakespeare's intentions in adding Jewish details to *The Merchant*. His general attitude toward Jews is also hard to determine, as he left no journals, letters, notes, or table talk to indicate his views. Instead, we have only this play and brief allusions to Jews in a half-dozen other plays.[17] Jewish characters appear nowhere else in Shakespeare's work outside of *The Merchant*. Some scholars propose that he wrote the work to furnish his company, the Lord Chamberlain's Men, with a play that would exploit current interest in the case of Roderigo Lopez, Queen Elizabeth's Jewish-born physician, who had been tried and executed for his alleged participation in a Spanish plot to poison the queen. When the rival company, the Lord Admiral's Men, revived Marlowe's *The Jew of Malta*, it seems not unreasonable to speculate that Shakespeare's troupe asked their chief poet for a play about a villainous Jew.[18] Scholars are still debating whether Shakespeare's Jewish moneylender was performed with a false nose, as Marlowe's Barabas seems to have been, and with a red wig, believed to match the color of Judas Iscariot's hair.[19]

The title page of the first quarto (published in 1600) of *The Merchant* bears a long subtitle, a kind of publisher's blurb to promote sales at bookstalls. We have no idea who wrote it, but the author invoked the common tropes of Elizabethan prejudice against Jews. The subtitle refers to "the extreme cruelty of Shylock the Jew toward the said Merchant, in cutting a just pound of his flesh," and then alludes to "the obtaining of Portia by the choice of three caskets."[20] Not a word about Shylock as victim. No one would use such language today to market the text or advertise a production of the play.

Whoever wrote the blurb, the play itself presents a much more complicated depiction of the Jew. Shakespeare, following Fiorentino, portrays his Jew primarily as a generic comic villain, whose function it is to thwart the successful union of romantic lovers. Such blocking agents are necessary structural elements in many romantic comedies, and Shakespeare's characterization of Shylock includes stock features of the stage miser and the oppressive father. But Shakespeare also made Shylock into a victim of Christian antisemitism, as well as a homicidal avenger, devoid of mercy and intent on cutting a pound of flesh from the breast of another human being.

Printed in the first folio (1622) under the rubric of "comedies," *The Merchant* focuses on Bassanio's courtship of Portia, which is financed by Shylock's loan to Bassanio's friend Antonio, who is, in fact, the eponymous merchant of Venice. When Antonio unexpectedly defaults on his loan, Shylock, whose daughter has recently eloped with a Christian, demands his collateral: a pound of Antonio's flesh. In his willingness to sacrifice his life for Bassanio, Antonio, the friend, threatens to usurp Portia's role as the one who loves Bassanio the most. Portia finds a way to break Antonio's moral hold on Bassanio by breaking Shylock's legal hold on Antonio, first by pointing out that the bond stipulates collateral of a pound of flesh but says nothing about blood, and then by citing a statute making it a crime for an alien to seek the life of a Venetian citizen.

From a structural standpoint, Shylock, who appears in only five scenes, is simply a "blocking agent," a comic villain who stands in the way of true love and is then either readmitted into the community or ejected from it, but Shakespeare also made him a complex amalgam of avenger and victim. Somewhere along the way, Shakespeare seems to have become intrigued with this outsider, who is reviled by the Venetians until his final exit and who can be absorbed only by religious conversion. Shakespeare also gave him fleeting moments of sympathy, as he does to other comic villains, as well as a distinctive voice.

THE MERCHANT OF VENICE AFTER SHAKESPEARE

History has played strange tricks on this romantic comedy. Quite apart from whatever qualities Shakespeare endowed Shylock with, the Jewish moneylender has, for many readers and playgoers, displaced the lovers as the center of interest and turned the play into something other than a romantic comedy. This shift in perception of Shylock, from avenger to victim, began in the nineteenth century, as Jews assimilated into the host cultures of the West and became playgoers, theater artists, and even professors of literature and drama, a process unimaginable in Shakespeare's day.[21] In general, after the nineteenth century, the more a given production or adaptation stressed Shylock's Jewish identity, the harder it became to keep the audience sympathetically engaged in the union of the lovers.

As always, there were countercurrents. Not everyone who produced the play in modern times sought to make Shylock more sympathetic. In 1898, William Poel tried to re-create what he imagined was the original Elizabethan Shylock, "a grotesque, unsympathetic figure in a red wig."[22] At the New Jersey Shakespeare Festival in 1984, Paul Barry opted for a villainous outsider in the name of historical authenticity, assigning the role of Shylock to an Israeli actor with a heavy accent, and received heavy protests from his audiences.[23] While the Nazis evidently discouraged productions of *The Merchant* for fear they might evoke pro-Jewish sentiments, as often happened on the German-speaking stage, they finally commissioned a viciously antisemitic production in Vienna in 1943, starring Werner Krauss, who had played the role of Jew Süss, a nasty court Jew in the film of that name, to celebrate the deportation of the city's last remaining Jews.[24] As English productions of the late 1930s frequently avoided responding to the worsening plight of Jews on the continent, John Gielgud expressed his wish "to keep the play from becoming the tragedy of the Jews." One critic described his Shylock as "puling, remorseless, toothless—utterly revolting in the remains of a ginger wig," while another critic noted his "gummy, blinking eyes that suggested some nasty creature of the dark."[25]

These examples are exceptions to the general tendency, starting with Edmund Kean in 1814, to find ways to present a more human Shylock than the melodramatic villain made famous by Charles Macklin in the previous century.[26] Since Kean, actors have sought and found moments in the play when Shylock evokes sympathy. One such moment is Shylock's realization that the ring his daughter stole from him and traded for a monkey is the very same turquoise ring "I had from Leah when I was a bachelor" (3.1.101). For some, revisions and fleeting moments of sympathy do not outweigh what they see as the fundamental antisemitism of the original text. Others have argued that the play does not *endorse* but rather *represents* antisemitism in action and may even be regarded (and produced) as exposing such attitudes to criticism. Still others might agree that although Shakespeare himself may have been innocent of bias, it was wrong to enact and display antisemitism on the stage so soon after the Shoah.

Such was the feeling of Orson Welles, who in 1960 announced he would not be making a film of the play. As he explained in an article in the *Morning Post* under the headline "Why I Won't Play Shylock . . . At Any Rate Not Just Now," "the picture of a Jew to be published just now is not Shylock. The Jewish story to be told just now is not the one about the pound of flesh. Not so long ago, 6,000,000 Jews were murdered." A decade later, Welles did start to film a version of *The Merchant* but it was never completed and only a few scenes survive.[27]

There are still theater artists and spectators who cannot help but see the Shoah lurking at the heart of *The Merchant.* Moreover, productions that refuse to acknowledge recent Jewish history may paradoxically make audiences especially aware of it, like the proverbial never-to-be-mentioned elephant in the room. Barbara Gaines's first Chicago production in 1997 tried to dodge the problem of implicit but nonetheless intrusive Holocaust associations by setting the play in New York City in the Roaring Twenties.[28] It opened on a party scene, with "flappers" on swings and couples dancing the Charleston to lively 1920s Dixieland tunes, which gradually morphed into mournful klezmer music. Despite Prohibition, or perhaps because of it, cocktails were in abundance. Other scenes in Belmont were staged as if at the seashore, with girls in bathing suits, men in gaudy beachwear, and more alcohol. Spectators were transported to the Hamptons at a time when "nice" people like Portia could think it appropriate to treat Jessica, the daughter of a Jew, with icy disdain. She was the immigrant daughter trying awkwardly to fit in with her new husband's sophisticated friends. Some of their same genteel upper-class antisemitism is captured in St. John Ervine's sequel to *The Merchant* entitled *The Lady of Belmont,* published in 1924, a decade before, a sardonic friend of mine once quipped, Hitler began to give antisemitism a bad name.

Rather than keeping the potentially disruptive presence of the Holocaust outside the world of the play, as Gaines tried to do, many directors have taken the opposite tack, making or allowing the Holocaust itself to seem to break into the text of Shakespeare's romantic comedy. Perhaps the boldest example of such disruption occurs in Don Selwyn's 2002 New Zealand film *The Maori Merchant of Venice,* which could also be considered an ethnic remapping. The film is based on a theatrical production Selwyn had directed the previous year, which used Maori actors speaking the Maori language to perform a translation done by Pei Te Hurinui Jones in 1945. Selwyn's film followed Shakespeare's play very closely, but he inserted an intrusive episode in which two of the characters visit an art gallery. Valerie Wayne describes the inserted scene: "The setting for this scene is an art gallery . . . and the paintings on the walls present images of 'the sacking and burning of the Maori Parihaka community by the government in the 19th century.' All the paintings are by the contemporary artist Selwyn Muru and as the scene ends the camera reveals the artist himself working on a large canvas across which is scrawled the word 'holocaust.'"[29] The two men return to their village and the plot resumes, but the romantic comedy has been temporarily fractured by an allusion to the Shoah and to what the Maori community considers its own "holocaust."

FRAMING AS DISRUPTION: *THE SHYLOCK PLAY* BY JULIA PASCAL

Julia Pascal's 2008 adaptation, which raises disruption to a fine art, merits detailed consideration.[30] It was first performed in 2007 at the Arcola Theatre in London under Pascal's direction and published the following year. Pascal employs several techniques to disrupt Shakespeare's romantic plot: cutting Shakespeare's text, inserting new scenes to underscore Jewish identity, inventing tableaux, and creating an intrusive frame.

Pascal cuts the story of the wooing of Portia significantly. Shakespeare devotes much time to the lottery scheme of Portia's dead father, in which the successful suitor must choose the casket (lead, gold, or silver) that contains her picture. In Pascal's version, the choice of caskets, featured on the title page of the first quarto, is radically de-emphasized. Bassanio's two rival suitors make their choices in a few parallel speeches in the same scene (rather than in separate scenes), while Bassanio's wooing of Portia is condensed from two scenes to one, a scene split with Jessica's conversion so that the music accompanying Bassanio's choosing turns out to be Jessica singing "Ave Maria" (62). Finally, supposedly in the interest of saving time, Pascal has the actor playing "the stage manager" order the actors to run the final scene—the lovers' reunion in Belmont—at double-speed, further subverting the romantic plot.

In another set of disruptive episodes designed to expand Jessica's role, Pascal underscores her and Shylock's Jewishness, as well as his devotion as a Jewish father. One such episode opens with a vignette of domestic piety, as Shylock and Jessica welcome Shabbat by blessing candles, challah, and wine, but the scene goes on to bristle with tension between father and daughter when Jessica heaps scorn on the Hebrew Bible and seems to resent Shylock's sentimentality in recollecting his dead wife, Leah. In other domestic episodes, Pascal shows us Shylock as a dutiful Jewish father, hemming his daughter's coat and bleaching her hair with fresh lemon juice to make her blond and help conceal her Jewish identity. In another invented father-daughter scene, Shylock gives Jessica the turquoise ring given to him by Leah before their marriage, the same ring Jessica later steals and trades for a monkey.

Pascal paradoxically brings additional focus to the characters' Jewishness with a tableau inserted to illustrate the power of Christianity in Venice: a Catholic procession with a line of priests and nuns carrying a statue of the Virgin (27). She also stages the conversions of Jessica and Shylock, neither of which Shakespeare dramatizes. Pascal invents other tableaux or episodes to heighten the power of antisemitism. In one, Jessica falls asleep on her father's roof, where she is tormented by dreams, enacted by the cast, of Jews being hunted down by barking dogs, tortured by the Inquisition, and forcibly converted (40). In a tableau after the trial scene, Jews appear wearing yellow stars.

Pascal's most forceful and original disruption is the intrusion of a contemporary frame around Shakespeare's love story. Before we hear a word of Shakespeare's text, we are transported to present-day Italy when two rival African street vendors come onstage, argue, and flee at the sound of a police siren. We then meet Sarah, a middle-aged, Polish-born Jew on vacation in Venice. (In the original London production, Sarah was played by Ruth Posner, herself a survivor of the Warsaw Ghetto, to whom Pascal dedicated the play for having "inspired so much of my work" [6]). Sarah meets Valentina, her tour guide, and as they await the rest of their tour group, they talk about themselves and their families. Sarah reveals that at age eleven, she and an aunt escaped the Warsaw Ghetto; her father, who remained behind and later died in Treblinka, furnished her with false papers that enabled her to survive by passing as a Catholic. Valentina reveals that her parents loved both the Catholic Church and Mussolini and tells Sarah about the origins of the Ghetto.

While waiting for the other members of their tour, Sarah and Valentina encounter a group of actors about to rehearse *The Merchant of Venice*. Invited to watch, Sarah has no trouble recognizing the piece: "It's the Shylock play . . . I wish it had never been written" (27). In this moment, and whenever Sarah disrupts the rehearsal, spectators are reminded of links between *The Merchant* and the Shoah, which shatter the plane of illusion of Shakespeare's romantic comedy.

An even more striking disruption occurs a few scenes later, when Sarah intrudes into the play to urge Jessica not to abandon her father and elope with Lorenzo:

SARAH: Don't go!
JESSICA: Who are you?
SARAH: Your mother.
JESSICA: No you're not.
SARAH: I could be.
JESSICA: My grandmother?
SARAH: If you like.
JESSICA: What do you want of me?
SARAH: Stay. He needs you.
JESSICA: Leave me alone you old witch.

(46)

Having made her first intrusion into the world of *The Merchant*, Sarah is immediately driven offstage by actors dressed as Venetian masquers, who, in the words of the stage direction, "*taunt her using the long nose on the Venetian masque to make antisemitic gestures*" (46). But Sarah returns, this time to intercede by warning Jessica that Lorenzo, whom we will soon see consorting with a prostitute, is unfaithful to her, will make his wife his "meal ticket" (48), and will squander her father's money (47–48). In a later scene with Jessica, Sarah continues to disparage Lorenzo by matching each of Jessica's troubled recollections of her lover's blandishments with the smutty words she remembers spoken by the Polish peasant who raped her after her escape from the Warsaw Ghetto.

Sarah intervenes yet again when she tries to prevent Jessica from converting. Pascal presents Sarah's entreaties on a split stage, where they alternate with moments of Bassanio wooing Portia. In these episodes, when the Inquisitor asks Jessica to accept the blood of Christ, Sarah urges her to decline: "Don't do that . . . Don't betray your father. You are all he has" (60–61). Sarah is ignored. Jessica arrives in Belmont, wearing, as the stage direction tells us, "*a large crucifix around her neck*," as well as a large natural-looking yellow wig, "*as a symbol of assimilation*" (64). Together with Jessica, who is seen by her father, Sarah silently witnesses the trial scene.

Sarah returns for the final scene of Pascal's play. As the stage directions to the previous scene tell us, "*Shylock is forcibly converted with his back on a plank*" and "*says the Shema in Hebrew to try and drown out the Inquisitor's conversion*" (93). In the short final scene of Pascal's play, Sarah and Shylock meet onstage. As the stage direction puts it, "*They cross and acknowledge one another*" (94). They have no lines, but the encounter could not help but be highly charged. Valentina then informs Sarah that the other tourists are now en route and they go off to begin the tour, closing the frame that had enveloped and disrupted Shakespeare's romantic comedy.

In *The Shylock Project*, Sarah's intrusions into Jessica's scenes, along with all of Pascal's other disruptive strategies, do not totally derail *The Merchant of Venice* so much as they reshape, augment, and refocus it. In any case, Shakespeare's full text will always be there for us to read and produce. Like other post-Shoah versions, Pascal's play expands Jessica's role and resets the play within a contemporary frame. But its originality lies in its strategic disruptions, which, in my view, remind us that we are not Elizabethans but live in the twenty-first century, still in the shadow of the Shoah.

Such reminders took visual form for the audience of the 2016 Venice production of *The Merchant*, as Clive Sinclair notes elsewhere in this volume: entering the Ghetto, spectators had seen "squads of soldiers . . . stationed at the Ghetto's entrances, while other teams patrol[led] its two squares" and passed within sight of the Holocaust memorial, "with its brick wall, barbed wire, and metal reliefs of humanity in extremis," reminders that the shattering of the plot of Shakespeare's romantic comedy is nothing compared to the shattering of millions of lives in the Shoah.[31] Like Sinclair's comments, Pascal's play, and other versions of *The Merchant* that disrupt Shakespeare's romantic comedy, are reminders that recent events, such as those that took place in Charlottesville, Pittsburgh, and San Diego, grow out of the same antisemitism Shakespeare held up for scrutiny in his own day.

NOTES

1. William Shakespeare, *Twelfth Night*, in *The Norton Shakespeare*, ed. Stephen Greenblatt, Walter Cohen, Jean Howard, and Katharine Eisaman Maus (New York: W. W. Norton, 1997), 5.1.115–16. All subsequent citations to Shakespeare refer to this edition and are cited by act, scene, and line.
2. Edna Nahshon, "New York City, 1947: A Season for Shylock," in *Wrestling with Shylock: Jewish Responses to "The Merchant of Venice,"* ed. Edna Nashson and Michael Shapiro (Cambridge: Cambridge University Press, 2017), 140–67. See also Yael Chaver, "Writing for the Jews, Writing for the Goyim: Adaptations of *The Merchant of Venice*," *Jewish Social Science* 17, no. 2 (2011): 28–47. John O'Connor mentions three early productions, one in London in September 1946 (339n76); a Yiddish version in 1946 at the Folk House in Stepney, a district in the East End of London then heavily populated by Eastern European Jewish immigrants; and one in Stratford in 1947 with John Ruddock as Shylock (132). See O'Connor, *Shakespearean Afterlives* (Cambridge, UK: Icon Books, 2003).
3. Margaret Kidnie, *Shakespeare and the Problem of Adaptation* (London: Routledge, 2009), 134.
4. Nahshon, "New York City," 146.
5. Nahshon, 160.
6. Nahshon, 167. Earlier studies of post-Shoah productions include Michael Shapiro, "*The Merchant of Venice* after the Holocaust, or Shakespearean Comedy Meets Auschwitz," *Cithara* 46 (2006): 3–23; Arthur Horowitz, "Shylock after Auschwitz: *The Merchant of Venice* on the Post Holocaust Stage—Subversion, Confrontation and Provocation," *Journal for Cultural and Religious Theory* 8 (2007): 7–19; and Michael Shapiro, "*The Merchant ON Venice* [Boulevard, Los Angeles] (Chicago, 2007): Universalizing Shakespeare's Play," *European Judaism* 51 (2018): 223–25.
7. Shishir Kurup, *Merchant on Venice*, in *Beyond Bollywood and Broadway*, ed. Neilish Bose (Bloomington: Indiana University Press, 2009), 91–158.
8. Quotations in James Bulman, *"The Merchant of Venice" in Performance* (Manchester: University of Manchester Press, 1991), 120–21; see also Miriam Gilbert, "Jewish Directors and Jewish Shylocks in Twentieth-Century England," in Nahshson and Shapiro, *Wrestling with Shylock*, 291–316.
9. Michelle Ephraim, "Jessica's Jewish Identity in Contemporary Feminist Novels," in Nahshson and Shapiro, *Wrestling with Shylock*, 337–58.
10. Elizabeth Klein and Michael Shapiro, "Shylock as Crypto-Jew: A New Mexican Adaptation of *The Merchant of Venice*," in *World-Wide Shakespeares: Local Appropriations in Film and Performance*, ed. Sonia Massai (London: Routledge, 2005), 31–39.
11. Sabine Schülting, "Evoking the Holocaust in George Tabori's Productions of *The Merchant of Venice*," in Nahshson and Shapiro, *Wrestling with Shylock*, 227–32, and Gad Kaynar-Kissinger, "*The Merchant of Venice* on the German Stage and the 1995 'Buchenwald' Production in Weimar," in Nahshson and Shapiro, *Wrestling with Shylock*, 260–72. See also Zeno Ackerman and Sabine Schülting, *Precarious Figurations: Shylock on the German Stage, 1920–2010* (Berlin: de Gruyter, 2019), 110–7 and 180–83. For Clive Sinclair, see chap. 5 in this volume, "The Ghetto of Venice: Clive Sinclair Discusses Venice, Judaism and Shylock."
12. Michael Shapiro, "Two Merchants: The Glow of the Roaring Twenties and the Shadow of 9/11," in *Chicago Shakespeare Theater*, ed. Regina Buccola and Peter Kanelos (DeKalb: Northern Illinois University Press, 2013), 236–45.
13. The words inserted were: "*Sh'ma Yisroel Adonai Eloheinu Adonai Echod*" [Hear, O Israel, the Lord is our God, the Lord is One]. In her 1997 production, Gaines inserted the same prayer but used it as Shylock's exit line in the trial scene.

14. Miriam Gilbert, "Jewish Directors," 310–14. Nahma Sandrow describes a weeklong workshop held in New York City in October 2015, funded by the Shakespeare Society and led by Stephen Burdman, artistic director of the New York Classical Theatre. Its goal was to create, for a future production, a text of *The Merchant of Venice* in which Shylock regularly "lapses—or rises—into Yiddish." See Sandrow, "Shylock's Jewish Way of Speaking," in "There's a Jewish Way of Speaking: Essays in Honor of David Roskies," ed. Avraham (Alan) Rosen and Jillian Davidson, special issue, *In Geveb: A Journal of Yiddish Studies* (July 2020): 1–8, https://ingeveb.org/articles/shylocks-jewish-way-of-speaking.
15. Toby Lelyveld, *Shylock on the Stage* (London: Routledge, 1961), 71.
16. No early modern translation of Fiorentino's tale has been found. For a modern translation, see Geoffrey Bullough, *Narrative and Dramatic Sources of Shakespeare* (London: Routledge and Kegan Paul, 1975), 1:463–76. See also Jay Halio, introduction to *The Merchant of Venice*, by William Shakespeare, ed. Jay Halio (Oxford: Oxford University Press, 1993), 13–19.
17. The following are Shakespeare's references to Jews in his other plays:
    1) In *Macbeth*, one of the ingredients mentioned by the Weird Sisters as they concoct their witches' brew is "liver of blaspheming Jew" (4.1.26);
    2) In *Henry IV, Part I*, Falstaff tells a tall tale of how he and his companions captured and bound the initial wave of imagined robbers he claims attacked them and then tries to authenticate this account by asserting "or I am a Jew else, an Hebrew Jew" (2.5.164–65);
    3) In *Much Ado about Nothing*, Benedict declares, "If I do not love her, I am a Jew" (2.3.231–32);
    4) In *Two Gentlemen of Verona*, Launce tells his fellow servant Speed that if he does not accompany him to the alehouse "thou art an Hebrew, a Jew, and not worth the name of a Christian" (2.5.44–45);
    5) In the same play, Launce complains that his stone-hearted dog, Crab, was unmoved at their departure from home, even though "a Jew would have cried at our parting" (2.3.9–10);
    6) In *Midsummer Night's Dream*, in the rehearsal of the artisans' playlet, "Pyramus and Thisbe," Flute, as Thisbe, calls Bottom, as Pyramus, "Most bristly, juvenile, and eke most lovely Jew" (3.1.82);
    7) In *Love's Labour's Lost*, Costard says farewell to the page Mote with "my sweet ounce of man's flesh, my inconny Jew" (3.1.124).

    Some of these allusions are mildly disparaging references to Jews as unfeeling or hard-hearted; others serve as touchstones to complete the rhetorical formula "Well, I'll be . . . [a monkey's uncle]"; others may simply be based on the aural similarity between Jew and another syllable—JU-venal or a-DIEU.

18. Halio, introduction, 28. James Shapiro, *Shakespeare and the Jews* (New York: Columbia University Press, 1996), 71–73, discusses the Lopez case but suggests that the play might have also appealed to a more general Elizabethan curiosity about (if not an obsession with) Jews. Shapiro's work has recently been supplemented by Sarah Coodin, *Is Shylock Jewish?* (Edinburgh: Edinburgh University Press, 2017), 26–84. On the Lopez case, see David Katz, *Jews in the History of England* (Oxford: Clarendon Press, 1994), 76–106. On its possible influence on Shakespeare, see Emma Cox, "Was Shakespeare Jewish?," *Shakespeare Quarterly* 64:192–96; and Stephen Greenblatt, *Will in the World* (New York: Norton, 2004), 273–80.
19. On the color of Shylock's hair and/or beard, see Lelyveld, *Shylock on the Stage*, 7–8. See

also Stephen Greenblatt, "Shylock and Shakespeare," *New York Review of Books*, September 30, 2010; James Shapiro, "Shylock in Red?," *New York Review of Books*, October 14, 2010; and Greenblatt, "Shylock on Stage and Page," *New York Review of Books*, December 9, 2010.

20. Halio, introduction, 84.
21. For discussion of the change, see Lelyveld, *Shylock on the Stage*, 39–95; Bulman, *"Merchant of Venice" in Performance*, 25–52; and John Gross, *Shylock: A Legend and Its Legacy* (New York: Simon and Schuster, 1992), 125–64.
22. Charles Edelman, introduction to *The Merchant of Venice* (Cambridge: Cambridge University Press, 2002), 36.
23. Harry Keyeshian, "The 1984 New Jersey Festival *Merchant* Production and Response: A Case Study," *On Stage Studies* 9 (1985): 11–29.
24. Kaynar-Kissinger, "*The Merchant of Venice* on the German Stage," 254–56. See also Ackerman and Schülting, *Precarious Figurations*, 57–62.
25. Gielgud quoted in Patrick Stewart, "Shylock in *The Merchant of Venice*," in *Players of Shakespeare: Essays in Shakespeare Performance by Twelve Players*, ed. Philip Brockbank (Cambridge: Cambridge University Press, 1985), 18–19; critics quoted in O'Connor, *Shakespearean Afterlives*, 125.
26. For an account of Macklin's Shylock, see Lelyveld, *Shylock on the Stage*, 20–37.
27. *Morning Post*, January 16, 1960, quoted in O'Connor, *Shakespearean Afterlives*, 137–38. O'Connor questions Welles's motivation: "A cynic might also suggest that he is putting a moral gloss on an economic decision."
28. Shapiro, "Two Merchants," 233.
29. Valerie Wayne, review, "Te Tangata Whai Rawa o Weniti: *The Maori Merchant of Venice*," *Contemporary Pacific* 16, no. 2 (2004): 425–29, Project MUSE, https://muse.jhu.edu. See also Emma Cox, "Te Reo Shakespeare: Te Tangata Whaì Rawa o Wenìti / The Maori *Merchant of Venice*," *Kunapipi* 28, no. 1 (2006), https://ro.uow.edu.au/kunapipi/vol28/iss1/10.
30. Julia Pascal, *The Shylock Play* (London: Oberon Books, 2008). All subsequent citations to this play will be given parenthetically in the text. Pascal is also the author of the late twentieth-century plays *The Yiddish Queen Lear* and *The Holocaust Trilogy*, a work discussed by Phyllis Lassner in *Anglo-Jewish Women Writing the Holocaust* (Basingstoke: Palgrave Macmillan: 2009), 156–85.
31. Clive Sinclair, "The Ghetto of Venice," this volume, 134.

CHAPTER FIVE

THE GHETTO OF VENICE

Clive Sinclair Discusses Venice, Judaism and Shylock

CLIVE SINCLAIR

In my time I have seen many Shylocks, but never before had I seen seven Shylocks on a single day, as I did this summer in Venice. The first was in the Doge's Palace, scene of the infamous "pound of flesh" trial, and its vexing conclusion; the second was in the Scuola Grande di San Rocco, an equally unlikely venue; while the remainder were all in the Ghetto, exactly where you'd expect to find a man like Shylock.

Taken together these three locations formed the stations of an extraordinary day at the end of July, the climax of a summer of events orchestrated by Professor Shaul Bassi of Ca' Foscari University to mark the quincentennial of that Ghetto, the mother of them all. On March 29, 1516, the then Doge—Prince Leonardo Loredan—signed the decree setting aside an area designated to segregate La Serenissima's "precious" Jews (precious because of their necessary role as moneylenders), at that time primarily refugees from the Iberian Peninsula. This may not sound terribly hospitable, but it was a big improvement on what Spain and Portugal had to offer. And the Doge's Palace remains the best place to commence a crash course in Ghetto-ology, currently being host to an exhibition, "Venice, the Jews, and Europe, 1516–2016," which runs until November 13. Shylock, as impersonated by Sir Laurence Olivier, is an integral component. Flickering on a screen like some shade in Hades, he is condemned

First published in *TLS*, October 21, 2016, https://www.the-tls.co.uk/articles/freelance-766. Reprinted with permission.

endlessly to repeat his most famous speech. And what a beautifully constructed thing the speech is, its architecture fully exposed by Olivier's precise intonation. First there comes anger, which apparently cools and mellows into a lesson on shared humanity, but then fizzes up again into revenge with menace: "The villainy / you teach me, I will execute, and it shall go hard but I / will better the instruction." Watch out Antonio!

Later in the afternoon F. Murray Abraham delivered the same lines—but in the flesh—in the Chapter Room of the Scuola Grande di San Rocco. His rendition, no less affecting than Olivier's, tends to emphasize its demand for equal rights, not to mention the speaker's religion: "I am a Jeeeeew. Hath / not a Jew eyes? hath not a Jew hands, organs, / dimensions, senses, affections, passions? Fed with / the same food, hurt with the same weapons, subject / to the same diseases, healed by the same means, / warmed and cooled by the same winter and summer, as / a Christian is? If you prick us, do we not bleed?" A wise move, given that Shylock is present in the Chapter Room as the Appellant in a Mock Appeal against the play's original verdict: no pound of flesh, no repayment; on the contrary, forfeiture of property and fortune and forced conversion.

The Scuola Grande di San Rocco was completed around 1560, a few years before Shakespeare's birth. Tintoretto won the commission to decorate its inner walls. The canvases in the Chapter Room on the top floor were completed in 1581. The three dominant paintings on the ceiling each depict a scene from the journey of the Israelites to the Promised Land. Surrounding them are numerous panels illustrating further dramatic moments from the Old Testament. White of hair and beard, old Abraham stands center stage, his arms outstretched, as if posing for a version of the Crucifixion—except that his left hand rests on the shoulder of his naked son, downcast on the sacrificial pyre, and his right clutches a murderous blade. The latter is primed to deliver the fatal blow, only to be disarmed at the last by the gentle touch of an angel, a sort of Portia *avant la lettre*.

While the ceiling belongs to the Old Testament, the walls are the province of the New, featuring episodes from the life of Christ. Thus the Chapter Room itself is an emblem of one of the major conflicts of *The Merchant of Venice*: between the religion of the Son and that of the Father. Another source of friction is, of course, the conflict between mercy, a quality in which Shylock, as a Jew, is supposedly deficient—and justice. Greeting Antonio at the commencement of the trial, the Doge (retitled Duke by Shakespeare) has this to say:

I am sorry for thee: thou art come to answer
A stony adversary, an inhuman wretch
Uncapable of pity, void and empty
From any dram of mercy.

The large audience has come to hear a less partial consideration. Indeed, when the justices enter at 5 pm and we are all instructed to rise, I cannot help but remember those ancient days when I accompanied my father to Raleigh Close Synagogue on Yom Kippur (always sweltering in my memory), and we men (and boys) in our prayer shawls rose as our rabbi lifted the holy scrolls from the Ark and paraded them down the aisles. The jurists who march down the aisle of the Chapter Room are almost worthy of similar respect. First among them is the Honorable (and diminutive) Ruth Bader Ginsburg, associate justice, Supreme Court of the United States. She is followed by four others: John R. Phillips, US Ambassador to Italy; Professors Laura Picchio Forlati of Padua and Richard Schneider of Wake Forest University; and finally Avvocato Fabio Moretti of Venice. They take their seats before a structure that looks strangely like the Ark of the Covenant.

A Florentine, Manfredi Burgio, represents Shylock. His chief weapon is anachronism, comparing the Alien Statute (Portia's invention, he concludes, having found no evidence for its existence outside the play), under which Shylock is sentenced to death for threatening the life of a native Venetian, then paupered, to Mussolini's Racial Laws, which deprived Shylock's co-religionists of their rights, jobs, assets, and lives. The judgment against his client, he concludes, "should therefore be reversed *in parte qua*." Jonathan L. Geballe, speaking on behalf of both Antonio and Portia, will have none of this: "The Court needs to question the fairness of measuring the legal correctness of the proceedings in the sixteenth-century court by standards developed over the hundreds of years which have passed." Besides, he adds, Venice was "markedly tolerant and accepting towards Jews for its time," permitting them religious freedom, albeit within the confines of the Ghetto. He points to the finale of Shylock's great speech and argues that the Appellant attended the trial with murder in mind. Why else, he asks, "whet his knife so earnestly?" Mario Siragusa, lawyer for both the Republic of Venice and Antonio, is of a like mind: "My first comment is that it would not be appropriate to approach the matter with our contemporary sensibility, schooled by history to the atrocious outcome of anti-Jewish prejudice and persecution in the twentieth century." Instead he proposes sticking to Venetian law circa 1570.

While the judges retire to deliberate, the platform is given over to two professors, James Shapiro and Stephen Greenblatt, who have twenty minutes in which to turn the spotlight from law to literature, from the court to the theatre. They prove to be a fine double act. Their discussion leads, via a consideration of Portia's motives once she has heard her new husband Bassanio declare that he would gladly sacrifice his life and that of his wife to save Antonio, and the anxieties that contemporary productions of *The Merchant* create, especially in the United States, to the recollection of a production by the Cameri Theatre of Tel Aviv, which was in rehearsal when Baruch Goldstein massacred nearly three dozen Muslims at prayer in Hebron. This prompted the recasting of Shylock as a West Bank settler who, becoming radicalized, turns both rabbinic and rabid. Jan Kott was right, as if there were any doubt: Shakespeare is our contemporary.

We all rise again when the judges return. Their ruling is unanimous, according to Justice Ginsburg: the bond—the pound of flesh—is dismissed as a jest, one that no court in its right mind would grant; Antonio is ordered to repay his loan (though he is spared interest on it); Shylock's fortune is restored; and his conversion is revoked, on the grounds that Antonio, as defendant, had no right to demand it. What can I say? It is Shylock's lucky day. Furthermore the court has a particularly harsh reprimand for Portia (though here there is one dissenting voice), perhaps because she acquired her doctorate in less than a week. Anyway, she is required to attend law school at the University of Padua and to further pursue a Master of Law degree at Wake Forest.

We repair to the Ghetto for the evening performance. Greenblatt and Shapiro are right; any given production of *The Merchant* causes disquiet, especially when that production takes place in the Ghetto. On this occasion the fear does not concern possible charges of anti-Semitism, but actual charges by armed anti-Semites. To protect the audience, squads of soldiers are stationed at the Ghetto's entrances, while other teams patrol its two squares. In addition a permanent observation post has been established immediately before the Holocaust memorial, with its brick wall, barbed wire, and metal reliefs of humanity in extremis. Stands of seats have been erected in the Campo del Ghetto Nuovo.

To my mind the most notable feature of the production by the Compagnia de' Colombari, apart from its setting (which itself is enhanced by the fading of day into twilight, and the merging of twilight into night, whereupon the chorus of cicadas ceases its chirping), is the fact that Shylock's role is taken by five different actors. It almost makes sense of Portia's question on entering the courtroom, "Which is the merchant here, and which the Jew?," because we are not 100 percent sure ourselves. Shylock's most famous lines are lent to Jenni Lea-Jones, who would have us believe that her character has been driven to the breaking point, an impression confirmed when she discovers that her daughter has eloped with a Christian and her keening causes lights to go on in the Ghetto's darkened windows.

The performance concludes, not with the traditional harmony in Belmont, but with each cast member repeating Shylock's challenge: "Are you answered?" Actually an answer of sorts does appear, like the writing on the wall, spread across several of the Ghetto's tenements: the Hebrew word *Rahamim*, which means mercy. It is all very well for Portia (in this instance Linda Powell) to recite her beautiful lines on how "The quality of mercy is not strain'd, / It droppeth as the gentle rain from heaven," but precious little of it falls on Shylock. Is there one law, then, for Christians, and another for Jews? Are we to be granted justice, but no mercy, because mercy is so alien to us? You could even argue that such a distinction inspired the very first ghetto, with its unique rules (including a curfew and locked gates). And now we are back there again, in some numbers, insisting that mercy is an essential component of Judaism.

SEX, DEATH AND JEWS. This trio of muses were a constant throughout Sinclair's career, reflected—in both his fiction and nonfiction—through the lens of his extensive travels. His fifteen books and innumerable essays for the *TLS, Observer, Jewish Chronicle,* and *Playboy* (among many others) took readers to Stockholm, Cuzco, Jerusalem, Cairo, Texas, California, Hendon, and Venice. The heroes and villains of these stories range from August Strindberg to Captain Haddock, Odysseus, Mephistopheles, the Golem, Davy Crockett, Wyatt Earp, and the Marlowesque private detective (Sinclair's smart-aleck alter ego) Joshua Smolinsky.

Born in London in 1948, Sinclair was winner of the Somerset Maugham Award, the PEN Silver Pen, and the Jewish Quarterly Award and was selected, in 1983, as one of Granta's original Best of Young British Novelists. He was a fellow of the Royal Society of Literature and held a doctorate from the University of East Anglia. He taught there, at the Uppsala University in Sweden, and at the University of California at Santa Cruz, where his son, Seth, was born.

Clive lived in London with the artist Haidee Becker until his death on March 5, 2018. His final collection of short stories, *Shylock Must Die,* published posthumously, was a series of reincarnations of Shakespeare's most alluring antihero. Through these stories, Shylock—as a man, a ghost, and an idea—travels through time and across continents, through comedy and tragedy, awaiting that final judgment between mercy and revenge.

Seth Sinclair

PART III

FIGURE 10. Jacopo de' Barbari, *View of Venice*, 1500, woodcut on six sheets of paper.
—Purchase from the J. H. Wade Fund, Cleveland Museum of Art, https://clevelandart.org/art/1949.565.1. CC0 1.0.

THE MAP
A MEMORY SPACE THAT TRAVELS

AMANDA K. SHARICK AND KATHARINE G. TROSTEL

In Jacopo de' Barbari's famously intricate *View of Venice*, published in 1500, the mapmaker attempts to represent each and every structure in the landscape of the city. The task was a monumental one: "No single vantage point would have been sufficient, so a large team of surveyors climbed various towers and tall buildings to record small sections of the city. These individual views were combined to form the map that follows a single, though inconsistent, system of perspective."[1] The aerial view presented by the map is so large that the finished product had to be pieced together, a composite of six individual, oversized sheets of paper. Many viewers of the resulting map are both struck by the panoramic view of the city and entranced by the level of detail captured by de' Barbari: they can zoom in closely and trace the minute contours of buildings, count the number of gondolas depicted on the canals, and even admire the architectural details of Venice's iconic buildings. *View of Venice* is a remarkable attempt to capture the three-dimensional reality of a living and breathing city on a two-dimensional plane.

As a technology, mapmaking collapses spaces that are dynamically lived and more fluidly experienced. A map, by its very nature, is a flattened representation of place—one that does not take into account how the inhabitants of the geographic reality experience the city and does not record the stories and collective memories that animate, circulate through, and lend importance to these cartographic points. A map must be connected to acts of storytelling to illuminate a city's psychogeography. Israel Zangwill, one of the most prominent Anglo-Jewish literary voices of the late nineteenth and twentieth centuries, makes a similar claim about the cartographic discourse of maps, using Venice as a prime example. Zangwill reminds us that "old maps," with their allegorical depictions of Neptune in the sea, as de' Barbari's map features, show the viewer not only where a culture or society has been, or the limits of inhabitants' knowledge, but also how cartographers account for those limits and gaps for their imagined audience. "In truth," Zangwill reminds his Anglo-American readers, "the Orient, like heaven, is not a place but a state of mind."[2] The interplay between de' Barbari's precision and his incorporation of mythological figures serves as a reminder that maps are interspersed with culturally significant stories that, not unlike a legend, situate the viewer in place as much as any coordinate.

The essays in this section explore a process of thick mapping,[3] whereby dimensions of memory, nostalgia, and imagined geographies fuse with the contours of the static map within the space of fiction, animating the layers and levels of the ghetto as palimpsest. The Venice Ghetto is the catalyst—a memory space codified around an identity. As Robert Bevan has suggested, the built environment can prompt a call to remember, and layered memories represent "a continuity of successive experiences, setting down layers of meaning, [that] can . . . result in an especially strong power of place—a psycho-geography, an 'awareness' of the past (rather than an architectural avatar of a petrified spirit) that is dynamic, handed down by the people rather than recorded on the very stones . . . If the touchstones of identity are no longer there to be touched, memories fragment and dislocate."[4] In this section of the collection, we argue that the Ghetto functions both as a touchstone of identity and as a metaphor for navigating how transhistorical memories have shaped and continue to inform Jewish identity as plural and dynamic, serving as keys or legends for specific moments in time. These are points that exceed boundaries and that push us toward the edges of the map. We conceive of these "maps" as snapshots of history that work to preserve the built environment at a given place and time, even as these historical sites are inherently unstable. Cartographic projects become placeholders and legends for past communal experiences that no longer exist in the present moment. Entering the map becomes a way to return to the past while maintaining the lens and perspective of the present. As we will see from the essays, layering past and present is critical for a practice of cultural wayfinding, allowing both authors and audiences to chart potential futures.

Both essays in this section utilize twentieth-century texts to expose tensions between the Jewish ghetto, as it existed materially and discursively, and the ghettos that were imagined out of necessity to provide alternate realities to war or exile. This practice of using the ghetto to map and process the experiences of individual and collective trauma has connections to nineteenth-century Jewish traditions that use literature to map and imagine layered histories. In particular, the practice of reimagining the ruins and architecture of former Jewish spaces, especially the Ghetto, was a useful literary device for some writers to both grapple with long histories of violence and generational trauma and to construct new narratives of collective Jewish identity for the future.

In a 2015 special topics issue of *Partial Answers*, titled "The Ghetto as a Victorian Text," Murray Baumgarten, the guest editor, summarizes the impact of the historic Ghetto for modern Jewry: "What the force of the Italian city-state had imposed upon the Jews in the sixteenth century had become at the end of the nineteenth a psychological phenomenon."[5] We see this in the nineteenth-century writings of famous Anglo-Jewish authors Lady Katie Magnus, Amy Levy, and Israel Zangwill; they use historical ghettos in their writings as portals so as to imagine how past generations not only survived in but also changed their worlds. In essays like Magnus's "Story of a Street" (1886); Levy's "The Ghetto at Florence" (1886); or Zangwill's "Child of the Ghetto" (1898), for instance, the historical portraits of these physical places and heritage sites are illuminated by what Levy calls "inherited" memories—a term she uses to name the affective impact of these spaces on the descendants of the communities that once lived there.

This practice that Levy describes has an antecedent: Levy translated some German verses for Magnus's *Jewish Portraits*, first published in 1888.[6] The collection of essays provides snapshots of important Jewish figures with lessons for modern Jewry. In her chapter "Story of a Street," Magnus offers a sketch of one of England's most distinguished Jewish families: the Rothschilds. The piece is, in sum, a Jewish immigrant success story—detailing how the impoverished ancestors of the Frankfurt Ghetto became the wealthiest Jewish family in England. Though bordering on hagiography, Magnus provides a unique reframing of the well-known story, most notably by writing from the perspective of the very cobblestones that made up the *Judengasse*, the "Jewish street," another term for the Ghetto of Frankfurt. The sketch compresses the history of the Frankfurt Ghetto, from 1241 to 1880, into three paragraphs that are offset by the permanence of the stones, which themselves play the integral role of the imagined witnesses to the paradox of the ghetto, both a "prison" and a space of "protection" from the outside world. They witnessed, for instance, the "alchemy of domestic life," especially the power of the Sabbath preparations to transform the poverty and seeming crudeness of the ghetto into a place of dignity, compassion, and learning (38). Magnus's imaginings of everyday life within the Frankfurt Ghetto culminate with a nod to generational progress, something that is not guaranteed but must be reconstituted with each generation. And while Magnus, Levy, and Zangwill lived during a period in England of increased civil liberties for Jews of a certain station, their engagement with the legacies of the physical Ghetto helped them reframe the creation of new ghettos that emerged at the turn of the century due to increasing imperial expansion and emerging nationalisms. In this way, these nineteenth-century essays are precursors for thinking through the memory frameworks explored in this collection. They are examples of how the physical spaces of the ghetto have inspired communal place-based memory practices that were then mobilized at moments of historical transition—often violent and traumatic—to renegotiate multiple, conflicting pasts for the purpose of forging new possible futures.

Drawing on Marianne Hirsch's idea of "connective histories in vulnerable times," we find nineteenth-century Jewish writers like Magnus and Levy penning histories of "connectivity" rather than of comparison between sixteenth-century ghettos and nineteenth-century London.[7] These connective histories are themselves examples of the way place-based memory is activated through instances of creative production. Below, we offer a brief final theoretical detour through writer Amy Levy's essay "The Ghetto of Florence" to provide a navigational lens through which to read the pieces in this section. This work serves as a case study that demonstrates how Jewish writers of the nineteenth century utilized the methodology of place-based writing as a tool for memory work.

In March of 1886, Levy wrote "The Ghetto at Florence" as a travel essay for a London-based Jewish newspaper, *The Jewish Chronicle*. The piece served as a personal reflection on the space as it appeared while she visited Florence during Carnivale, just two years before it would ultimately be destroyed in 1888. We argue that Levy offers a working theory of memory that weaves together the physical ruins of the Florence Ghetto with a proto-Benjaminian formation of messianic history, which is redeemed only when seized through a connection to a specific present. As Benjamin writes, "A historian who takes this as his point of departure stops telling the sequence of events like the beads of a rosary. Instead, he grasps the constellation which his own era has formed with a definite earlier one. Thus he establishes a conception of the present as the 'time of the now' which is shot through with chips of Messianic time."[8] With the material ruins of the Florence Ghetto foregrounded, Levy's text is primarily focused on her experience of the historic space, her observations and internal wrestling with both the haunting features of the collapsing ruins and the ghostly affective feeling she describes as her "inherited memory."[9] This has deep resonances in the way she explores the ghetto's past, present, and future in what Richa Dwor describes as an "encounter with the imagined experience of segregation . . . [where the] ghetto presents to the emancipated Jew both the origins of modern Jewish identity and also a material reminder of how memory works to transfigure 'bars' and 'fetters' into an internalized form of difference."[10] Levy's attention to memory, space, and identity as linked to her contemporaries' use of the ghetto illustrates these generational and cultural conflicts that have given rise to new forms of Jewish expression in a post-emancipation England.

In Levy's opening lines, she emphasizes the bleak future awaiting the stone walls of the Florence Ghetto: they will "pull down" the seven-story ruin (518). The space neither speaks to her of a relatable past nor carries an intrinsic message for the future; rather, the "innumerable sashless windows [appear] like the vacant eyes of the blind" that cannot see the horizon (518). It is at this point in the article that Levy imagines the distinct contrast between the "tricked-out Ghetto palace" decorated for Carnivale and the now-sacred ruin haunting her thoughts, as she thinks she sees "faces of ghosts" and hears the "sound heard in a dream" while walking in the dilapidated alley pathways of the Ghetto (519). Levy offers a lament: "Poor-old Palace-Prison! You are very splendid, but it is only a funeral pomp, after all. The lamps flicker, the people stream out, the musicians play louder and louder—'that when he dies he makes a swan-like end, Fading in Music'" (520). Here we see that Levy's complex relationship to the Ghetto is underpinned with guilt for the destruction of this tie to the past and angst about a new, untethered future. Her last line confirms this proto-modernist feeling, as she misquotes a scene from Shakespeare's *Merchant of Venice*. The play, as Linda Hunt Beckman has noted, held a special place in Levy home theater productions, with Amy Levy notably cast as Shylock.[11] Shakespeare's line reads:

> Let music sound, while he doth make his choice;
> Then if he loses he makes a swan-like end,
> Fading in music.[12]

In contrast, Levy's last lines of her essay close in on the certainty of the Florence Ghetto's finality: Levy's substitutions are telling, for as she replaces the original subjunctive "if" with a seemingly fatalistic "when," it is no longer a "choice" but "death" that is certain. While walking about she observes that "it is true that the Jews have ceased to dwell in the Ghetto, but they have by no means ceased to dwell in the city" (520). Alex Goody has argued that Levy sees the city as a "force which not only allows transgression but itself crosses borders between private and public, interior and exterior." The city's "intersections, interchanges, and subversions make it impossible to maintain the division of self and other, object and subject."[13] Levy seems to confirm this reading as she remarks to herself that the facial characteristics of native Florentines make them indistinguishable from Jews. Her comment is not so much about literal confusion over the identity of Jews and Florentines as it is a wider observation about how the city provides opportunities for these slippages between self and other through a new social contract created, she assumes, through the Ghetto's destruction. The Ghetto was the product of an old social contract, a way for Jews to remain a part of the city in an early modern city-state. In the late nineteenth century, Levy hopes, the continued presence of the Jewish population in the city will confirm a new contract for the future, one filled with potential. The Ghetto must die, she explains, but the city, as an equally rich site of Jewish identity, past and present, remains.

Levy's mapping of the Ghetto of Florence fuses the discrete place with the psychic effects of segregation that although not gone are manifested differently for her contemporary Jewish community. The ghetto is no longer a place of the past but a vehicle for remapping the Jewish people's past as defined not by their former confinement but by their enduring connection to the larger urban fabric of the city. In this way, Levy demonstrates something akin to what Todd Presner, David Shepard, and Yoh Kawano have described as the purpose of countermaps and counterhistories: a way of "curating places, conjuring and caring for ghosts" already in our midst.[14]

In "Primo Levi, the Ghetto, and *The Periodic Table*," Murray Baumgarten demonstrates how the German Nazi-created ghettos reveal the dark underbelly of nationalist projects and how this space can then also be reclaimed as a restorative laboratory to imagine new and more hopeful futures. Emanuela Trevisan Semi and Dario Miccoli's essay, "What the Mellah Was: Imagining the Moroccan Jewish Quarter," demonstrates how the imagined ghetto in literature, when remapped onto a space grappling with the missing historical artifacts of the mellah, can revive communal memories entangled within complex and enduring postcolonial legacies.

For Baumgarten, Trevisan Semi, and Miccoli, the Nazi ghetto and Moroccan mellah are physical spaces with opposing significance that shape the meaning of Jewish experiences for the authors of the works they discuss. Whether real or imaginary, then, the ghetto is transformed by memory into a laboratory for its inhabitants to change their worlds—from Primo Levi's metaphorical chemistry laboratory to escape the Nazi Lager to the nostalgic dream of returning to past places and times of the mellah that no longer exist. The ghetto remains a critical part of Jewish history but not as it existed historically; the ghetto space is less important than the transmogrification of its significance for generations past and present. As Daniel B. Schwartz reminds us, it is useful to think of the ghetto "not as a neat conceptual package, but as a changing and contested conglomeration of diverse elements, brought together by the contingencies of history and the projection of memory."[15] Building on this idea, Trevisan Semi and Miccoli suggest in their essay that literature becomes a "cartographic catalog" by which we remember places as boundary monuments to a community whose access to spaces is mediated by cross-generational memories.[16] Sounds, smells, tastes, and daily routines that marked generations of the lived community are now encoded on pages of text, and literature becomes the map by which to explore and navigate complex legacies of contested, ghettoized spaces and histories.

NOTES

1. Jacopo de' Barbari, *View of Venice*, Cleveland Museum of Art, https://clevelandart.org/art/1949.565.1.
2. Israel Zangwill, *Italian Fantasies* (New York: Macmillan, 1910), 306, 309.
3. See Todd Presner, David Shepard, and Yoh Kawano, *Hypercities: Thick Mapping in the Digital Humanities* (Cambridge, MA: Harvard University Press, 2014): "Thick maps are conjoined with stories, and stories are conjoined with maps, such that ever more complex contexts for meaning are created. As such, thick maps are never finished and meanings are never definitive. They are infinitely extensible and participatory, open to the unknown and to futures that have not yet come. And perhaps most importantly, thick maps betray their conditions of possibility, their authorship and contingency, without naturalizing or imposing a singular world-view. In essence, thick maps give rise to forms of counter-mapping, alternative maps, multiple voices, and on-going contestations. Thick maps are not simply 'more data' on maps, but interrogations of the very possibility of data, mapping, and cartographic representational practices. In this sense, 'thickness' arises from the never-ending friction between maps and counter-maps, constructions and deconstructions, mappings and counter-mapping" (19).
4. Robert Bevan, *The Destruction of Memory: Architecture at War* (London: Reaktion Books, 2007), 16.
5. Murray Baumgarten, "Israel Zangwill and the Afterlife of the Venice Ghetto," special issue, "The Ghetto as a Victorian Text," ed. Murray Baumgarten, *Partial Answers* 13, no. 1 (January 2015), 79.
6. Lady Katie Magnus, *Jewish Portraits* (London, 1888), 15. References to Magnus's work refer to this edition and will henceforth be cited parenthetically in the text.
7. Marianne Hirsch, "Presidential Address 2014—Connective Histories in Vulnerable Times," *PMLA* 129, no. 3 (2014): 330–48.
8. Walter Benjamin, *Illuminations*, ed. Hannah Arendt, trans. Harry Zohn (New York: Schocken Books, 1968), 263.
9. Melvyn New, ed., *The Complete Novels and Selected Writings of Amy Levy, 1861–1889* (Gainesville: University Press of Florida, 1993), 520. References to Levy's work refer to this edition and will henceforth be cited parenthetically in the text.
10. Richa Dwor, "'Poor Old Palace-Prison!': Jewish Urban Memory in Amy Levy's 'The Ghetto at Florence' (1886)," special issue, "The Ghetto as a Victorian Text," ed. Murray Baumgarten, *Partial Answers* 13, no. 1 (January 2015): 156, 158.
11. Linda Hunt Beckman, *Amy Levy: Her Life and Letters* (Athens: Ohio University Press, 2000), 14.
12. William Shakespeare, *The Merchant of Venice*, ed. Cedric Watts (Ware, Hertfordshire: Wordsworth Classics, 2000), 3.2.43–45.
13. Alex Goody, "Murder in Mile End: Amy Levy, Jewishness, and the City," *Victorian Literature and Culture* 34, no. 2 (2006): 469, 461.
14. Presner, Shepard, and Kawano, *Hypercities*, 15.
15. Daniel B. Schwartz, *Ghetto: The History of a Word* (Cambridge, MA: Harvard University Press, 2019), 5.
16. Emanuela Trevisan Semi and Dario Miccoli, "What the Mellah Was," this volume, 166.

CHAPTER SIX

PRIMO LEVI, THE GHETTO, AND THE PERIODIC TABLE

MURRAY BAUMGARTEN

GHETTO AS CULTURAL TROPE AND THOUGHT EXPERIMENT: AN INTRODUCTION

The specter of the ghetto hovers over Primo Levi's *The Periodic Table* (1975). The hybrid memoir captures the haunting atrocities of World War II and, instead of shuttering them away, invites them into the experimental space of the chemist's former laboratory, re-created from a series of memories. Each memory of Jewish experience, tied to different moments of space and time, functions in Levi's mind like an element, with the potential to be combined and recombined as in a chemistry experiment. Every moment explores and clarifies new structures of understanding of difficult and interlinked pasts. The results of these moments reveal how the lived experience of Jewish people across time and space has been shaped by rolling traumas, external elements, and processes. The ghetto becomes the blueprint—the formula—against which we can test different moments of experience, determining what is known and unknown about Jewish historical trauma. This scientific approach allows Levi to face the unknown in a productive way, defining a framework that makes it possible to systematically uncover missing traces. The ghetto is a portal into the lives of a people and a community. It functions as a literary trope and thought experiment, as Levi explores how this traumatic experience articulates a fateful and as yet incomplete account of a people's history and future. For in *The Periodic Table*, the ghetto now maps a dynamic memory space that travels, whose destinations serve as a container for memory, cartography encoding remembrance. From a contemporary perspective, the history of the ghetto is both haunted and shaped by our understanding of the spaces and places that in the modern era have carried this name.

We can trace the image of the ghetto in this book beginning with the legacy and continuing influence of the original Venice Ghetto, established in 1516. That powerful beginning was followed by the process of ghettoization that swept through the principalities of Renaissance and Baroque Italy and led among others to the Ghetto of Turin—Primo Levi's hometown—which was consolidated in 1679. The ghetto story did not end there: despite Risorgimento and Jewish Emancipation in the eighteenth century, as well as national unification in the last quarter of the nineteenth century, ghettoization emerged once more with Mussolini's 1938 racial laws. Then the Nazis seized on the name of "ghetto" and, transforming it, made it into an instrument for genocide. Primo Levi's writing attests to the murderous program of the Lager of Auschwitz, where he was an enslaved laborer from 1943 until liberation in January 1945. He spent three of those months in a laboratory in the Auschwitz subcamp Buna, participating in the effort to develop synthetic rubber. His book explores the continuing impact of personal and communal trauma in the tumultuous postwar era. Implicit in *The Periodic Table* is the question of what kind of recovery might be possible following the Nazi transformation of Europe. The ghetto spaces and times—of the Venice Ghetto, Turin Ghetto, and Nazi Lager—are all singular examples of forcible Jewish sequestration and control that came together in the twentieth century to generate and reinforce the humiliating stereotype of the Jews as aliens: the ghetto, we now know, prepares the way for the murderous purpose of the lager.

And, in the aftermath, in the space of memory, recombinations of these historical experiences prompt Levi to create a map of Jewish life under these conditions, demonstrating how despite attempts to contain them, their impact exceeds their moment in time and provides a pathway into understanding the historical events that lead to moments of freedom and creativity even under extreme repression. Pieced together, these different experiences of historical segregation echo Walter Benjamin's concept of messianic time: "The past can be seized only as an image which flashes up at the instant when it can be recognized and is never seen again . . . For every image of the past that is not recognized by the present as one of its own concerns threatens to disappear irretrievably."[1] By mapping the relation of these different versions, transformations, and reiterations of the original Venice Ghetto, Levi invites us to learn about their significance for his present. How can this historical understanding of the way in which these interlinked pasts work together allow us to forge a path toward a more positive future?

The image of the ghetto raises questions about how Jewish identity and Jewish life has been and may continue to be constructed. Together, the Venice Ghetto, the Turin Ghetto, and the Nazi Lager elaborate a defining image of a people and their place in modern European history, which Levi describes and to which he crafts a powerful response, charting the totalizing impact of the ghetto now reinforced by the lager. This claim leads the reader to entertain the possibility that after the defeat of the Nazis there is a way out of the trauma of the Shoah. That possibility is embedded in the narrative discourse of the text's twenty-one chapters, *The Periodic Table* having been named for the chemical elements in narrative counterpoint to the autobiographical coming-of-age account of the protagonist, Primo Levi, whom we must distinguish from the author of the same name.

SPATIAL MAPPING AND IDENTITY FORMATION: TRAUMA AND SHAMING

Reading *The Periodic Table*, we hear a person choosing his words carefully in an unusual narrative that crystallizes a modern literary tradition. *The Periodic Table* brings to mind the personal narratives of Charles Darwin and Richard Feynman, the letters of Albert Einstein and Oliver Sacks, and the autobiographical account of the difficult work history and lived experience of Primo Levi's cousin and fellow citizen of Turin, the Nobel Laureate Rita Levi-Montalcini, in *In Praise of Imperfection: My Life and Work* (1988). Like these writers, Levi articulates connections between scientific discoveries, personal experiences, and ethnographic insights into scientific intellectual communities. Readers will also think of Jorge Luis Borges's stories and the philosophical fiction of Rebecca Goldstein that reveal how individuals inscribe themselves in "mattering maps."[2]

Similar to those narratives, which at times read like parables, Primo Levi's narrator speaks directly to us, building an intimate relation with the reader. We are invited into the chemist's world to hear personal stories of his trade in everyday language: the successes and failures of the young chemist Primo Levi unroll before us. No one pulls rank on us or scolds us for not knowing the atomic weights of elements or the bonds binding electrons into molecules, and no one is scorned for a dislike of calculus. This narrative does not charge an entrance fee.

From Static Argon to Dynamic Carbon

Chemical practice and personal experience interact and generate an intimate dialogue. The narrative builds on the role of witnessing central to Primo Levi's first book, *Survival in Auschwitz*, and reaches through the language of testimony to elaborate a lexicon for ethics. How to approach a book named for the chart of the central building blocks of matter organized by modern chemistry has disconcerted and surprised many readers. For what could the generic expectations be of a book that deploys twenty-one chemical elements to recount, among others, the complicated and tangled experiences of a Piedmontese Jewish family; the education of a chemist who just manages to get into graduate school in the era of the anti-Jewish racial laws; the responses of his friends; his brief failed partisan adventure; his eleven months as an enslaved laborer in Auschwitz; and his postwar life and work after returning to his family and hometown. Primo Levi tells us of his family history, beginning with "Argon." In what follows he connects life experiences and chemical elements, a natural linkage for the history of the education of a Jewish chemist singled out by the racial laws of 1938 and relegated once again to ghettoization in twentieth-century Italy. *The Periodic Table* responds to his situation as he explores some of the meanings of re-ghettoization and enslavement in the lager: note how the first chapter of the book opens with a succinct discussion of argon, one of "the so-called inert gases in the air we breathe," which by the beginning of the second paragraph quickly turns comparative: these sentences lead readers into the realm of metaphor.[3] Each spatially and temporally rooted memory is mapped back onto an element on the periodic table with similar properties, an exercise that will allow him to experiment with recombinations of these memories.

First, Levi lists the characteristics of argon: a gas "so inert, so satisfied" with its condition that it does "not interfere in any chemical reaction," does "not combine with any other element, and for precisely this reason" has "gone undetected for centuries" (3–4). The narrator then begins his second paragraph by telling us "the little that I know about my ancestors presents many similarities to these gases." These "noble gases" are often also designated as "rare," while "one of them, argon (the Inactive)," is "more abundant than carbon dioxide; without that there would not be a trace of life on this planet" (3–4). Chemical analysis aims for precision, so we learn immediately of a social nuance: Primo Levi's ancestors were not all "materially inert," for they had to be "quite active, in order to earn a living." Nevertheless, the narrator continues, "there is no doubt that they were inert in their inner spirits, inclined to disinterested speculation, witty discourses, elegant, sophisticated and gratuitous discussion" (4).

These characteristics of argon, especially its inertness, define his ancestors: "It can hardly be by chance that all the deeds attributed to them, though quite various, have in common a touch of the static, an attitude of dignified abstention, of voluntary (or accepted) relegation to the margins of the great river of life. Noble, inert, and rare: their history is quite poor when compared to that of other illustrious Jewish communities in Italy and Europe" (4–5). Will Primo Levi, the protagonist of this narrative, be static and passive like his relatives?

The first two chapters offer descriptions of negative situations whose sting is somewhat ameliorated, even qualified, and yet leave the reader perplexed. They take us from "inert gases" to inert "inner spirits" that generate, even so, "witty discourses" having no outcome in action and thus are unsatisfying. The people of his family are relegated to the "margins of the great river of life," it bears repeating. They are "quite poor" by comparison to those living in the "illustrious Jewish communities of Italy and Europe." Comparing his family to argon, the narrator sets the chemical periodic table into motion as a familial mapping.

It is a charming and amusing comparison of a familial inheritance that hinders achievement even as it offers the security of established habits. These qualities deserve to be acknowledged, if not applauded. But note that *The Periodic Table* concludes with carbon, already mentioned in its first sentences, that most active and welcoming of elements, which drives the action of writing, as we discover in the final sentence of the book. Carbon—with its traits of flexibility, the building block of life—embodies Benjamin's call to recognize the potential of messianic time.

A paragraph later, after the mention of carbon, this amusing, ironic, and self-deprecating comparison leads into a series of events that brand his family and shame them in their Jewishness. That shame, whose dimensions and ongoing power we will discover in the course of this account, is the operating force relegating them to their inert status. Like the conversos—the Jews who stayed in Spain after 1492 by converting, hoping they would not be noticed (*de no ser notado,* as the Spanish phrase has it, "to go undetected")—so too these immigrants to Turin. And even emancipated, the power of the many faces of their shaming keeps them inert. This first chapter, providing the defining experience of this narrator's family, maps its familial range and extent. In the process of this investigation we will build a case for the power of this book as a defining map of modern and contemporary Jewish life as well.

Lurking in the shadows of the opening chapter of *The Periodic Table,* shame defines a Jewish family's experience from the first sentences, which briefly describe a family's arrival in Turin in the sixteenth century: the Jews—a tiny minority—bring not moneylending but silk making to Piedmont. They are neither welcomed nor excluded; the phrase will be echoed in Giorgio Bassani's *The Garden of the Finzi-Continis*[4] and carries the impact of the ghetto, which made Jews invisible in daily life except when visibility was of benefit to their "betters."

In a riveting paragraph, Primo Levi encapsulates their shamed experience. His father's generation is mocked for its Jewish piety in a song that focuses on the *tzitzit,* the tassels of prayer shawls, which, wrapped around their fingers, Jews use to kiss the letters of the Torah scroll they unfurl in the synagogue on market days and the Sabbath. That history of derision becomes the mockery of the SS, which some decades later makes underwear of the prayer shawls, the *taleysim* of Jewish practice, in the vicious degradation of the Jews and their world-historical shaming by the Nazis. Threaded throughout this account of the chemist's trade, shame drives the narrative of *The Periodic Table* (*Il Sistema Periodico*), published in 1975. Eleven years later, in 1986, Primo Levi elaborated its psychic and social impact in *The Drowned and the Saved* (*I Sommersi e i Salvati*).

Primo Levi's ethnographic and autobiographical account is worth looking at in further detail as he elaborates the ways in which the ghetto hovered over his family and set their central gesture: that of being ashamed. This narrative of indirection ranges from the arrival of Jews in Turin early in the sixteenth century to the Era of Emancipation beginning in 1848, as it tells us of the impact of the Shoah on his life and the postwar reconstruction of Italian Jewish communal life.

The third paragraph of "Argon" begins by shifting to the reception accorded the Jews of Turin: "Rejected or given a less than warm welcome in Turin," the narrator notes, reminding us of their difficult if not totally negative situation. Yet even "in their most flourishing periods," these Jews were an "extremely tiny minority." Like argon, hardly noticed, his ancestors were "never much loved or much hated" and do not have stories of "unusual persecutions." And now he unpacks the implications of their almost unwelcome: nevertheless, "a wall of suspicion, of undefined hostility and mockery, must have kept them substantially separated from the rest of the population, even several decades after the emancipation of 1848, if what my father told me of his childhood in Bene Vagienna is true" (4–5). Note that this is the first and only mention of Primo Levi's father, Cesare, in this chapter, so centered on family matters and names. The mention of Cesare's hometown is taken up by Levi's biographer, Ian Thomson, who followed this lead and filled in the family history.[5] That generational experience bears the imprint of the controlling ghetto, a spectral, powerful, and continuing force in their lives in Turin.

The prosperity of the grandfather's family, Thomson notes, "had profited greatly" from the "secular liberalism that followed the Savoy edict" of the 1848 Jewish Emancipation. Cesare Levi was born in 1878; there were to be two more sons. "Jews were now able," Thomson tells us, "to trade," even "with the Church," one of the largest economic powers of that era. Thomson continues: "Records at Bene Vagienna indicate that [the family] owned at least fourteen properties, many of them formerly church lands." Levi Company, the family business, "was also a bank." Thomson indicates its importance in the next sentence: "One could almost say that the Levi bank was the National Bank of these lands." However, prosperity was not certain, and "in the summer of 1888 a rumour (of unknown origin) spread that 'Levi & Sons' had run out of credit, leading to a run on the bank by angry creditors." Thomson's sources indicate that "they intended to lynch Michele Levi and his father Giuseppe."[6]

In a throwback to earlier times, these once-respected financiers were now seen as despised Jewish moneylenders. One of the mob, a priest with savings of eleven thousand lire, "raised such an outcry as he tried to recover them that 200 peasants assembled in the street outside the bank." The priest, Canon Pietro Dompé, "had no difficulty in whipping up anti-Jewish passions," and "the crowd had to be pushed back by carabinieri and the Levi house cordoned off to avoid 'further troubles.'" Fleeing Bene Vagienna on "Tuesday 24 July 1888, Michele Levi made it to Turin." The "frightened engineer" found refuge, "according to a newspaper," with his wife's relatives, "staying in Turin's former ghetto."[7] Note that Michele was Primo Levi's uncle; Michele is Primo's middle name.

There were consequences to the shift in public opinion. "In the weekend edition of July 26–27, the Turin *Gazzetta del Popolo* reported the suicide of Engineer Michele Levi of Bene Vagienna, aged 40," who at two o'clock in the morning "threw himself out of a window from the second floor of a residence at 18 Via San Francesco da Paola into the courtyard below." An hour later, in the hospital, he was declared "dead on arrival."[8]

Thomson reports that the "Levi company" was never actually bankrupt but "had been forced to close down by the efforts of an 'anti-Jewish priest.'" Thomson also notes that "soon after the Levis were hounded out of Bene Vagienna, Canon Dompé founded a replacement bank in the town."[9] The unstated ironies indicate some of the continuing sources of Jew-hatred. As we see, even in emancipated 1888, the ghetto continued to function not only as the diasporic home of the Jews—more than neighborhood, almost a sanctuary—but also as their stereotyped status as despised moneylenders.

The ghetto, Dana Katz tells us, "created an architecture of vision that situated the Jew in a unique spatial relationship with the city." As Katz emphasizes, the ghetto gave "physical form to the subordination of Jews and Judaism," and its "spatial practices" indeed "disenfranchised Jews with the perpetual gaze of surveillance embedded in the Jews' enclosure."[10] Michele Levi's escape to the ghetto and his suicide there reinforced the branding of his family as Jews.

Their displacement unsettled notions of place, even as "the establishment of the ghetto preserved the Jews' position as a legally constituted community." Note the psychic impact of the geography instituted by the ghetto: the "politics of place . . . required their subordinated status." Furthermore, incorporating "the ghetto into the built environment created an urban matrix of shifting borders and delimiting places of private life that draws attention to the unstable divide between center and periphery."[11] Instead of the anonymity of the metropolis, the ghetto marked the urban fabric as "infected zones where all kinds of monstrosities are possible, and where a different man is born, an aberrant from the prototype who inhabits the center of things."[12]

Primo Levi's account is dynamic, moving from the muddles of first-person relationships to the mastery of third-person narration: it includes the struggles of his personal experience, which he renders in a first-person narrative, and the magisterial voice of a chemist's judgment noting the takeaway at the conclusion of an experiment. Grounded in first-person telling of the narrator's experience as he becomes a chemist and grows into manhood, Primo Levi reflects on his unfolding life experiences. And in the third-person narration, the narrative elicits a series of coming-of-age accounts of a young, middle-class Italian Jew. Inviting the reader to join in the comparison of chemical elements and family history, *The Periodic Table* establishes an unusual and powerful combination for making metaphors.

Fundamental scientific insights coalesce into communal and personal discoveries: in *The Periodic Table* the reader joins the narrator in constructing the dialogue of action and reflection that this book articulates. Literary art and chemical analysis reframe living experience to generate unfolding insights—as if we were observing a photographic image emerging in developing fluid. As we read the book it engages us in thinking with and feeling for Primo Levi, Italian Jew, chemist, partisan, enslaved laborer of the lager, young man, life writer.

Reading *The Periodic Table*, we discover how aspects of Primo Levi's life story parallel the elements of the periodic table: the methods of chemical analysis elicit the pressure of racist stereotyping, cultural trauma, personal terror, and political oppression. We learn of their impact on familial behavior, minority experience, and cross-cultural economic and social interaction. Primo Levi's action, inflected by his Jewish experience, becomes a lens into mainstream culture: his book sifts, examines, weighs, and assesses the range of harsh totalitarian experiences of the twentieth century as it also separates them into their various elements.

The Holocaust survivor's shame is reinforced by the stereotyping that inscribes historic shaming imposed by ghettoization from 1516 onward and generates an exponential trauma that pervades his experience. The different episodes form the chapters of his various efforts to recuperate from, if not fully to overcome, this defining trauma and make it possible for him to practice the chemist's trade as a Jew and an independent-minded young Italian navigating a dangerous, complex, and difficult economic and political landscape.

At the crossing point of the chemist's trade and the writer's craft, we encounter the speaker of this text.

"BECAUSE YOU NEVER KNOW"—SHAME: THE AFTERLIFE OF THE GHETTO AND THE LAGER

The deep reserve of the Turin community expressed in familial and communal privacy, which many observers have underlined as characteristic, is seconded by Primo Levi in his preface to the celebratory exhibit and catalog of the Turin Synagogue in 1984 on its one hundredth birthday.[13] Instead of accepting that reserve as a given—as if Turin's Jews were afflicted with the English habit of knowing your place that its social structure enforced—it is worth asking what instigated and reinforced such reserve. Reading this introduction leads me also to ask to what extent that reserve figures as a notable feature of the social, political, cultural, and psychological landscape of his community as well as of his writing, even after emancipation, which came to Piedmont only in 1848 and more than two decades later to the rest of a unifying Italy.

Even emancipation, Primo Levi noted on the occasion of "the centenary of the inauguration" of "our Synagogue, which took place on 16 February 1884," did not bring the Jews of Turin out of "our double traditional dual reserve." That "well-known Piedmontese reserve," which "leads some to see us as the least Italian of Italians," he comments, continued to be "superimposed on the age-old reserve of the Diaspora Jew, forever accustomed to living in silence and suspicion, listening a great deal and saying little, not drawing attention to himself, because 'you never know.'"[14] The dangling phrase with which his sentence concludes functions as a personal reaching out: you, too, the reader, may not want to draw attention to yourself. Better to listen in "silence and suspicion, listening a great deal," and keep your views to yourself, "because you never know."

As he describes the "age-old reserve of the Diaspora Jew," speaking of the "double traditional dual reserve" of the Jews of Turin, I cannot help but think of the ghetto and the lager. Together they are the engine driving this reserve: what the Venetians devised in 1516 that spread quickly and lasted until 1848 in Piedmont and until the 1870s throughout Italy, was reinforced in the twentieth century by the Fascist racial laws of 1938. Five years later, the Nazi invasion of Italy and the imposition of the hegemony of the lager system inscribed it in the Italian and Jewish psyche. Israel Zangwill's dictum that the ghetto is the "law of Jewish being" would continue to be the defining algorithm of Jewish life, perhaps until the reclaiming of the Old City of Jerusalem by Israeli forces in the Six-Day War.[15] Ghetto history, twentieth-century racial laws, Nazi imposition of the lager—together they set the context for the literary tone, nested gesture, and hidden subtexts of this writing.

The subtlety of Levi's introduction is characteristic; it is easy to pass over the modest narrative voice and the care with which words were chosen that is evident in the phrasing. Keen readers quickly notice that the Piedmontese reserve is layered on and reinforces an older strategy of reticence and self-protection that derives from the Jewish community's historical experience. Living in Diaspora, the Jews existed at someone else's whim and desire, and even the contract the Jews (implicitly) agreed to in moving to the Venice Ghetto made them participants in a political arrangement—if reluctantly so—subjecting them to a hostile sovereign power. And that experience even after emancipation reached an intense pitch as a result of the Fascist racial laws of 1938; it turned murderous under the Nazi assault. Implicit in Primo Levi's phrasing in his preface to the commemorative volume *Ebrei a Torino: Ricerche per il Centenario della Sinagoga (1884–1984)* (Jews in Turin: Research for the centenary of the synagogue, 1884–1984), we find a gesture toward the social control of the Jews exercised by the majority. Even in 1884 and still resonant a hundred years later at the publication of the catalog, the specter of the ghetto hovers.

Again, tone counts: Primo Levi does not write an exultant communal congratulation but instead reminds us of the "Piedmontese reserve" that reinforces and, as if in a chemical formula, is superimposed on "the age-old reserve of the Diaspora Jew, forever accustomed to living in silence and suspicion, listening a great deal and saying little, not drawing attention to himself, because," as he phrases it, "'you never know.'"[16] Note the complexity of the Italian phrasing with which he begins:

> In occasione del centenario dell'inaugurazione della nostra Sinagoga, avvenuta il 16 febbraio 1884, noi ebrei torinese abbiamo risoluto di venir meno, per una volta, al nostro duplice tradizionale riserbo. E il ben noto riserbo piemontese, legato a radiche geografiche e storiche, per cui c'e' chi vede in noi i meno Italiani fra gli italiani, sovrapposto al millenario riserbo dell'ebreo diasporico, avvezzo da sempre a vivere nel silenzio e nel sospettto, ad ascoltare molto ed a parlare poco, a non farsi notare, perche "non si sa mai."[17]

It is worth underlining the penultimate phrase, *a non farsi notare*, which echoes the private mantra of the Spanish converso, *de no ser notado*, "not to be noticed." And that leads into the punctuating phrase with which this paragraph ends: "*perche 'non si sa mai,'*" which the translator Sharon Wood writes as "because you never know."

Note that the Turin Ghetto was established in 1679 and abolished in 1848. But in 1938 with the promulgation of the racial laws and then the takeover of Italy by the Nazis in 1943, the new ghetto was established all over Europe, along with the killing centers massacring the Jews as an industrial production. Primo Levi's preface to the centenary of the Turin Synagogue is a general statement about the Jews of Turin and also a personal description resonant with his experience as an enslaved laborer in Auschwitz.

Celebrating the synagogue's centenary by glancing at numbers, he comments that "there have never been many of us: barely four thousand in the 1930s, and that was the highest figure we ever reached, while today—1984—there are just over one thousand." Note how his doubled reserve leads to a muting of the celebratory tone and informs the next sentence: "And yet we don't feel we are overstating the case if we say that we have counted for something, and we still count for something in the life of this city."[18] We hear the sense of limits in his phrasing. There is a striking modesty with which he regards his and his Jewish community's success.

Numbers count yet don't tell the whole story. With the exception of just about two years when he was in succession a prisoner of the Fascists and Nazis and then a liberated survivor seeking to return home, Primo Levi lived his entire life in Turin, where he was born in 1919, living in the same house on Corso Re Umberto 75 until his death in 1987. By that time, Turin had become a dynamic and progressive northern Italian industrial hub, home not only to Fiat but Olivetti, which stamped Italian industrial production with a reputation for design.

And there is little mention that Primo Levi's Turin was the city that had led the way in the second half of the nineteenth century to Italian unification under the deft leadership of Cavour (the prime minister) and King Carlo Alberto. And it was in Turin that Garibaldi organized his expedition of the Thousand that captured Sicily and Naples and completed Italian unification by taking over the Vatican, thus making Rome the capital of the new Italian nation-state in 1871. The House of Savoy had close ties with revolutionary France and had resisted the example of other Italian cities, including Rome, that had embraced ghettoization.

The ghetto reluctantly established in Turin not far from the city center was abolished by royal decree on March 29, 1848, exactly 332 years to the day from the establishment of the Venice Ghetto in 1516.

A stroke of the pen, and King Carlo Alberto emancipated the Jews and made them citizens of Piedmont. The Jews of Piedmont celebrated, placing plaques in their synagogues praising the king and expressing their thanks privately. Unlike the Jews of Rome, who built a magnificent cathedral-like synagogue in the historic ghetto across the Tiber from the Vatican, the Turin Jews sold their new building (the *Mole*), the elaborate monument, which their architect kept building to commemorate emancipation, to the city fathers. "We too of course," Primo Levi notes, "like everybody from Turin, harbour a certain affection for the *Mole*, but our love for it is ironic and polemical and we do not allow it to blind us. We love it as we love the walls of our homes, but we know it is ugly, presumptuous and of little use." If the operation had not succeeded, he notes, "we would today be faced with a melancholy spectacle: the few hundred Jews who go to the Temple on solemn feast days, and the few dozen who go for daily services, would be almost invisible in the enormous space enclosed by Antonelli's dome."[19]

JEWISH IRONY AND DOUBLE-VOICED DISCOURSE: THE JEWISH DIALECT

The ironic stance evident in the preface underlines the structural ambiguity of the historic Jewish experience in Turin. It is already used in *The Periodic Table*, when Primo Levi begins by commenting that the Jews were "given a less than warm welcome in Turin." Introducing "the technology of making silk, they were never much loved or much hated, stories of unusual persecution have not been handed down" (4). How to tell their complex and perplexing story that includes their participation in the Risorgimento, the optimism of nation building, and the trauma of the Nazi deportations that multiplied the historic weight of ghettoization?

Primo Levi tells us that "Post-Risorgimento Italy" turned "its Jews into a class of good citizens who respected the law, who were loyal to the State and far removed from corruption and violence." From "this point of view, the integration of Italian Jewry is very unusual; more unusual still, perhaps, is the equilibrium of Turinese-Piedmontese Jewry, which integrated easily without losing its own identity." And it is not surprising that this small group of people fully aware of their own identity devised "a curious Judeo-Piedmontese language" that "our fathers and mothers used on a daily basis": it became the "language of family and of the home."[20]

Speaker of several languages and explorer of the properties of chemical elements, metaphors, and analytic skills, Primo Levi includes a comment on his community's dialect worthy of attention. Using it on a daily basis, the Jews of Turin "were nonetheless aware of its intrinsic comic force." That comic force "sprang from the contrast between the layer of language that was rustic and laconic Piedmontese dialect, and the Hebrew interpolations which derived from the language of the Patriarchs, remote but revived each day by public and private prayer, the reading of the Texts, worn smooth by the millennia as the river bed by the glacier."[21]

Language fusion leads us to history and culture: "this contrast mirrored another, the essential contrast of Judaism dispersed amongst the peoples, the Gentiles, stretched taut between divine vocation and the wretchedness of their daily lives; it mirrored another contrast also, on a much larger scale, one intrinsic to the human condition, since man is bipartite, a dough made of divine breath and earthly dust. After the Diaspora the Jewish people lived this conflict painfully, and from it, along with its wisdom, has acquired its laughter, which is not to be found in the Bible and the prophets." There is little assertion of self or community in this phrasing. Even as he cites the Jewish participation in the resistance to the Nazis, "higher than their mere numbers would suggest; and the 800 deportees, of whom nothing more remains than a tombstone in our cemetery," he does not deviate from his elegiac tone. With "this exhibition," Primo Levi notes, "we perform an act of filial piety," in order "to show to our friends in Turin, and our children, who we are and where we have come from." On this occasion of the commemoration of the centenary of the synagogue, Primo Levi notes, "we did not wish to speak of victories, defeats, struggles, and massacres." The task is, rather, to "remember, to invite others to remember, to introduce ourselves before it is too late."[22]

The task set by this writer is to braid the facts of history into the seductive context of literature. The situation, the discourse—"because you never know"—foregrounds the experience in the second person and grammatical present tense that cannot be evaded. With the narrator, the reader participates in the process of imagining the Shoah: she becomes with the narrator its witness, the one who, attesting to its truth, tells the story. For, as he says, "because you never know."

ETHNOGRAPHY AND *HIER IST KEIN WARUM*

To grasp the originality of *The Periodic Table*, we need to look briefly at Primo Levi's first book, *Survival in Auschwitz*, which forms its personal and political context. There, shortly after his arrival in Auschwitz, he encounters a situation that punctuates the fact that in the lager, normal logic does not apply. I call it the scene of the "*Hier ist kein warum*," and it becomes the dominating situation of his lager experience. There is no why here: it is a singular example of how trauma shapes thought and action. Primo Levi charts the impact of the violent, power-driven effort by Nazis to redefine modern Western culture in a "gigantic biological and social experiment."[23]

For while this book recounts personal experiences in the hell of Auschwitz, unlike other accounts, it does not remain personal. Instead, personal experience directs the reader to the parameters of the general situation. After the horror of the train ride from Fossoli to Auschwitz, Primo Levi's thirst becomes a lesson in the Nazi social system. It was cold, there had been snow, he reaches out from the barracks for an icicle that will slake his thirst. But the guard knocks it out of his hand. In his "*povere Tedesco*" ("poor German," Primo Levi calls it), he asks, "*Warum?*" And the guard answers, "Hier ist kein warum." It is a brief exchange: like much of his writing it deserves a second look, in Italian, in whatever language with which you are most comfortable. And he records and then translates this German phrase that hits like a slap across the face—even more, a body blow: "Hier ist kein warum."

Our second look at this exchange leads Primo and the reader, now in dialogue with him, to understand that this "Hier ist kein warum" is not just a personal insult, a blow at Primo Levi, Italian Jew, marked to be killed in Auschwitz, but only after all possible usefulness for the Nazi Reich is wrung out of him. Now he, along with the reader, also recognizes that this is a central parameter, a defining dimension of Auschwitz: "Hier ist kein warum" is the new normal. Now both he and the reader know that this is what the lager is about. "Hier ist kein warum" is the System of the Lager, of this Nazi world. Primo Levi has now glimpsed and can begin to understand the defining parameters of the environment to which he must adapt if he is to live, survive, and tell of the horrors and the senseless work and random viciousness of this realm.

Note that this account is not just autobiographical but also, as Gregory Feldman notes, ethnographic: "I do not want to trivialize this profound work by saying that it is simply the best ethnography that this anthropologist has ever read. Ethnography is a mode of research and writing that captures not the local per se, but rather the particular: that which appears, and can only appear, through historically contingent events. Levi obtains such phenomenal descriptive insight into what made Auschwitz tick not because he understood racism and bureaucratic management, but because he grasped how the plurality of ordinary people—capable of making choices and of initiating actions—integrated those features of modern society into their daily lives."[24] Furthermore, as Feldman makes clear in his analysis, Primo Levi and his colleagues in the scenes at the end of the book evaded the teleological death vectors of Auschwitz by collaborating and constituting a social world in opposition to the Hobbesian war of all against all of the Nazi Lager.

Feldman directs us to Levi's careful narrative of the last ten days of Auschwitz, asking the reader to focus on Levi's use of biblical imagery as the three survivors of his infirmary ward work together, finding two bags of potatoes and a working stove that Primo manages to wrestle into a wheelbarrow and bring to their ward, where they cook the potatoes. In Levi's words, "we were broken by tiredness, but seemed to have finally accomplished something useful—perhaps like God after the first day of creation." Feldman underlines the meaning of this action, for the survivors have reclaimed their humanity through mutual action: "They had no other choice; they would likely have perished if they had reverted to the old law of the camp: 'Eat your own bread and, if you can, that of your neighbor.'"[25]

Feldman's discussion of the actions taken by Primo Levi and his bunkmates in the infirmary ward highlights their reversal of the conditions of Auschwitz. Feldman's analysis recalls Hannah Arendt's account of the lager in *The Origins of Totalitarianism,* especially part 3, "Total Domination."[26] Working together, the bunkmates put into play the possible way out of their death world through reversing its defining conditions. Feldman directs us to a parallel vector that Hannah Arendt would articulate and elaborate on in a different discursive genre in *On Revolution* (1990) and *The Human Condition* (1958).

Different genres generate different kinds of knowledge, and Feldman's comment leads us to ask what field of vision and what horizon of expectations await the readers of Primo Levi's writing. To that we add Primo Levi's awareness of the perspective of the narrator and his position in relation to the narrated. As a scientist, Primo Levi follows here some of the key insights of modern physics and includes the situation of the observer in that which is being observed. That account informs us as to how religious othering prepared the way for the modern hatred embodied in the Italian racial laws of 1938 and the Nazi reinvention of ghettos as concentration camps for the starvation and murder of the Jews. These Jews do not resist their stereotyping, preferring to imagine they can evade stereotyping by simulating invisibility. They do not even speak out against their scapegoating, for they lack the power of agency; theirs not the forceful assertion of the Gedalists, the band of fighting Jewish partisans whom Levi will track in *If Not Now, When*. Naming them with the Hebrew name of their leader, the Gedalists prepare us for the arrival of the Israelis and the Zionist importance of the Hebrew speaking at the concluding section of *If Not Now, When*.

These later works can be traced back through the literary map of *The Periodic Table*. The stories of argon, the images and metaphoric resonances, encapsulate centuries of Jewish shaming. It sets their history on a spectrum of sequestration, from the founding of the Venice Ghetto in 1516 and even to their emancipation, first in 1848 in Piedmont by King Carlo Alberto, when they left their enclosures and entered its cities, and then in a unified Italy in 1870. That spatial marking was internalized, becoming intrinsic to Jewish identity, in response to the engine of a continuing antisemitism. Furthermore, it alerts us to the power and importance of this urban geography and its Jewish located-ness. For the ghetto defines the field of vision of the Jews and leads us to inquire into their horizon of expectations, defining the line of sight and the angle of vision of Primo Levi's narrative.

NOTES

1. Walter Benjamin, "On the Concept of History," https://www.sfu.ca/~andrewf/CONCEPT2.html. See also Primo Levi, *The Drowned and the Saved*, trans. Raymond Rosenthal (New York: Summit Books, 1988).
2. See Rebecca Newberger Goldstein, "The Mattering Map," video lecture, Smithsonian

Magazine, The Future is Here Festival, May 9, 2016, https://www.smithsonianmag.com/videos/category/future-is-here/mattering-map/.

3. Primo Levi, *The Periodic Table*, trans. Raymond Rosenthal (New York: Schocken Books, 1984), 3. All future references to this text refer to this edition and will be cited parenthetically in the text.
4. See Murray Baumgarten, "Primo Levi's 'Small Differences' and the Art of *The Periodic Table*: A Reading of 'Potassium,'" *Shofar* 32, no. 1 (2013): 60–78.
5. Ian Thomson, *Primo Levi: A Life* (London: Macmillan, 2004).
6. All quotations in this paragraph are from Thomson, *Primo Levi*, 8–9.
7. Thomson, 10.
8. Thomson, 10.
9. Thomson, 10–11.
10. Dana E. Katz, *The Jewish Ghetto and the Visual Imagination* (Philadelphia: University of Pennsylvania Press, 2008), 1, 13, 8.
11. Katz, *Jewish Ghetto*, 34.
12. Piero Camporesi, *The Incorruptible Flesh: Bodily Mutation and Mortification in Religion and Folklore*, trans. Tania Croft-Murray (Cambridge: Cambridge University Press, 1988), 79.
13. Primo Levi, preface to *Ebrei a Torino: Ricerche per il Centenario della Sinagoga (1884–1984)*, ed. Umberto Allemandi, in Levi, *The Black Hole of Auschwitz*, ed. Marco Belpoliti, trans. Sharon Wood (Cambridge: Polity, 2005).
14. Levi, preface, *Black Hole of Auschwitz*, 151.
15. Israel Zangwill, *Dreamers of the Ghetto* (London, 1898), quoted in Murray Baumgarten, "Israel Zangwill and the Afterlife of the Venice Ghetto," *Partial Answers* 13, no. 1 (2015): 80–81.
16. Levi, *Black Hole of Auschwitz*, 151.
17. Primo Levi, *Opere*, ed. Marco Belpoliti, 2 vols. (Torino: Einaudi, 1997), 2:1251.
18. Levi, *Black Hole of Auschwitz*, 151.
19. Levi, 151.
20. Levi, 154.
21. Levi, 154.
22. Levi, 154–55.
23. Primo Levi, *Survival in Auschwitz*, trans. Stuart Woolf (New York: Touchstone, 1996), 87.
24. Gregory Feldman, "Politics in Particular: From Primo Levi to Freedom and Being in the Works of Hannah Arendt and Baruch Spinoza," *Contours* 8 (Spring 2017): 1–2.
25. Feldman, "Politics in Particular," 2–3.
26. See Hannah Arendt, *Origins of Totalitarianism* (New York: Harcourt, 1973).

CHAPTER SEVEN

WHAT THE MELLAH WAS

Imagining the Moroccan Jewish Quarter

EMANUELA TREVISAN SEMI AND DARIO MICCOLI

Neither the word nor the concept *ghetto* was born in the Arab Muslim world. This does not mean, however, that forms of urban segregation for the Jews—as well as for other minority groups—were alien to the region or that Jewish quarters did not exist in this part of the world. Of course, such quarters had different characteristics and names from those of early modern Europe: the most significant and best-known example is the Moroccan *mellah*. Initially the name of a Fès neighborhood where salt—in Arabic, *milh*—was stored, the word "mellah" came to identify any Jewish neighborhood in Morocco where Jews were forced to live beginning in 1438.[1] In other North African countries, the term *hara* (neighborhood) was utilized, which referred to all Jewish quarters in general. The word "ghetto" has a similar story: at first it was the name of the Venice quarter where a foundry (*geto*) was located; then it came to signify and label every Jewish quarter in the West; and in time, it referred to all neighborhoods inhabited by any marginalized or excluded minority, to the point where the term has become synonymous with exclusion. In the globalized world of the twenty-first century, however, we do not speak of "mellahization" or "haratization" but rather of ghettoization, and the term *mellah* remains largely unknown, except to experts in the field. This might be because Jewish ghettoization was far stricter and more repressive in the West than in North Africa. Morocco, in contrast to Venice, was not an important center for trade and cultural exchange during the seventeenth and eighteenth centuries, and therefore we might postulate that an originally local term of Venetian origin could be more readily globalized and pass into common usage. But how did the mellah begin? Furthermore, what are the origins of its contemporary incarnations and the state of its memorialization, when only some of its ancient vestiges remain in the cities of Morocco and all the Jews have left for such disparate places as Israel, France, and Canada?

In this chapter, we are interested in the examination of the Moroccan mellah insofar as it is reimagined and reenacted through literature produced by the Jews who have left Morocco since the 1960s and today live in Israel or the Western world, writing in languages such as Hebrew, French, or English. Reconstructing a space through the imagination, so as to fill the gaps in history and memory, is something that many Jewish, as well as non-Jewish, writers share; that seems of particular significance in an age of diaspora and migration like the twenty-first century. Think of the Egyptian-born André Aciman, who in his numerous novels and essays imagines Alexandria in ways that go well beyond the assumed reality of that Mediterranean city, or of Jonathan Safran Foer's *Everything Is Illuminated* (2002), set in an imaginary shtetl whose contours reflect the author's fantasy more than anything else, an attempt to resurrect the vanished world his ancestors came from. In the case of Morocco, since the second half of the twentieth century, the space of the mellah has changed and lost not only its Jewish population but also some of its tangible markers, like street signs. Thus, literature has stepped in as an important repository for the collective memory of neighborhoods that once existed. It has become a cartographic catalog that allows us to re-create and then preserve the past in original ways: a narrative of the mellah might be presented from a positive perspective (the mellah as a familiar and intimate quarter) or from a negative one (the mellah as a space of exclusion and closure), depending on the author's personal point of entry and life story. The mellah becomes a metaphor that represents an entire bygone world brought to an end by Jewish migration—one that resurfaces through literature or, as we shall see in the conclusion of this essay, thanks to various kinds of heritage-related activities that in recent years have begun to take place in Morocco.

THE JEWS OF MOROCCO AND THE MELLAH

The Jews historically formed a very important sector of the Moroccan population and had resided in the country since ancient times: they were the so-called *toshavim* (inhabitants/residents). During the fifteenth and sixteenth centuries, Jews of Sephardic origin, the *megorashim* (expelled), arrived from the Iberian Peninsula, which led to the birth of a heterogeneous yet well-integrated diasporic population. Even though until 1438 no mellah existed, the Jews were already subject to an Islamic charter that governed minorities (*dhimmi*). This discriminatory status granted some rights and protections to the so-called People of the Book (Jews, Christians, and Zoroastrians) while simultaneously imposing limitations on activities that ranged from riding horses to building new places of worship to matters of inheritance. This charter did not lead to the complete marginalization of the Jews, however, who managed to navigate between Islamic law and the *halakhah* in original and creative ways.[2] As for urban segregation, Islam does not explicitly prescribe the segregation of non-Muslims living in the *dar al-Islam*. On the contrary, some Islamic jurists and theologians even argued that daily contact and cohabitation could induce them to convert.[3]

In Morocco, until the onset of colonialism, the Jews shared a traditional societal structure with their non-Jewish neighbors, at the top of which stood the *shaykh al-yahud* (head of the Jews/Jewish community), who oversaw the relations with the Makhzen, the Moroccan royal household. The local rabbis and rabbinical tribunals further regulated Jewish life, particularly in areas such as family life and personal status law. Since the Jews lived in villages situated in regions such as the Atlas Mountains and in the urban centers of southern and northern Morocco, they were an integral part of the entirety of Moroccan society and occupied a significant position in many sectors, including craftsmanship and goldsmithing.[4]

The mellah originally formed a part of the largest and most important Moroccan *medinas*, the neighborhoods that structured the complex architectural and ethno-social fabric of the city. Its history is directly connected to that of the Moroccan rulers: the first Jewish quarter was established in Fès in 1438 by the Marinid sultan, while the second—the mellah of Marrakech—was built by the Sa'adians when that city became the capital. Moulay Isma'il (1672–1727) then ordered the creation of the mellah in his capital, Meknès. Lastly, the mellahs of cities like Tetouan, Rabat, and Essaouira (also known as Mogador) were established in 1807 following Moulay Slimane's decree, an act generally attributed to his pro-Wahhabi ideas.[5] On the other hand, some cities, like Tangier and Safi, never had a mellah. In the case of Fès or Meknès, the proximity of the mellah to the casbah simplified the collection of the *jiziyah* (the Islamic poll tax paid by non-Muslims) and the provision of royal protection in return. But, as Emily Gottreich explains, "the origins of the *mellah* are also connected to many of the broader historical themes of the sixteenth-century Mediterranean world. A general rise in population, the expulsion of Jews and Muslims from Spain and the gradual institutionalization of the walled Jewish quarter" were all elements that further contributed to the concept of the mellah's diffusion from Fès to Marrakech and beyond.[6]

Although until the colonial period only Jews and European visitors resided in the mellah, Muslims and others always had been a visible presence during the day, when many went there to buy and sell goods, to collect rent—as in Marrakech, in whose mellah Muslims could own buildings but not reside—or to drink alcohol, gamble, and visit Jewish prostitutes. The mellah was traditionally locked at night, but this hardly meant that it was a space wholly estranged from the rest of the city. Even from an architectural point of view, walls encircled only some of the Moroccan Jewish quarters, such as in Fès.[7] As Daniel Schroeter writes, "At night, the Jews would shut their shops in the *medina* and return to their private residences, like all other inhabitants of the town. Jews were able to maintain their distinctiveness precisely because the division between the world of family and religion and the world of business was so clearly demarcated in the wider urban context."[8] The world of family and religion revolved around the mellah, maintaining the boundaries deemed necessary by both Muslims and Jews.

JEWISH QUARTERS (*HARA*) IN THE ARAB MUSLIM WORLD

Just as in Morocco, in most of the other Arab Muslim countries until the colonial period, Jews tended to concentrate in a specific quarter of the city, known as the *hara* or *harat al-yahud* (the Jewish neighborhood). However, the hara's origin was not connected to ad hoc legislation as in the case of the mellah, and even non-Jews could live there. The hara of

FIGURE 11. The Mellah of Meknès in a 1919 postcard.
—Wikipedia, https://fr.wikipedia.org/wiki/Fichier:Le_Mellah-Meknès_1919.jpg.

Cairo, for instance, existed beginning in the Fatimid period and by the early twentieth century was known as one of the poorest areas of the old city, where less than 8 percent of the local Jews still lived. Divided into a Rabbanite and Karaite section, it has been described by the twentieth-century Arabophone Jewish writer Maurice Shammas as "my birthplace" and "the source of my deep-rooted Egyptianness"—an area where Jews and Muslims lived and worked together.[9] This image remains even today in Egyptian popular memory, as is testified by the television series *Harat al-Yahud*, broadcast with great success in Egypt during the month of Ramadan of 2015.[10] That said, for a middle-class Egyptian Jew, like the writer Jacqueline Kahanoff, the hara constituted a faraway space inhabited by Jews in need of help and lacking education, one that contrasted with modern neighborhoods like Abbasiyah, Garden City, and Zamalek where many had resided since the early twentieth century.[11]

The hara of Tunis originated at the time of the Almohads, around the end of the tenth or the beginning of the eleventh century. As in Egypt, the Tunisian hara did not have clear-cut or fixed boundaries and—from an urban perspective—could be considered a quarter just like any other in the old medina. What distinguished this (and any other) hara was the presence of synagogues and other Jewish-related buildings, as well as

Jewish-owned stores. As in Cairo, in Tunis, too, from the late nineteenth century onward, most of the Jews began to reside and buy houses outside the hara. The former space remained as a traditional and generally overcrowded lower-class quarter, where poor Jews, as well as Muslims and Christians, lived.[12]

THE TWENTIETH-CENTURY MELLAH

The disruptions of the early twentieth century that decentered the Moroccan mellah as the center of Jewish life began with the onset of French colonialism and its accompanying social and economic changes. There were also shifts internal to Jewish society (such as the migration of rural Jews to the cities) and to the Moroccan economy.[13] By the interwar years, many Jews had left the mellah; the more affluent ones especially had moved to the modern neighborhoods of Marrakech or Fès. In the 1950s, most Moroccan Jews did not live in the mellah, except in the case of Meknès, where a new, more modern, and spacious mellah had been founded in 1912 to host affluent members of the Jewish population.[14]

The history of cohabitation between Jews, Arabs, and Berbers halted only in 1948 when, after the foundation of Israel, the first Jewish migratory waves occurred. From that period and throughout the 1950s and 1960s, the vast majority of the roughly 250,000 Jews who lived in Morocco left the country for Israel and other destinations such as France, Canada, and the United States owing to the worsening regional political situation and the community's deteriorating living conditions.[15]

Those Jews who emigrated to Israel faced social and urban segregation, first in transit camps and then in development towns often situated in the north or south of Israel. As in the case of many other *Mizrahim* (Eastern [Jews]), this situation often led to an idealization of the lost Moroccan homeland and the development of resentment toward the Israeli state and its establishment.[16] This is evident both in political movements—think of the protests that occurred as early as the 1950s and 1960s or the development of *Ha-panterim ha-shehorim* (Black Panthers) in the early 1970s—and in nostalgic cultural production by Moroccan migrants and their descendants. In addition, in the case of Moroccan Jews who emigrated to other countries in the Diaspora, the migration was a difficult and sometimes traumatic process. Beginning in the

1980s, the experience was frequently described in literature and autobiographical writings, as well as represented in museums and through the activities of heritage groups.[17]

CONTEMPORARY MOROCCAN JEWISH LITERATURE

Here, we focus on literature, particularly self-writing, so as to examine representations of the mellah—and the creation of an imagined mellah—by contemporary Jewish Moroccan writers who left Morocco in the 1960s and 1970s.[18] We deal particularly with authors who left Morocco as children or adolescents and emigrated to Israel, France, and the United States. Fifty years later, these writers are returning through memory to the neighborhoods where they grew up or which they have come to know intimately only by thinking of them as their homeland in miniature. All of these authors share a similar migration story and can be said to belong to what Susan Rubin Suleiman, a scholar who has dealt with post-Holocaust literary writing, calls the "1.5 generation," people writing about experience they lived directly as children or adolescents, thus producing a particular kind of memory in which imagination and creativity play a greater role.[19] With the exception of Carlos de Nesry, all of the authors we discuss left Morocco for Israel, France, or the United States at a young age between 1950 and 1960 but generally began to write and publish as adults at a temporal distance of decades, during the 1990s or later. Some of them emigrated more than once, first from Morocco and then, for instance, from France to Israel (Haim Shiran) or Israel to France (Mickaël Parienté). After the migration, the majority of these writers moved back and forth, returning to Morocco only for short periods of time.

In this section, we specifically examine Gabriel Bensimhon, Erez Biton, Ami Bouganim, Shlomo Elbaz, David Elmosnino, Uziel Hazan, Mickaël Parienté, and Haim Shiran, who emigrated to Israel; Daniel Sibony, Marcel Bénabou, and Pol-Serge Kakon, who emigrated to France; and finally Michel Emile Bensadon and Ruth Knafo Setton, who emigrated to the United States. Depending on the country in which they reside, some of them write in French, some in Hebrew, and others in English. These writers left Morocco during a period of profound political and social turmoil that witnessed the birth of the State of Israel; the end of the French colonization and protectorate; the economic crisis that followed the departure of the French; the development of Moroccan nationalism, the Arabization of the country and consequent feelings of insecurity; and the attraction felt by many Jews to France and its culture thanks to the education received in the schools of the Alliance Israélite Universelle.

Writing the Mellah, 1950s to Today

The mellah was both a place of protection and of privilege, as it was often built next to the sultan's palace. Rather than a place of marginalization, it was an integral part of the city and an extension of the Muslim area. Last but not least, it was seen as a place of exchange and socialization, allowing Jewish society to preserve its own social and traditional life,[20] and so even in the literature of contemporary Moroccan Jewish writers, the mellah is represented as both a place of protection and intimacy as well as of marginalization.

Before expanding on this contradiction, we wish to begin with Carlos de Nesry's 1950s description of the Casablanca mellah. It is to de Nesry —a significant figure of the 1940s and 1950s, described by the Jewish press of the time as the Albert Memmi of Morocco—that we owe some of the finest pages devoted to the Casablanca mellah.[21] Those pages, written by a Jew hailing from Tangier, a city where no mellah existed, are of interest not so much because of the style (though it is remarkable) but because of the fact that they were written in medias res, as a sort of documentary. Even today they are, so to speak, a documentary charting a time of great change, from political transformation (the end of the French Protectorate and the return of King Mohammed V, exiled by the French, to Morocco) to changes in identity (the long years of colonialism and French influence) to social shifts (the twentieth-century migrations of Moroccan Jews).

The Case of Carlos de Nesry

Carlos de Nesry wrote his text in one afternoon toward the end of Shabbat while at the Place de France in Casablanca, next to the mellah. He was clearly struck by the comings and goings of the local populace. The mellah he describes, which he interestingly calls the "ghetto," fascinates him first and foremost because of its atemporal dimension: "Coming from a city with no ghetto, I have always been fascinated by this world beyond time," a world that can give a "sensation of immutability"

(10, 9). He is particularly struck by its spatial dimension, placing the mellah at the intersection of two worlds and two ages, between past and present, the elderly and the young. The area of the mellah seems to him sacred, to the extent that he defines it as "a kingdom of God," protected by frontiers (12). The mellah of de Nesry, above all, was able to preserve its traditions, local color, and ancestral customs, described by de Nesry as atavistic, even during the great crisis that marked the 1950s, when the book was written. It is a world with its own inner fissures, particularly between the older and younger generations, with the latter influenced (or emancipated, to use the author's terms) first by France and then the United States through their cinema—he mentions Marlon Brando's hairstyle—and soldiers parading arm-in-arm with the splendid girls of the mellah. The older generation, with its "happy-in-their-own-way Diogenes" and "long beards, dark *djellabas* and opprobrious skullcaps," seems far from de Nesry's preoccupations (10, 11).

Indeed, his most pressing concerns were with the massive Jewish emigration from Morocco and Jewish integration into that country's new social and political reality. De Nesry dwells on the language of conversations ("I hear the same popular, guttural, resonant Arabic") and on the bilingualism of young people who "walk by, mixing French and Arabic speech" (9, 16). He was struck by the atmosphere of Shabbat that persisted among the older generations: "The holy day will get them through to evening, enveloping them in its warm protective weave. You would surprise them by talking of other worlds and joys. Theirs suffices. I understand that they feel out of their element even in Israel" (11). Yet he worries about the younger generation, one he defines as a hybrid, fearing that "the children of the ghetto have disowned the *mellah* and its symbols. They have disowned by the same token its virtues and timeless values" (13).

The impact of this remark is mitigated by his idea that one cannot divest oneself so easily of the "atavism" of the mellah, which "persists tenaciously under a pseudo-modern cloak . . . it lasts in a certain way of thinking, speaking and behaving" (13). The writer trusts that the lessons of "modesty and discretion peculiar to the *mellah*" may be preserved for the future. De Nesry closes his remarks optimistically, noting the charm of the feminine beauty circulating in the mellah, which for an instant takes him to any alameda of northern Andalusia and makes him exclaim: "Where are the problems set by the new Morocco, the dramatic issues of our destiny in this country? Where are the questions of conscience we would expect the Jews to debate in this country? For a community which said it was threatened and which some believed to be in grave difficulty, what a proud admission of vitality!" (16)

For Carlos de Nesry, the mellah is, above all, a place able to protect, preserve, and perpetuate a traditional culture and the society living there, with all its fissures, hybridity, and contradictions. It is a place of vitality, a generator of morality, and a symbol of modesty and discretion, values the writer wishes to preserve (even though modesty and discretion may lead us to think of issues linked to the lasting status of dhimmi in Moroccan society). His secular viewpoint takes in a space which he believes to be sacred because it is unchangeable, a little realm of God that he describes as outside time and ahistorical. It is a condition that de Nesry seems as much to wish for as to fear. The mellah is therefore a quarter conceived of as a place of contradictions and conflicting visions, just as we find it to be in the autobiographies of today.

MOROCCAN JEWISH WRITERS: DIFFERENT ATTITUDES TOWARD THE MELLAH

Many of the Moroccan Jewish writers that we study lived and grew up in the mellah, a quarter that has become a metaphor for home and that has been turned into a space of intimacy, family affection, and identity formation. Other authors we examine write of the site without ever having lived there, either because there was no mellah (as in the case of Tangier) or, as in the cases of de Nesry and Marcel Bénabou, because they come from a wealthy family background. The wealthy did not tend to live in the mellah, a place of exclusion that produced differences in identity within Moroccan Jewish society itself.

Daniel Sibony warns us against considering Moroccan Judaism as a uniform entity even within a single city; it was riven by profound contrasts. For example, Sibony writes that in Marrakech, the distance of the mellah from the world of Jewish notables was so great as to create widely differing identities among the same Marrakech Jews. In the Jewish space of that city, the mellah was just one part. Michel Emile Bensadon speaks of the stigma attached to living in the mellah and explains that when his family suddenly became poor, the organization of his bar mitzvah ceremony had to be drastically modified: "Would my entry into manhood resemble that of the poorer Jews of the mellah, the squalid Jewish neighborhood we were forbidden to frequent?"[22]

Positive Views of the Mellah

It is Shlomo Elbaz who describes the mellah of Marrakech as a substitute for Jerusalem, both a state within a state "and first and foremost that warm, familiar enclosure, like a mother's breast: the *mellah*! . . . an autonomous kingdom, a bubble cut off from the rest of the town."[23] To anyone raised in the mellah, that quarter could be a maternal breast, warm and protective, but also an autonomous, independent realm.

Marcel Bénabou knows the old mellah of Meknès only because he used to go there to buy kosher meat with his mother and to see his old Aunt Zahra. He describes the layout of his aunt's house, a courtyard with a well overlooked by three musty, windowless rooms. This aunt was also famous for her delicious cakes and the mysterious practices she engaged in, of which all the women of the family took advantage, "more or less magic remedies, gestures and formulae adapted to life's most diverse circumstances."[24] Hence Bénabou's mellah was an unknown place, full of allure and mystery.

In a poem entitled "Simhah ba-mellah" (Joy in the mellah), written in Moroccan Arabic and Hebrew, the Israeli poet Erez Biton celebrates the joy and cheer associated with the scale of the libations—the spicy olives and the hallah (Shabbat bread) with cinnamon washed down with *'araq*.[25] David Elmosnino paints us a familiar picture of the mellah of Essaouira in "The Day of the Couscous": "If the Muslims had not had the idea of building the *mellahs* . . . the tradition of the 'day of the couscous' could not have been born and I would not have had the chance of learning how to know better the people and their thoughts."[26] The mellah has also been depicted as a living theater full of humor in which strange characters move. Fools, madmen, wizards, sorcerers, and rabbis both holy and bizarre acted on the stage where folkloric and traditional rituals took place, such as is found in the pages of *Récits du mellah* by Ami Bouganim or in *Rica la vida* by Pol-Serge Kakon.[27] The warmth, protection, magic, joy, good cheer, traditional dishes, and familiar climate of intimacy—all this is represented by the mellah.

Negative Views of the Mellah

The mellah also meant poverty and discrimination. For Mickaël Parienté, who, unlike Bénabou, actually lived in the old Meknès mellah, this

FIGURE 12. The mellah of Meknès, 2018. —Photograph by Emanuela Trevisan Semi.

FIGURE 13. House interior in the mellah of Meknès, 2012. —Photograph by Emanuela Trevisan Semi.

quarter produced a stigmatized identity. Parienté tells of how in less than a decade, he moved from the mellah of Meknès, which he describes as "a miserable, primitive village," to a modern prosperous city (Geneva), having spent years on a kibbutz.[28] Parienté associates the mellah with his father, who, next door to the mellah's entrance, had a small shop that made ice and lemonade, a business he later built up to become the mellah's supplier of fish.[29] Nonetheless, for this writer, who lives between Israel and France, the mellah remains primarily a synonym for poverty and precariousness, a stigmatized place par excellence. "In Morocco I was just a Jew from the *mellah*," he writes, one of the many indistinct Jews stigmatized simply because they were inhabitants of that quarter, "while in Israel I was taken for a Moroccan. In France, on the other hand, I feel myself first and foremost Israeli."[30] According to Parienté, he suffered unfair treatment and stigma for the rest of his days.

Ruth Knafo Setton experienced a similar situation even in the absence of a mellah. An emigrant from Tangier to the United States, she writes that between Jews and Muslims there was a barrier even with no mellah, a wall both real and symbolic: "In Tangiers, Jews and Arabs lived side by side, but still, there was the wall—always the wall between them."[31] Later, Knafo Setton dwells on the figure of Lalla Suleika, the Jewess from Tangier kidnapped by a Muslim—who then fell in love with her and sent to her death because she would not deny her Judaism: "Suleika was a trespasser. She crossed from the Jewish world to the Arab world. In those days there was no *mellah* in Tangiers, but still the separation was distinct, an invisible wall. I used to wonder how long it takes to cross from the Jewish house to the Arab house. An eternity. Or a second. A breath, and you're there, in the other world."[32] In this passage, the mellah works metaphorically, the space representing the everyday systems of cross-cultural exchange.

AN AMBIGUOUS AND POROUS SPACE

As Gabriel Bensimhon tells us, the mellah was grey, but its inhabitants, full of invention, gave it color through the space of their imagination. A search for the color green, part of a school assignment in Israel, reminds the protagonist of the lack of green in the mellah, where "colors were missing and everything was grey; however, even if green were missing, imagination made up for that." In the mellah, neither trees nor flowers would grow, but even if the color green was lacking this was made up for by imagination.[33] For Ami Bouganim, a Francophone Israeli author of Moroccan origin, the mellah of Essaouira gives us the opportunity to reflect on Israel, to which he emigrated: "We did not barter the dusty, worm-eaten ghettos and *mellahs* for a supreme ghetto-*mellah* where military justification matters more than reason of state and messianic unreason more than political reason, to the extent that Israel has no more moral lessons to give anyone either in terms of human charity or social justice."[34] He remembers the mellah as a space of isolation—and is horrified to find himself in another, pejorative version of this space.

A number of authors dwell on who closed the doors of the mellah, monumental doors made of iron or wood. It is one thing to imagine a mellah being closed in the evening by its own inhabitants; it is quite another if it was closed from the outside by the Muslims. Whether locked from the outside or the inside, they offered shelter and safety. Elmosnino recalls that the doors of the Mogador mellah were closed by the inhabitants so that the "only entry to the *mellah* was defended by a heavy iron portal which was carefully bolted and padlocked at sunset with iron cross bars set into the sides of the double doors, from one *mezuzah* to the other, with the result that all entry and exit was forbidden."[35]

According to Uziel Hazan, the closing of the mellah's doors in Casablanca was carried out by Muslims: "At midnight the Rue du Patio doors of rotten wood were padlocked. The Muslim watchman fitted the cross members into their slots and secured a heavy padlock to them. Then he lay down on his flea-ridden straw mattress and fell asleep."[36] In the description of the Meknès mellah, Haim Shiran speaks of a "protected and confined citadel" and conveys the notion of protection by evoking the doors of the quarter. Shiran mentions the monumental door closed every evening in defense against the Aissauas, a confraternity that organized its violent rituals, whose sanctuary was near the doors of the mellah, and whose very mention made one shiver.[37]

CONCLUSION

Considering these descriptions and the emotions that they convey, what remains of the Moroccan Jewish quarter today? Has the mellah become a *lieu de mémoire*, deprived of a proper history, filled only with contrasting memories scattered across the Diaspora, Israel, and Morocco? Has it been forgotten altogether, except by those Jews who experienced it directly and who now write about it?

It is undisputed that in the cities of Morocco, where hundreds of thousands of Jews lived until not so long ago, from Meknès to Marrakech, the mellah has been transformed into a quarter like any other in the medina. The memories of its Jewish inhabitants did not vanish, however; elders still remember a time when Jewish tradesmen lived and worked there. Since the 1990s, though, the Moroccan authorities have begun to be interested in the restoration and preservation of Jewish heritage, from synagogues and cemeteries to the mellahs themselves, an interest only strengthened by the promulgation of the Moroccan constitution in 2011. Even though these projects did not involve all Moroccan cities, they nonetheless led to the creation of small museums and the restoration of several buildings from Essaouira to Fès and Casablanca, often with an eye toward attracting tourists and the many Moroccan Jews living in Israel or in the Diaspora who might visit their homeland.[38] This contrasts with the previous period, from decolonization until the 1980s, when there was a general lack of information about the mellah, at least at a public and official level; in the case of the two mellahs of Meknès, even the street names were changed. The new names referred to Palestine or to Muslim personalities: Rue Petahia Berdugo became Rue Salah el-Din and Rue de Jérusalem was transformed into Boulevard al-Quds (the Arabic name for Jerusalem).[39]

When it comes to literary production, though not all of the texts examined contain Moroccan memories or regrets in the style imagined by Carlos de Nesry, Shlomo Elbaz, or other writers, most of the writers concur in remembering the mellah as a symbol of vitality. It is a space surrounded by an atmosphere of protection and intimacy, even if colored gray. These narratives contribute to the creation of an imagined mellah for new generations of individuals who do not know the Jewish quarter as their forefathers did but, based on these authors, can fantasize about it as a way of finding connection to and meaning for their own identities—often in ways that shift traditional notions and discourses of the Jewish Diaspora. Given the absence of (or perhaps too limited space assigned to) the memory of Jewish Morocco in Morocco as well as in the Jewish world, literature may therefore constitute more than a privileged lieu de mémoire where the past can be reconstructed and reinvented.

Self-writing ends up producing a mellah that is both fictional and real, where the reminiscences of the past intermingle with the present lives of the authors who live in the Western world or in Israel.

Without idealizing or presenting it too rosily, the descriptions of Elmosnino, Shiran, and others enable us to see the differences between the mellah and European ghettos. The proliferation of closed Jewish quarters in Europe since the establishment of the Venice Ghetto in 1516 was not mirrored in the Arab Muslim world. In a context where the cohabitation, more or less harmonious depending on the epoch and region, of different ethnic and religious groups was not infrequent, the idea of a closed Jewish neighborhood was unique to Morocco. It reflected the history of its Jews, its cities, and the ways in which various ruling dynasties managed to assert power over them.

That said, in Morocco, just like in Venice, the Jewish quarter was established not for religious reasons—as was the case of the ghetto of Rome, created in 1555 by Pope Paul IV—but as a practical means of coping with and governing a (useful) ethno-religious group that lived in the city permanently.[40] The boundaries between the mellah and the outside world perhaps were more porous than those between the European ghettos and the city that surrounded them. Nonetheless, in both cases, today we notice a shared tendency to remember the Jewish quarter as a familiar space where, as Salo Baron famously argued, aside from segregation and episodes of violence, "Jewry was enabled to live a full, rounded life, apart from the rest of the population . . . The Jew, indeed, had in effect a kind of territory."[41] If the French Revolution and Napoleon's emancipation were the main factors that brought about the opening of the European ghettos, in the case of the mellah, we would attribute this opening to the effects of colonialism and the changes that occurred in the socioeconomic structure of Morocco in the course of the late nineteenth and early twentieth centuries.

This shifting Jewish identity, along with the abrupt migration of the Jews from Morocco in the 1950s and 1960s, explains why what was originally a space of urban segregation like the mellah metonymically came to symbolize an entire Moroccan (Jewish) landscape of familiar faces, smells, and sounds that were eventually lost. In other cases—think of Ami Bouganim—the mellah is also a metaphor for the experience of marginalization felt by many Moroccan Jews after their migration to Israel. Beneath these metaphorical readings lies the idea of the mellah as a "memory space that travels" and that today binds together several generations of Moroccan Jews who live in countries as different as Israel, the United States, and France but who still feel a sense of nostalgia, or at least affection, for a world that some experienced for only a short period of time or, in the case of the younger generations, know solely through the stories of their parents and grandparents.[42] In other words, a physical place like the mellah structures and becomes a hub for memories both real and imagined, leading to the production of a rich memorial literature by the Jews of Morocco—an extraordinary way to pay homage to a bygone world in which they had lived for centuries.

NOTES

This chapter was written jointly by Emanuela Trevisan Semi and Dario Miccoli. Miccoli is the author of the sections "The Jews of Morocco and the Mellah," "Jewish Quarters (*Hara*) in the Arab Muslim World," "The Twentieth-Century Mellah," and the conclusion; Trevisan Semi is the author of "Contemporary Moroccan Jewish Literature," "Moroccan Jewish Writers: Different Attitudes toward the Mellah," "Positive Views of the Mellah," "Negative Views of the Mellah," and "An Ambiguous and Porous Space."' The introduction was written collectively by the two authors.

1. However, according to Muhammad Al-Manuni's *Civilisation Mérinide*—which quotes the fourteenth-century Arabic chronicle *Rawd al-Qirtas*—some Jews were living outside the old city from a much earlier epoch: "In the 677 *hijra* [1278 AD] the Jews were moved to the *mellah* next to Fès *el-gedid* (New Fès) and so were banished from Fès Idrissiya, after they had been relieved of their goods and a large number of them had been killed." See Al-Manuni, *Civilisation Mérinide* (n.p.: Kulliyat al-Adab bi-al-Rabat, 1996).
2. See Jessica Marglin, *Across Legal Lines: Jews and Muslims in Modern Morocco* (New Haven, CT: Yale University Press, 2016). As an introduction to the history of the dhimma, see Bernard Lewis, *The Jews of Islam* (Princeton, NJ: Princeton University Press, 1984), esp. 21–66.
3. Emily Gottreich, "Jewish Quarters," in *Encyclopaedia of Jews in the Islamic World*, ed. Norman A. Stillman (Leiden: Brill, 2010), 3:26.
4. Shlomo Deshen, *The Mellah Society: Jewish Community Life in Sherifian Morocco* (Chicago: University of Chicago Press, 1989).
5. Mohammed Kenbib, *Juifs et Musulmans au Maroc* (Paris: Tallandier, 2016), 24–35, and Daniel Schroeter, "How Jews Became 'Moroccans,'" in *The Sephardic Experience East and West: Essays in Honor of Jane S. Gerber*, ed. Federica Francesconi, Stanley Mirvis, and Brian Smollett (Leiden: Brill, 2012), 224. We should note that even after the establishment of the local mellah, some affluent Jewish families in Essaouira were allowed to live in the casbah. See Daniel Schroeter, *The Sultan's Jew: Morocco and the Sephardi World* (Stanford, CA: Stanford University Press, 2002).
6. Emily Gottreich, *The Mellah of Marrakesh: Jewish and Muslim Space in Morocco's Red City* (Bloomington: Indiana University Press, 2006), 38.
7. Emily Gottreich, "Rethinking the 'Islamic City' from the Perspective of Jewish Space," *Jewish Social Studies* 11, no. 1 (2004): 118–46. See also Susan Gilson Miller and Mauro Bertagnin,

eds., *The Architecture and Memory of the Minority Quarter in the Muslim Mediterranean City* (Cambridge, MA: Harvard University Press, 2010).

8. Daniel Schroeter, "The Jewish Quarter and the Moroccan City," in *New Horizons in Sephardic Studies*, ed. Yedidah K. Stillman and George K. Zucker (New York: State University of New York Press, 1993), 73.
9. Maurice Shammas, *'Azza, Hafidat Nifirtiti* (2003), quoted in Deborah Starr, "Sensing the City: Representations of Cairo's Harat al-Yahud," *Prooftexts* 26 (2006): 146. On the Jews of Egypt, consider Jacob Landau, *Jews in Nineteenth-Century Egypt* (New York: New York University Press, 1969); Gudrun Krämer, *The Jews of Modern Egypt, 1914–1952* (London: IB Tauris, 1989); and Dario Miccoli, *Histories of the Jews of Egypt: An Imagined Bourgeoisie, 1880s–1950s* (London: Routledge, 2015).
10. Among the many reviews that appeared in newspapers at the time, see, for example, Roula Khalaf, "Cairo Soap Opera Casts Islamists as the Bad Guys," *Financial Times*, July 1, 2015, https://www.ft.com/content/2db617e8–1fd9–11e5-ab0f-6bb9974f25d0 (no longer available), and Eyal Sagui Bizawe, "How 'The Jewish Quarter' Became the Talk of Cairo," *Ha-'Aretz*, July 5, 2015, https://www.haaretz.com/life/television/.premium-how-the-jewish-quarter-became-the-talk-of-cairo-1.5375242. On Jews and cinema in post–Nasserist Egypt, see Yaron Shemer, "From Chahine's *Al-Iskandariyya . . . leh* to *Salata Baladi* and *An Yahud Masr*: Rethinking Egyptian Jews' Cosmopolitanism, Belonging and Nostalgia in Cinema," *Middle East Journal of Culture and Communication* 7, no. 3 (2014): 351–75.
11. Jacqueline Kahanoff, "Europe from Afar," in *Mongrels or Marvels: The Levantine Writings of Jacqueline Shohet Kahanoff*, ed. Deborah Starr and Sasson Somekh (Stanford, CA: Stanford University Press, 2011), 100–113.
12. Paul Sebag and Robert Attal, *L'évolution d'un Ghetto Nord-african: La hara de Tunis* (Paris: PUF, 1959).
13. Susan Gilson Miller, "The Mellah of Fez: Reflections on the Spatial Turn in Moroccan Jewish History," in *Jewish Topographies: Visions of Space, Traditions of Place*, ed. Julia Brauch, Anna Liphardt, and Alexandra Nocke (Aldershot: Ashgate, 2008), 113.
14. Michel Abitbol, "De la Tradition à la Modernité: Les Juifs du Maroc," *Diasporas* 27 (2016): 19–30. See also Emanuela Trevisan Semi and Hanane Sekkat Hatimi, *Mémoire et Représentations des Juifs au Maroc: Les Voisins Absents de Meknès* (Paris: Publisud, 2011).
15. Consider Haim Zafrani, *Deux Mille ans de Vie Juive au Maroc* (Paris: Maisonneuve & Larose, 1998); André Lévy, *Il Était une Fois les Juifs Marocains* (Paris: L'Harmattan, 1995); and Yigal Bin-Nun, "La Négociation de l'Évacuation en Masse des Juifs du Maroc," in *La Fin du Judaisme en Terres d'Islam*, ed. Shmuel Trigano (Paris: Denoel, 2009), 303–58.
16. Sami Shalom-Chetrit, *Intra-Jewish Conflict in Israel: White Jews, Black Jews* (London: Routledge, 2010).
17. Orit Ouaknine-Yekutieli and Yigal S. Nizri, "'My Heart Is in the Maghrib': Aspects of Cultural Revival of the Moroccan Diaspora in Israel," *Hespéris-Tamuda* 51, no. 3 (2016): 165–94, and Emanuela Trevisan Semi, "La Mise en Scène de l'Identité Marocaine en Israel: Un Cas d''Israélianité' Diasporique," *A Contrario* 5 (2007): 37–50. On Francophone Maghrebi Jewish literature, see Ewa Tartakowsky, *Les Juifs et le Maghreb: Fonctions Sociales d'une Littérature d'Exile* (Tours: Presse Universitaires François Rabelais, 2016).
18. We use the term "self-writing" to refer to a wide range of texts, not just autobiographies, but also memoirs, semiautobiographical novels, and the like.
19. Susan Rubin Suleiman, "The 1.5 Generation: Thinking about Child Survivors and the Holocaust," *American Imago* 59, no. 3 (2002): 277–95.
20. Trevisan Semi and Sekkat Hatimi, *Mémoire et Représentations*, 295–303.
21. Carlos de Nesry, *Les Israélites Marocains à l'Heure du Choix* (Tangiers: Editions Internationales,

1958), http://library.lclark.edu/rabatgenizahproject/items/show/325 (no longer available). Further references to de Nesry's text refer to this edition and will be cited parenthetically in the text.

22. Daniel Sibony, *Marrakech, le Depart* (Paris: Odile Jacob, 2009); Michel Emile Bensadon, *Where the Wind Blew: A Boyhood Lost in Tangier* (New York: Lilibooks, 2013), 199.
23. Shlomo Elbaz, *Marrakesh-Jérusalem: Patrie de Mon Ame* (Neufchâteau: Avant-Propos, 2013), 107.
24. Marcel Bénabou, *Jacob, Ménahem et Mimoun une Épopée Familiale* (Paris: Seuil, 1995), 91–92.
25. Erez Biton, *Sefer ha-nana* [The mint book] (Tel Aviv: Eked, 1979), 32–33.
26. David Elmosnino, *Palais et Jardins* (Ashdod, Israel: Brit Kodesh, 2008), 14.
27. Ami Bouganim, *Récits du Mellah* (Paris: Lattès, 1981); Pol-Serge Kakon, *Rica la Vida* (Paris: Actes Sud, 1999).
28. Mickaël Parienté, *Rue de la Grande Chaumière* (Montrouge, France: Stavnet, 2011), 51.
29. Mickaël Parienté, interview by Emanuela Trevisan Semi, May 16, 2013, Paris.
30. Parienté, *Rue de la Grande Chaumière*, 177–78.
31. Ruth Knafo Setton, *The Road to Fez* (Washington, DC: Counterpoint, 2001), 119.
32. Knafo Setton, *Road to Fez*, 118.
33. Gabriel Bensimhon, *Ne'arah be-hultzah kehulah* [The girl with a blue shirt] (Tel Aviv: Yediot Aharonot, 2013), 20.
34. Ami Bouganim, *Es-Saouira de Mogador* (Matanel: Louven, 2013), 242.
35. Elmosnino, *Palais et Jardins*, 15.
36. Uziel Hazan, *Armand* (Tel Aviv: Sifriyat Poalim, 1982), 121.
37. Haim Shiran and Fabienne Bergmann, *Le Rocher d'Origine* (Paris: La Compagnie Littéraire, 2013), 92, 59.
38. Emanuela Trevisan Semi, "Entre lieux de mémoire et lieux de l'oubli au Maroc: Quelle politique et quels acteurs pour la mémoire juive?," *Ethnologies* 39, no. 2 (2017): 69–80. On Moroccan Jewish memory tours, see Emanuela Trevisan Semi, "Revenir pour écrire: Le livre d'or, un nouvel espace de communication dans le pèlerinage des Juifs au Maroc," *Diasporas* 8 (2006): 153–61.
39. Yolande Cohen and Noureddine Harrami, "From Synagogue to Mosque: My Grandfather's House in the Old Mellah of Meknès," in *Homelands and Diasporas: Perspectives on Jewish Culture in the Mediterranean and Beyond*, ed. Dario Miccoli, Marcella Simoni, and Giorgia Foscarini (Newcastle: Cambridge Scholars, 2018), 36. More generally on the current Moroccan attitudes toward the country's Jewish past, see Aomar Boum, *Memories of Absence: How Muslims Remember Jews in Morocco* (Stanford, CA: Stanford University Press, 2013).
40. See Marina Caffiero, *Storia degli Ebrei nell'Italia Moderna* (Rome: Carocci, 2014).
41. Salo W. Baron, "Ghetto and Emancipation," in *The Menorah Treasury: Harvest of Half a Century*, ed. Leo Schwartz (Philadelphia: Jewish Publication Society, 1964), 55.
42. On the case of second- and third-generation Mizrahi writers, see Lital Levy, *Poetic Trespass: Writing between Hebrew and Arabic in Israel/Palestine* (Princeton, NJ: Princeton University Press, 2014), esp. 238–84; Yochai Oppenheimer, "Be-shem ha-'av: 'Edipaliyiut ba-sipporet ha-mizrahit shel ha-dor ha-sheni" [In the name of the father: Oedipal themes in second-generation Mizrahi literature], *Te'oriah u-viqoret* 40 (2012): 161–84; and Dario Miccoli, *La Letteratura Mizrahi: Narrazioni, Identità, Memorie degli Ebrei del Medio Oriente e Nord Africa* (Florence: Giuntina, 2016), 69–96.

PART IV

SCARPA
SCARPA
CARLO SCARPA
AFTER
CARLO SCARPA
CARLO SCARPA
AFTER
CARLO SCARPA
CARLO SCARPA
AFTER
CARLO SCARPA

THE TOURIST
THE FUTURE OF MEMORY

AMANDA K. SHARICK AND KATHARINE G. TROSTEL

FIGURE 14. Sharick and Trostel touring Venice in summer 2016. —Photograph by Katharine G. Trostel.

In this collection's closing section, "The Tourist: The Future of Memory," we ask important questions about what lessons the Venice Ghetto might carry for the twenty-first century. How do we resist thinking about the Ghetto as a static site and instead embrace it as a dynamic place of cultural interchange? How do we work toward preserving the physical space while simultaneously accepting the ongoing process of collective memory making? Memory, just like the environment, functions within a fragile ecosystem. And in the context of Venice, the indiscriminate pursuit of instant gratification and profit has jeopardized both, unleashing natural catastrophe and creating an uncertain future for the city. The figure of the tourist becomes a metaphor for understanding the challenges of interacting with local memory in meaningful ways in the context of a city dependent on global travelers. The essays in this section reimagine the relationship between tourist and built environment. They model acts of situated engagement that counter the negative effects of consumer-driven or extractive mass tourism.

In November 2019, as overlapping forces—both global and local—caused record-breaking floods to engulf Venice, Shaul Bassi reminded us of the fragility of memory: "The flooding is all but a natural catastrophe, caused by the indiscriminate tampering with an ecosystem nurtured by Venice for centuries, the impact of cruise ships, threatening new and intrusive excavations of the lagoon and the rapacious investment in tourism."[1] The devastating effects of climate change add another dimension to the necessity and urgency for sustainable, place-based memory work. We consider how place-based memory work can help us to refigure our relationships to heritage sites through acts that situate our own personal experiences and utilize creative labor to generate dialogue between the tourist and the local communities. In this way, the act of tourism might be transformed by encouraging artist-scholars to cultivate deep relationships with the Venice Ghetto over extended periods of time. Their works become the doorway into physical sites, making them remotely accessible. This creative practice counters the "extractive" relationship between tourist and place by considering how we can productively create new meanings for memories as they interact within the experimental space of the endangered heritage site.

James E. Young asks us to contemplate the task of "saving" a heritage site in danger of extinction—of losing its relevance in the landscape or becoming disconnected from the lived, communal memory that lends it importance: "Rather than continuing to insist that the monument do what modern societies, by dint of their vastly heterogeneous populations and competing memorial agendas, will not permit them to do, I have long believed that the best way to save the monument, if it is worth saving at all, is to enlarge its life and texture to include its genesis in historical time, the activity that brings a monument into being, the debates surrounding its origins, its production, its reception, its life in the mind . . . In this view, memory as represented in the monument might also be regarded as a never-to-be-completed process, animated (not disabled) by the forces of history bringing it into being."[2]

The exceptional historical moment of quarantine in response to the 2019 global coronavirus pandemic is animating the Ghetto once again, compelling us to think about memory work differently. The public health crisis halted all aspects of communal life, disrupting both the fabric of personal and professional networks and the possibility of global exchange. The crisis threw into relief the way in which memory work in the Venice Ghetto sustains and exceeds the physical boundaries of the site itself. In the absence of the physical space, we have access to the realm of the imagination. In the closing section of this collection, the authors would like to consider their role in the future of memory of the Venice Ghetto, particularly the role of expanding ethical and meaningful engagement through acts that "enlarge its life and texture." How can scholars from multiple fields contribute to creating additional contexts for meaningful engagement with the Ghetto that challenge the more passive model of tourism through forms such as interactive exhibits, poetry, and documentary films, to name a few? We echo the call made by Bassi in a November 30, 2019, interview with NPR addressing unprecedented flooding: "We need to imagine what climate change is going to be like. And for that, you need the artist, you need the intellectual, you need the poets, you need philosophers, you need the historians."[3] The memory work of creative engagement is both an act of preservation and a portal—a guide to places that are otherwise inaccessible. We think through the fragility and resilience of memory, the impact of rising waters, the aftermath of the devastating coronavirus, the possibility of poetry, and the imperative to function as guardians and stewards of memory, both rooted and global, static and traveling, archival and digital, in the twenty-first century. In the essays that follow, two artists—Marjorie Agosín, Chilean American poet and human rights activist, and Margaux Fitoussi, anthropology PhD candidate and documentary filmmaker—consider what it means to create art from the site of historically segregated spaces.

In 2019, Agosín served as a writer-in-residence for the series "Reimagining the Ghetto" for two weeks at the invitation of Beit Venezia so as to think deeply in, with, and about the space. This experience reflects the initial intentions of Bassi's organization, whose mission is "to think of the heritage of the Ghetto neither as a mere celebration of the past nor as an exclusive patrimony reserved for local use but rather as a dynamic living memory to be continuously elaborated on through an interaction between insiders and outsiders, even blurring the distinction between the two groups."[4] In Agosín's resulting poems and creative essay, composed from within the space of the Venice Ghetto and published for the first time in this collection, she illuminates what it means to experience the Ghetto of Venice as a Chilean Jew whose family was profoundly affected by the Shoah, whose own life was marked by exile due to Pinochet's dictatorship. In an interview conducted by Katharine Trostel, it becomes clear that Agosín sees the Venice Ghetto as the testing ground—the laboratory—through which she can explore what it means to absorb both the beauty and the horror of the site and its global reverberations across time and space. Experiences filter through the Ghetto, or as Agosín phrases it in her essay, the past dwellers of the Venice Ghetto "intuit . . . the presence of those who might one day visit this place and find something within its walls they never would have imagined" as she, the artist, listens to "the sounds and the silences that together create a map of memories."[5] Agosín draws from the collective memories tied to place to create new narratives in the present. She engages with the Ghetto's past in order to craft works that are forward looking, co-constructing new meaning, inserting the Venice Ghetto as a central node in a network of stories.

Beit Venezia's project to bring writers-in-residence like Agosín into the space of the Venice Ghetto generates touchstones of memory for others to animate through a process of drawing connections between local, rooted memories and global experience. Margaux Fitoussi and Mo Scarpelli's film *El Hara,* on the other hand, becomes a form of interpolated engagement with the layered past of the Jewish Hara in Tunisia refigured through the memories of its most iconic resident: author and theorist Albert Memmi.

In 2016, as a master's degree student at the Harvard Divinity School, Fitoussi traveled to Tunisia to engage with a space formative to her family's Jewish Tunisian heritage: the Hara. She wanted to understand what it meant to be Jewish and Tunisian in the twentieth and twenty-first centuries and how this iconic space had shaped the identity formations of multiple generations. After connecting with family in Paris, the United States, and Israel, Fitoussi interviewed Tunisian Jewish author and theorist Albert Memmi in 2016. As a result of these conversations, she and codirector Mo Scarpelli produced the 2017 film *El Hara,* which traces the present-day Hara and serves as the catalyst for activating Memmi's memories about his experience and the literary representations of the Hara in his works.[6] In her interview for this collection, Fitoussi discusses what it meant to engage with the physical space of the Hara and the Hara of Memmi's memories that were shared during the making of the film. She becomes a tourist of Memmi's memories and subsequently of the "real" Hara as it exists today. Learning to navigate the gaps between the reality of the physical landscape and Memmi's memory prompts her to ask if we can tell a story about the past without the expectation or presumption of fully recovering it.

This question shapes the project as a whole and points us back toward the usefulness of the Venice Ghetto as a metaphor for understanding the transfer of intergenerational memories, both real and imagined. In her 2016 interview with Memmi, Fitoussi asks why Memmi used the language of "ghetto" interchangeably with "hara," an anachronism that scholars have been clear to distinguish. His reply to the question revolves around the complex relationship between the particularities of space and their affective legacies.[7] Fitoussi quotes Memmi in this section to explain this conflation as a telescoping of his experience of colonization with the symbol and significance of the Venice Ghetto: "Jews felt in danger in Venice and so they chose a piece of land where they could live out their lives . . . The ghetto is on the one hand a symbol that crushes Jewish communities and at the same time the sign of possible salvation, of a possible historical solitude."[8] The Venice Ghetto is once again situated as a node of connectivity: it models the way that heritage sites continue to leave an imprint on diasporic Jewish communities, serving as the visible touchstone and organizing framework for animating new networks of place-based collective memories.

Both Agosín and Fitoussi unravel what it means to represent and rewrite these spaces, breathing renewed life and forging new connections between the past and the present. What can the site of the Venice Ghetto mean in the twenty-first century, in a time challenged by global warming and rising sea levels, mass tourism, and global pandemics, and how do we engage its memory for the creation of more positive futures? What limitations must the "outsider" acknowledge so as to productively contribute to the site's network of collective memories?

As these authors demonstrate, emplaced methods matter. Elsewhere, Amanda K. Sharick, Erica G. Smeltzer, and Katharine G. Trostel have asked what it might mean to conduct memory research rooted to place: "The Ghetto of Venice is at once deeply entrenched in a specific, physical site (a point easily mapped cartographically) and characterized by its flexibility . . . The flexibility of allusion that the Venice Ghetto embodies and the importance of its geographic specificity calls for a kind of 'emplaced' memory work that we are calling 'reading in place.' Our practice of 'reading-in-place' was prompted by the site of the Venice Ghetto. We weave together the highly symbolic physical site with the many powerful stories, both real and imaginary, that orbit this locus. Reading-in-place—the act of joining stories and geography—added more texture and projected another fictional and imaginative layer onto the original site."[9] As Agosín and Fitoussi demonstrate, the act of reading, writing, and creating in place—what we are calling "emplaced methodologies"—helps us unpack the lessons that the Ghetto has to offer to memory-studies practitioners. It also prompts questions for further inquiry. What does it mean to practice these methods after a global crisis has transformed the way we live and work? What new lessons for the twenty-first century does the Ghetto of Venice have for scholars, for students, and for the general public alike? What are the parameters of this work? Does it change physical conditions in the built environment itself? Does the work's impact extend to the local residents? Does it live only in the collective imaginary?

Bassi and Isabella di Lenardo underscore the importance of engaging creatively with these spaces. Speaking specifically of the Venice Ghetto, they write that we should pay "a greater attention to local tradition and [have] a greater openness to the world at large" in order for it to be "possible to write (again) on the palimpsest of the Ghetto a story couched in terms of cultural renewal, of study, of coming together and the exchange of ideas. Spaces could be created in which to live and study in a unique historic context and—an essential proviso—to interact with the local population . . . as open-minded visitors with the time and the inclination to put questions and find answers. No longer mass tourism content to wallow in melancholy (if not sadistic) imaginings of decadence and death, but an open cultural traffic capable of stirring a new, vibrant, plural, international Jewish *life* in the ancient Ghetto."[10]

It is our hope that this collection engages with this conversation, recognizing that within the space of the Venice Ghetto is a laboratory that allows us to explore the connections between the local and the global, the past and the present. The Ghetto functions as a site of conscience, prompting us to question the legacy of this lived experience, to find "new words to retell its emblematic story, preserving a delicate equilibrium between the conservation and renewal of its local identity and its ability to speak to the whole world."[11] The essays in this section illustrate the infinite possibilities and ongoing mobility of the Venice Ghetto's legacy.

NOTES

1. Shaul Bassi, "Waters Close over Venice," *New York Times*, November 15, 2019, https://www.nytimes.com/2019/11/15/opinion/venice-flood-climate-change.html.
2. James E. Young, *The Stages of Memory: Reflections on Memorial Art, Loss, and the Spaces Between* (Amherst: University of Massachusetts Press, 2016), 16.

3. Sylvia Poggioli, "Rising Sea Levels and Mass Tourism Are Sinking Venice, Threatening City's Future," *All Things Considered*, NPR, November 28, 2019, https://www.npr.org/2019/11/28/783622529/rising-sea-levels-and-mass-tourism-are-sinking-venice-threatening-citys-future.
4. Shaul Bassi, afterword to this volume, 232.
5. Katharine G. Trostel, "The Poetry of Marjorie Agosín," this volume, 206–7, 206.
6. *El Hara*, directed by Margaux Fitoussi and Mo Scarpelli (2017), HD video, 16 min.
7. Amanda K. Sharick and Margaux Fitoussi, "Metaphor and Memory," this volume, 225–26.
8. Sharick and Fitoussi, 225.
9. Amanda K. Sharick, Erica G. Smeltzer, and Katharine G. Trostel, "Reading-in-Place and Thick Mapping the Venice Ghetto at 500," in *Doing Memory Research: New Methods and Approaches*, ed. Danielle Drozdzewski and Carolyn Birdsall (Singapore: Palgrave Macmillan, 2019), 134.
10. Shaul Bassi and Isabella di Lenardo, *The Ghetto Inside Out*, trans. John Francis Phillimore (Venice: Corte del Fondego, 2016), 35.
11. Bassi and di Lenardo, *Ghetto Inside Out*, 35.

CHAPTER EIGHT

THE POETRY OF MARJORIE AGOSÍN

Writing-in-Place in the World's First Ghetto

KATHARINE G. TROSTEL

INTRODUCTION

Within the fictional space of Marjorie Agosín's poetry, Venice is compared to a mirror that reflects our most intimate desires: "Only in that illusory Venice / Distinct from everyday geographies . . . Will it be possible to find ourselves without looking" (*"Tan solo en Venecia la imaginada / La extraviada de las geografías cotidianas . . . Será posible encontrarse sin buscarnos"*). For Agosín, Venice—and its ghetto—becomes a kind of portal, opening up our innermost secrets and inviting us to tell our own stories. As she states: "I have always loved Venezia . . . and loved the elusive and illusory world of this city of water, city of dreams and also nightmares."[1]

Agosín's own biographical experience allows her to connect intimately to this space—one that is simultaneously marked by rich, collective memories, by beauty, by life, and by the traumatic fragments of overlapping moments of difficult histories. A Chilean Jew exiled to the United States during the dictatorship of Augusto Pinochet (1973–90), she is a poet who understands how to listen for the reverberations and echoes of family traumas, uncover secrets, and trace the movement of collective memory passed through the generations. She captures in her poetry experiences of the Holocaust, of exile, of displacement—but also images of the beauty of place and landscape, of ties to home, and of the love that binds families and communities together. Poetry becomes an important way of housing fragile memories, a process that ensures that we

> keep their memories safe,
> to prevent all this
> from becoming a dictionary of oblivion,
> An almanac of forgetfulness.

> (guardar sus memorias,
> Para impedir que todo esto
> Sea un diccionario de los olvidos,
> Un almanaque desmemoriado.)

In May 2019, Agosín was invited to spend two weeks in the Ghetto as part of an artist-in-residency program through the efforts of Shaul Bassi, president of Beit Venezia. As the mission of the cultural organization states: "Venice was for centuries a focal point for Jewish life and culture. The Venice Ghetto was founded in 1516 as a place of segregation. Against all odds, it became a cosmopolitan crossroads of different Jewish communities and an influential site of cultural exchange between Jews and non-Jews. This is the vision that inspires Beit Venezia (from the Hebrew *bait*—home), which aims to promote Jewish thought and culture and serve as a bridge between people of all cultures and religions."[2] During her stay in Venice, Agosín was able to produce several poems that serve as witness to her interaction with the site of the Ghetto, four of which are printed in this essay. Her poetry reflects a particular emotional response to the space—one that braids together images of beauty, of sadness and loss, of remembrance, and of the process of uncovering strata of overlapping historical moments that serve as the Ghetto's layered foundation.

In an essay cowritten by members of the Venice Ghetto Collaboration (Amanda K. Sharick, Erica G. Smeltzer, and Katharine G. Trostel) in 2019, we developed the idea of how emplaced methods or approaches to memory studies could be applied to the field of literary studies—specifically in the context of learning from the space of the Venice Ghetto. In other words, by reading and creating "in place," intimately considering the relationship between the site of production and the literary or artistic work at hand, we engage in "the practice of close-reading text, which is so deeply entrenched in our discipline . . . reconnecting story to cartography and placing often conflicting versions of the past in proximity." We continued to develop this concept as we reflected deeply on our own work as literary scholars: "We weave together the highly symbolic physical site with the many powerful stories—both real and imaginary—that orbit this locus. Reading-in-place—the act of joining stories and geography—added more texture and projected another fictional and imaginative layer onto the original site."[3] However, "emplaced methods" could also include Agosín's practice of creative production, one we might describe as *writing-in-place.*

Agosín's poems explore memorials, museums, and tourist sites, but also the intimate spaces of her own family life and interior reflections pulled forth by her interaction with Venice. In doing so, she treats the space of the Ghetto as belonging to the world of the living, to the realm of creation and critical inquiry, and as relevant for vibrant cultural production in the present. Shaul Bassi and Isabella di Lenardo echo this call for productive creation, claiming that renewal of the site is possible with "a greater attention to local tradition and a greater openness to the world at large" and that "it should be possible to write (again) on the palimpsest of the Ghetto a story couched in terms of cultural renewal, of study, of coming together and exchange of ideas." They elaborate that "while trusting that the Ghetto can continue to be a normal *campo,* full of local life and children at play, we hope that it will also be able to reaffirm its role as a 'site of conscience,' finding new words to retell its emblematic story, preserving a delicate equilibrium between the conservation and renewal of its cultural heritage, between its local identity and its ability to speak to the whole world."[4]

Agosín's poetic pieces ask us to engage with the Ghetto in precisely this way and provoke a number of questions. Where does the memory of the Venice Ghetto come to rest? What kinds of memories does the geography call our attention to? What can poetry do to intervene and direct our gaze, perhaps drawing our focus back to the scale of the micro? Do "stepping stones"—a project of collective memory begun in 1992 in Germany consisting of bronze plaques known as *stolperstein* (stumbling stones) placed with the name of those taken by the Nazis outside of their last known place of residency—with their "strange stillness" echo the quiet and contemplative spaces of poetry?[5] How do we—as thinkers, readers, and creators—become the safety net, the keepers of life stories, renewing them with meaning for the twenty-first century?

INTERVIEW WITH MARJORIE AGOSÍN

KATHARINE G. TROSTEL: *Explain your connection to the Ghetto. How did writing and reading in place change the way you thought about the space? Does the five-hundredth-year anniversary carry symbolic resonance for you?*[26]

MARJORIE AGOSÍN: Living and experiencing Venice and life in the Ghetto became so different as I was living in close proximity [to it.] Every day I found something new—the color of the water, the colors of the trees and the wind. Nature was transformed. And then, I imagined all the people that lived there, throughout the centuries and now. Somehow, I no longer wanted to talk about the victimization of Jews, or the concept of Jews living in closed space. I wanted something that breathes new life, and of course, I wanted to imagine that in the Ghetto you could have a flourishing Jewish life, that the Ghetto was a space for love and life and creativity. The five-hundredth celebration was so important to me, but somehow [it] was not as important as thinking about the continuity of Jewish life.

KT: *What does it mean to be a "tourist" or to give guided tours of a space marked by a dwindling community, multiple traumas, lost dreams? What does meaningful, ethical, and engaged interaction with this place look like from your perspective? What is the role of the creative and scholarly community in ensuring a vibrant future for the Ghetto?*

MA: Locals and tourists were always there, but I was so much [in] my own imaginary and creative experience that nothing bothered me. I was interested in the life of children that play in the Ghetto. I was interested in the cooks of the Kosher restaurant and in the rabbis that are always looking at the world and praying. I was interested in all of them—even tourists—but mostly I was thinking about how I was going to speak of such beauty and such horror existing together and how I was going to speak about being Jewish [in this space] with thousands of years of history.

KT: *Explain this entanglement of times that you experienced in the Venetian Ghetto. You describe the space as a threshold—into what or to where are we transported when we enter this symbolic site? What possibilities are opened by crafting a poetic history while simultaneously inhabiting the site itself?*

MA: The idea of entanglement is a beautiful concept. I felt that to be entangled and living in a multiplicity of spaces was the essential idea of the Ghetto. You lived in layers of time and in history. As a poet, this came so naturally to me. Poetry inhabits time and space and has multiple synchronicities . . . I believe they are all there for a reason. They are all entangled.

The following creative essay was produced during Agosín's Napoleone Jesurum Residency in 2019.

THE VENETIAN GHETTO

Translation by Alison Ridley, Hollins University

From time to time I wonder if one day I will finally understand all of the voices that inhabit a single glance. Sometimes, a glance made without forethought can assign sacred value to an object, a random stone, like the ones we kick while walking from one place to another, or those that, as a child, I would pick up and take to the Jewish cemetery to pay homage to the dead whom we were never to forget. They were family members who now live only in the house of memory but whose graves we zealously protect from the ravages of time, from the beasts that lie in wait, and from the desecration wrought by men. Why do we put stones on those graves? What do the stones mean? I remember asking myself these questions as my small hands participated in a sacred act I did not fully comprehend. The ceremony of the stones used to make me sad, but I managed to understand, with my parents' help, the importance of that silent act of remembrance. Each step toward the graves, each word spoken by my elders, possessed a structure and a rhythm that made me feel safe as I learned about the ceremony's complexity and perfection, like certain songs whose notes build on one another in unexpected ways and that surprise the listener with each new sound.

What should I do now, so many years later, with my childhood questions that still seem relevant and that come back to greet me with the unique echo that time and distance imprint on them? Are they still important questions to ask? I think so, because they represent the type of questioning that allows my mind to take flight when I recognize in their vibrations the stillness of a sunrise or a twilight, like this one in far-away Venice where the light of day hides little by little, giving way to a new scenery made of memories and ceremonies enacted with the same stones that my small hands carried so many years ago.

Now I think that my childhood questions likely contained within them their own answers, perhaps hidden in the labyrinth created by their colors and brightness, in the echo of sunsets, where I see myself at my mother's side leaving the family cemetery. Perhaps, as the poet Rilke suggests, we should love our questions: those that allow our minds to imagine, if only for a moment, and to reach beyond the limits of our daily lives. Perhaps thinking about the infinite possibilities of experience, memory, and words, or the invisible transcendence of our actions and the intricate complexity of another's gaze, grants us the possibility of coming face to face with the seductive presence of the unfathomable and also with the possibility that maybe one day the answers will become clear.

At this very moment, my childhood questions reemerge as I watch the inhabitants maneuvering through this unique city that is shaped by its tangle of canals. As I walk, I remember something I read a long time ago by Richard Sennett about the physical space that exclusion has occupied in Europe. He wrote about the places to which people labeled "Other" were banished because society at large was incapable of understanding their mysterious aura.[7] Today, I am remembering those who occupied such a segregated space in this city that, at the height of the Renaissance, was already beginning to weave itself into the political and symbolic landscape.

In his book *Flesh and Stone*, Sennett discusses the segregated places in Venice where the Jewish people and others were confined—places like the Fondaco dei Tedeschi. That very building that stands before me now is where thousands of German Christians passed their nights locked up simply because they were different, because they represented the Other. They were perceived by the city's officials to be the cultural enemy for embodying Luther's reformist ideas and other forms of superstition. Sennett notes: "In that real Venice, the desire for Christian community lay somewhere between a dream and an anxiety. The impurities of difference haunted the Venetians: Albanians, Turks, and Greeks, Western Christians like the Germans, all were segregated in guarded buildings or clusters of buildings. Difference haunted the Venetians, yet exerted a seductive power" (215).

Later in his book, Sennett describes another segregated place, the Venetian Ghetto, where the Jewish population of the city was locked up at night during different periods in history. Despite the restrictive nature of the Ghetto, the Jewish people managed to thrive within its walls. Ironically, it was their separation from the rest of the populace that allowed them to preserve their unique culture. In this regard, the Ghetto is distinct from so many other segregated spaces where people have been robbed of their identities.

The Venetian Ghetto is a space, like so many others, that is indelibly connected to the history of the Jewish people who arrived in Italy in the Middle Ages as a result of pogroms that seem to have been happening since time immemorial. Sennett describes how, because of Venice's unique geography, it was easy to create a segregated space in which to confine the Jewish people: "In Venice, the physical character of the city made it possible finally to realize the rule prescribed by the Lateran Council—Venice a city built on water, water the city's roads which separated clusters of buildings into a vast archipelago of islands" (216).

In great measure the confinement of the Jewish people in this city was the result of changes in the trade routes during the sixteenth century. As new routes were discovered by Portuguese explorers, trading shifted to Africa and the East, making Venice and other parts of Europe less important in the world of trade. Despite the overwhelming evidence to explain the economic decline of the city, the Christian residents of Venice chose instead to interpret it as a sign of God's ire at the presence of the Jewish people.

The Ghetto became a significant place in the history of the nomadic and itinerant Jewish people who always carried with them, along with the scrolls of the Torah, the ancestral wisdom of those who had survived expulsion and confinement throughout the ages. The history of the Jewish people can be defined by its many bifurcations and fractures that led to a perpetual search for an alternative way of living. Despite constant setbacks, they exuded energy and creativity as they continued to search for a light in the darkness, a place to call home. For me, the Venetian

Ghetto is a space rooted in the history of the Jewish people that managed to develop thanks to its inhabitants who instilled their values within it. Sennett explains: "The formation of the Jewish Ghetto tells the story of a people who were segregated but who then made new forms of community life out of their very segregation" (216).

In spite of being a space confined within stone walls and surrounded by canals, it was nevertheless a place where creativity triumphed over confinement. There, the Jewish community built at least five synagogues in which religious devotions were carried out and where intellectual conversations and the composition and recitation of poetry could freely take place. In those large spaces, women could also display the beauty of their jewels without fear of being singled out by those who associated the luxury of Jewish women with the moral decadence of a Venice that was gradually losing power. Within the confined space of the Ghetto, the Jewish people figured out a way to celebrate themselves as Other. It became a symbolic space where a new understanding of the essence of being Jewish began to define itself. Within its walls, they perfected the sense of both belonging and not belonging to the city in which they were always subject to restrictions imposed by the authorities.

These and other reflections accompany me as I walk through Venice's old and new Ghettos, which are close in proximity while being far apart in time. Both represent a great human legacy sculpted by history but to an even greater extent by everyday stories, filaments of which populate the pages of encyclopedias but do not do justice to the experience of the citizens who lived there. I have always believed that the great deeds of humanity occur in everyday life, in daily chores. Here, in the Venetian Ghetto, there was always a sacred and a public life. The latter was a life lived outside where secondhand goods were traded and loans for large sums of money were made. Another life, the one lived within the Ghetto, was characterized by the aforementioned gatherings and religious ceremonies that year after year allowed the Jewish identity to evolve.

Now, I invite you to cross these fragile drawbridges with me and to enter the Ghetto where countless pages were written and subsequently forgotten about the exile of a people who managed to reinvent themselves. I encourage you to immerse yourselves in the vast creativity of those who grew up subject to a destiny that was imposed on the Jewish diaspora. The Ghetto was a distinctive place where magic emerged at night. It was a place where human genius managed, through the creative act, to transcend borders: those imposed by the Venetian officials, the borders of discourse, and, above all, the borders of ignorance.

In the silence of the night, the Jewish community produced a whole world of new ideas as well as a new imaginary that bolstered the Jews, allowing them to reimagine themselves time and again. By candlelight, they returned to the precepts that had defined their identity throughout the ages and allowed themselves to reemerge, resilient as ever. The Ghetto listens to us and also speaks to us. It tells us stories that we might ordinarily overlook, and once we leave its embrace, we realize we are no longer the same people. We discover that our imaginations and our identities remain within those walls that no longer confine but rather draw for us the historical context in which the Jewish people were able to imagine themselves anew. It was, without a doubt, a miracle bathed in the soft gold of the Venetian artisans. In the Ghetto we feel how this unique, intimate life manifests itself in the gait of the elderly, in the songs of the children playing in the half-paved square, in the doctor who leaves his house to heal, in the women who sweep and cook.

The music and the prayers that filter through the slits in the walls of the Ghetto's synagogues speak to us about a particular way of inhabiting the world, about one world existing within another. It is important to consider the Ghetto in this way, as a constructed space within a broader space and as a cultural apparatus where its inhabitants were able to rethink their condition as individuals and as a people as well as their relationship with the divine and the randomness of fate. It is a place that opens like a flower at dawn and then closes back up when night falls. However, as we have already noted, the closing up of the Ghetto was only partial. It was only in the eyes of the city's officials that the Ghetto was completely closed at night. Inside, after dark, the Ghetto was as vibrant as any other city in the world, and perhaps even more so because the night gave residents the opportunity to study and worship, and with the advent of coffee in sixteenth-century Europe, the days of reflection were extended. A groundswell of creativity manifested itself in prayers to artisans, in poetry, in activities such as caring for the body and the soul of others, cooking with saffron and almonds, and singing in Ladino or Yiddish, Italian, and sometimes also Spanish.

As darkness falls, the habitual melancholy of the sunset allows the blue and silent night to reflect in the undulations of the canals that surround the city. The Ghetto is blanketed with a soft golden light as though the oil lamps of those who worked in silence on the ancient manuscripts illuminate this night outside time. It is a night perhaps like those when an angelic presence saved the Ghetto's residents from being lynched by enraged mobs during Lent, when the Christian community, incensed once more before the figure of the Other, directed its tirades against the Jewish community whose only illumination in the darkness was the light of their studies. Fortunately, the light always returned to the Venetian Ghetto. Perhaps more than one of those persecuted Jews bowed down to pray, grateful for having survived one more incident of hatred. Perhaps more than one of them put on the tefillin. Perhaps another wrote a poem reflecting the fragility of time and life.

On this night that is different from all others, I listen to the world unfurl before me while the echo of my footsteps betrays my presence. I am an observer who has come to interrupt the memory of those who passed through these same streets and who are no longer here. I stop on the small square to remember those who were deported during the Shoah. Many left from here, and from other cities in Italy, never to return. However, I do not want to dwell on that somber and cruel memory. Rather, I prefer to think about the privilege of being alive, about the gift of being here and being able to communicate with my ancestors who prayed in the five synagogues. I want to celebrate what they could not, what they could not hide. I want to celebrate the continuity of our story here in the Ghetto, to see it as another piece of the memory of my people. It is, without a doubt, a memory of light and shadows, of eternal nights and dawns.

At night, the wind is sovereign in the Ghetto. It blows in and out of windows and carries on it stories and secrets from one house to the next. Nighttime in this space looks like a cluster of stars on the water. The stars light up the faces of those who gaze up at them, perhaps searching for something sacred, something divine, something to explain the origins of difference. Víctor Frankl once said that the essence of being human resides in our awareness of being tied to a story, a tale, a memory, a sense of responsibility to one's self and to the past. And the Jews, as a people, demonstrated that awareness by preserving their narratives, their memory. Tonight, the Venetian Ghetto is lit up thanks to the stars that shine down and show the way like they did in Jacob's dream, when

God told him that his people would experience wonders, like the stars on the horizon.

After a night in which couples sleep entwined like ancient trees, a man and a woman kiss as dawn breaks. In the purity of that kiss they find each other time and time again, as though they have known each other forever, as though they represent that primordial couple or an early spring flower without thorns. At that moment, they know nothing of hurt and even less of deceit. All they see is the promise of a new day. The young man dresses for the first prayers of the day that fill his mind with the speed of one who has yet to be affected by the vicissitudes of time or age. By his side, his wife prepares coffee and bread. The bread is fresh and tastes of so many journeys. It knows of entrapment but also flight. It remembers paths that in other times, generations ago, forked to lead us home. It reminds us of a grandmother who in dreams told us the secret for keeping the bread piping hot, always fresh on the table. The bread sits before these young people who look at each other, enraptured. It made its way to us thanks to those who fervently kept the traditions of the Jewish people alive. The young couple's prayers illuminate their delicate stone house, a living space that out of necessity kept growing toward heaven, without any other planning than that dictated by the need to survive. Or perhaps the house was built that way in an effort to reach God, like in the painting of that old Dutch painter.

The fragrance of the bread that tastes of almonds encompasses the aroma of life, of everyday objects that in the Ghetto become sacred as they represent the preservation of the Jewish identity. In the Ghetto, we experience the time of God in the stones, the texts, the words, and the sounds of leaves beneath the feet of a people who, despite the restrictions imposed on them, allowed diverse voices to be heard and a variety of languages to be spoken. In the Ghetto both Sephardic or Ashkenazi can be heard—languages so distant and different but, at the same time, linked through brotherly love and tales of so many confinements.

When dawn breaks, a different kind of life begins. Children head to school and people head to work outside the Ghetto's gates. While the Venetian authorities ensured that the Jewish population was segregated at night, they could not deny the importance of that same population to the city's economy during the day. The Jews were professional moneylenders and doctors whose trades contributed substantially to the economic growth of the port city. Sennett describes how the lives of Jewish and non-Jewish peoples intersected thanks to the professional talents of the former: "These high-status Jewish moneylenders and doctors became highly visible refugees, since their lives intersected more with Christians in the Venetian community" (222).

At dawn, I leave the Ghetto and cross the canals, those mirages of illuminated water. I head to the Lido, where I find myself before a statue of Sarra Copia Sullam. I also find her in my memory. She represents the proud presence of a woman who survived in the Venetian Ghetto. She wrote and sang in various languages: in Italian and Hebrew, and sometimes Greek. She also met in salons with important people associated with the arts. So much has been said about Sara. For instance, some people note her stunning beauty or the unique color of her hair, while others recount how she used to help boat owners financially in exchange for them giving her lessons. She wanted access to a higher level of education than women were able to aspire to at the time.

Sara was an essential part of the Venetian Ghetto. She lived there, loved there, and was also betrayed there. Her name transcends the Ghetto's walls and exists in a space where there are no borders, where she is recognized as one of the most important poets of the seventeenth century. Today, in this early morning hour, I am remembering her and other women who have been forgotten. I think about those who are never spoken of and those who have achieved great feats without needing acclaim, unlike their male counterparts who make sure their accomplishments are known and recorded in history books and in pictures depicting heroes astride a horse, but never on the ground next to the animal. I think of women who have been betrayed or who have been the object of malicious remarks or opinions laden with superstition and ignorance. One does not need to be too clever to realize that women have always been on the front lines in terms of being victims of discrimination. In the history of this city, they were associated with prostitution, moral decadence, the plague, and fickleness. Perhaps in the case of the Jewish women in the Ghetto, they were singled out because they aroused the curiosity of those who saw in their beauty a strange and seductive force that had to be confined and rendered invisible.

Today, in their honor, I pick up a few colored stones. I make my way to the Jewish cemetery where I will place them. I am not honoring one woman but thousands. I know the stones in my pockets represent something sacred. In the cemetery I am greeted by the spirit of Aldo Izzo, an angel for this century, the guardian of the dead and of the memory of this vibrant people. This stone is for you, Sara, my friend. This stone that bathed in the waters of the canals, that knows of countless journeys, of comings and goings, including your own, will keep the memory of your work alive as well as the works of so many others that have been lost. I leave this stone here to look after you and to contribute to the yearned-for refuge where other men and women, like you, can hide from terror. It will be a haven against fear and betrayal.

When I leave the cemetery, I let myself be carried by the sound of footsteps. They are footsteps like rivers, like the canals that snake through this city, footsteps that run into others and lead me once more to the Ghetto, that place that is so fluid like the city of Venice itself, like the way of being and living in the world. It is said that those who decide to love this city do not need maps or directions because the city always unfolds before them, dazzling them at every turn, surprising them with some etching that time has cut into the stone. Venice is like a great firefly that in the afternoons shows us the way to find ourselves within it. I think if someone were to blindfold me, I would always know how to get back to the Ghetto. I would cross the small bridges and sit on the verdant plaza replete with the sounds and the silences that together create a map made of memories.

Coming into contact with the Ghetto is like experiencing creativity, faith, prayers, and that enigmatic time between happenings. It is like experiencing a time that lives in other times, where everything mixes and flows, where the image of Sara reciting her poems accompanied by a single lyre appears time and time again. Around her are children playing with stones. Her poems describe men who appear as angels flying above the synagogues that are a heartrending red, that sacred and beautiful red of the bricks and of twilight—the red of the city of Venice.

For me, the Ghetto represents the search for a distinctive way of looking at things, as well as the opportunity to continue to live a life full of humanity regardless of the devastation history has left in its wake. I dare to say that here, in this space and time of history, bathed in a sacred light, my life coexists with the pain, martyrdom, persecution, happiness, and creativity of my Jewish ancestors. Here, people weave and embroider life. They draw, write, and cook. They pray and intuit the passing of life as well as the presence of those who might one day visit this place and find something within its walls they never would have imagined: a golden city, a city of water, a city of artisans, a city of illustrators and painters, of wise men and poets, a city where the Jewish people have continued the story of their traditions.

I walk away from the Ghetto in step with many others who inhabit my memory and who have accompanied me on this journey. As I pass through the gates, I feel the night as well as the trees and the shadows they project. I also feel the rays of the moon and remember the sound of the small stones I picked up on my way to the old cemetery where the dead awaited me in silence. The dead remember their people's story filled with forked roads and fractured time—a story in which the tenuous continuity of life, of awakening, of yearning, of feeling, and of being can be perceived.

After a while of walking the narrow streets listening to my footsteps, I find myself once more, inexplicably, back at the Venetian Ghetto. It calls to me. I tell myself it will always be here to safeguard the memory of the Jewish people who were expelled but who found themselves again in the ancient prayers of the Torah and in the rich, diverse culture that evolved within these walls. The diversity of Jewish identity, which has not always been acknowledged, is the result of my people's eternal wandering and their undying quest for freedom. The Ghetto is a place where, contrary to its intended purpose, Jewish exiles from distinct places were able to build a diverse community and a vibrant way of life, one that has persisted and will continue to persist thanks to the resilience of a people who refuse to be silenced.

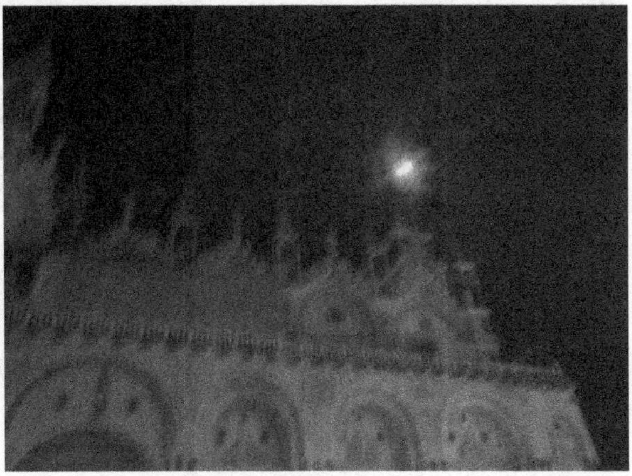

FIGURE 15. San Marco.
—Photography by Samuel Shats, May 2011.

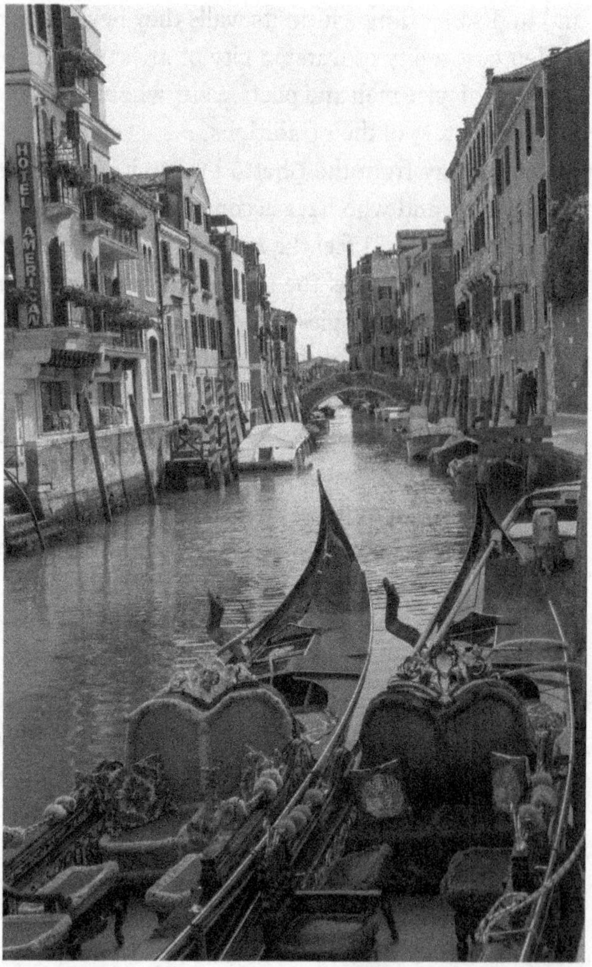

FIGURE 16. Canal with gondolas.
—Photography by
Samuel Shats, May 2011.

FIGURE 17. Canal in neighborhood.
—Photography by
Samuel Shats, May 2011.

POETRY OF THE VENICE GHETTO

Translations by Alison Ridley, Hollins University

En el gueto veneciano
En el gueto veneciano
Entrelazado en varios tiempos
Nos detenemos silenciosos como si el mismo lenguaje
Para rezar o conversar perdiera su presencia . . .
Se desvanecen los sonidos.

El guía con una extraña amabilidad y sensatez
Comenta que tan solo se llevaron a 222 judíos
De estas puertas clausuradas
Y que volvieron ocho . . .
"¿Ocho son muchos, no es cierto?"
Así habla con mesura de la desmesura acontecida
Y tan solo me quedo con las preguntas . . .
¿Cómo volvieron?
¿Se puede volver de Auschwitz?
¿Se puede hablar de aquellos umbrales
Entre la vida y la muerte?

"Nadie vuelve," le comento al guía . . .
Tan solo esos ocho con sus mortajas,
Con sus capas espesas de noche,
Con sus ojos vacíos,
Con las cuencas espantadas . . .
"Señor guía
Nadie vuelve de ahí."

Translation: In the Venetian Ghetto
In the Venetian ghetto
Entangled in various eras
We stand silent as though the language
We use to pray or converse has ceased to exist . . .
Sounds fade away.

The guide with peculiar amiability and wit
Remarks that only 222 Jews were taken from
Behind these closed doors,

And that eight returned . . .
"Eight is many, don't you think?"
He speaks with restraint about the most appalling events
And I am left only with questions . . .
How did they return?
Is it possible to return from Auschwitz?
Can one really speak of the thresholds
Between life and death?

"No one returns," I say to the guide . . .
Only those eight clad in their shrouds,
With their capes thick with night,
With their vacant gazes,
With their petrified eye sockets . . .
"Mr. Guide,
No one returns from there."

Tan solo en Venecia
Tan solo en Venecia la imaginada,
La extraviada de las geografías cotidianas,
Esa ciudad de pasos lentos,
De aguas que revelan la suavidad de los secretos,
Será posible encontrarnos sin buscarnos,
Reconocernos sin ser reconocidos
En la ciudad de los espejos que se bifurcan, que agudizan las formas.
Tan solo entonces nos veremos como una ráfaga de agua clara
Que pasa por nuestros ojos
Y nuestros ojos como cartas de agua,
Una infinita carta de agua,
Comenzarán a escribir esta historia de livianas palabras
Para nunca extraviarse,
Para estar en la lúcida luz del alma.

Translation: Only in Venice
Only in that illusory Venice,
Distinct from everyday geographies,
That city of measured footsteps,
Of water that reveals the lightness of secrets,
Will it be possible to find ourselves without looking,

To recognize ourselves without being recognized,
In the city of mirrors that fragment and refine figures.
Only then will we see ourselves as a squall of clear water
That passes through our eyes,
And our eyes, like letters of water,
An infinite letter of water,
Will begin to write this story of airy words
In order to never go astray,
To reside in the lucid light of the soul.

Gratitud

Solamente la gratitud
Por los días soleados
Cuando se enhebran historias
De luz y de paciencia.

Solamente la gratitud
Por el ruido de las campanas de Venecia
Cuando todas las campanas cantan a destiempo
Y por la imperfección.

Gratitud por los días de lluvia,
Aquellos grises y lentos
Cuando un fuego tenue nos acompaña
Así como la memoria de los otros.

Gratitud por haber nacido,
Por los padres perfectos e imperfectos
Que en el momento más lúcido del amor
Nos dieron vida.
Después nosotros los imitamos
Al darle vida a los que hoy son nuestros hijos,
A quienes queremos con una entrañable pasión,
A quienes protegemos de toda adversidad.

Gratitud por haber amado con dulzura y con impulsos,
Por haber sido impaciente y paciente.

Gratitud por haber encontrado en la vida
Un hombre que lee poemas,
Que es solitario en sus quehaceres . . .

Su invisible compañía otorga una tenue luz,
La del entendimiento que es la luz del deseo.

Translation: Gratitude
Only gratitude
For sunny days
When stories of light and patience
Entwine.

Only gratitude
For the sound of church bells in Venice
That peal out of sync,
And for imperfection.

Gratitude for grey, slow,
Rainy days,
When a soft fire accompanies us
Along with our memories of others.

Gratitude for having been born,
For perfect and imperfect parents
Who, in the most luminous trice of love,
Gave us life.
Later we emulated them,
Giving life to our own children
Whom we love with fathomless passion,
Whom we protect from all adversity.

Gratitude for having loved sweetly and impulsively,
For having been impatient and patient.

Gratitude for having found a man in this life
Who reads poetry,
Who is solitary in his tasks . . .
His subtle companionship emits a tenuous light,
The light of understanding that is also the light of desire.

Las baldosas
En los parques gloriosos de Europa,
Entre los canales de la majestuosa Venecia,
En los manicomios, en las casas señoriales,

En las plazas, en los parques cubiertos de lilas
Están ellas, las pequeñas baldosas,
Las baldosas que con las lluvias profundas
Poseen un distinto resplandor,
Una extraña quietud . . .

¿Quiénes eran? ¿Dónde vivían?
¿Por qué salieron de sus casas?
¿Quién los expulsó de sus hogares?
¿Dónde estaban las vecinas?
¿Por qué la policía los fueron a buscar
En el manicomio de Venecia?

Estas baldosas relatan sus vidas
Obstruidas, bifurcadas, robadas.
Te inclinas para pensarlos,
Para guardar sus memorias,
Para impedir que todo esto
Sea un diccionario de los olvidos,
Un almanaque desmemoriado.

Acércate a estas diminutas baldosas.
Contienen toda una vida,
Toda una historia sagrada y cotidiana
Ahora sin pasado o futuro,
Ahora una memoria de una gran vida truncada.

Acércate,
Escucha,
Siéntelos,
Haz una reverencia por los judíos muertos,
Por ellos que eran ciudadanos nobles,
Que no merecían morir
Ni saltar de los balcones
Para recibir una precipitada muerte . . .
Haz una reverencia,
Bésalos.

Translation: The Stepping Stones
In the glorious parks of Europe,

Amid the canals of the majestic Venice,
In insane asylums, in stately homes,
On plazas, in parks abloom with lilacs,
Small stepping stones can be found,
Stones that in heavy rains
Possess a distinctive gleam,
A strange stillness . . .

Who were they? Where did they live?
Why did they leave their houses?
Who banished them from their homes?
Where were their neighbors?
Why did the police search for them
In the insane asylum in Venice?

These stepping stones recount
Their thwarted, shattered, and stolen lives.
You bow your head and think of them,
To keep their memories safe,
To prevent all this
From becoming a dictionary of oblivion,
An almanac of forgetfulness.

Draw closer to these modest stones.
They contain a life,
A sacred and profane story
Now without a past or a future,
Now only a memory of a grand, truncated life.

Draw closer,
Listen,
Hear them,
Bow your head for the dead Jews,
For those who were noble citizens
Who did not deserve to die,
Or to jump from balconies
To ensure a swifter death . . .
Bow your head,
Kiss them.

NOTES

1. Marjorie Agosín, email correspondence with author, August 28, 2019.
2. "Home," Beit Venezia, Centro Veneziano di Studi Ebraici Internazionali, accessed February 10, 2021, http://beitvenezia.org/.
3. Amanda K. Sharick, Erica G. Smeltzer, and Katharine G. Trostel, "Reading-in-Place and Thick Mapping the Venice Ghetto at 500," in *Doing Memory Research: New Methods and Approaches*, ed. Danielle Drozdzewski and Carolyn Birdsall (Singapore: Palgrave Macmillan, 2019), 132, 134.
4. Shaul Bassi and Isabella di Lenardo, *The Ghetto Inside Out* (Venice: Corte del Fontego, 2016), 34–35.
5. "Home," Stolpersteine, Gunter Demnig, updated January 18, 2021, http://www.stolpersteine.eu/en/home.
6. Agosín, email correspondence with author. All questions and answers herein are taken from this correspondence.
7. Richard Sennett, *Flesh and Stone: The Body and the City in Western Civilization* (New York: W. W. Norton, 1994). All future references to Sennett's text refer to this edition and are cited parenthetically in the text.

FIGURE 18. Still shot from *El Hara*.— Photograph by Mo Scarpelli.

FIGURE 19. Still shot from *El Hara*.— Photograph by Mo Scarpelli.

CHAPTER NINE

Metaphor and Memory

A Conversation on the Making of the Film *El Hara*

AMANDA K. SHARICK AND MARGAUX FITOUSSI

In 2016, Margaux Fitoussi, a master's degree student at Harvard Divinity School, traveled to Tunisia over the winter recess to study a place that her family once called home. The visit was transformative and sparked more questions for her about the function of past places for communities shaped by diasporic currents of forced and elective migration from former colonies to metropoles of Europe. It was during her time in Tunisia that she reached out to her family, now living across the globe—in the United States, France, and Israel—to consider what they remembered and what they were willing to share about what it meant to be Jewish in Tunisia during the twentieth century.

El Hara is a coalescence of Fitoussi's academic studies and artistic pursuits as a filmmaker. The film traces her pivotal journey through an engagement with the story of the Hara of Tunis as described by past and current residents, including an interview with the Hara's most famous former resident, Tunisian Jewish author and theorist Albert Memmi (1920–2020) in the summer of 2016. The film opens with the sounds of French music and street noises of Paris as the camera pans over Memmi's home in the Marais neighborhood of Paris. We hear Fitoussi speaking French with Memmi and she asks: "Could you describe to someone like me who never experienced the Hara, what is the Hara?"

The question drives the film forward through a sequence of the medina in present-day Tunis, where the current and predominantly Muslim community resides. It cuts back to Paris, where Memmi is seen staring into the camera—as if contemplating where to begin. English subtitles to a French monologue of excerpts from several of Memmi's novels and essays play over a contemporary display of life filling the narrow alleys of the Hara, now known as the Hafsia. Often referred to during the French colonial period as the "Jewish ghetto of Tunis," the Hara remains a rich site of Jewish and Islamic history. The slippage between the two historically discrete Jewish spaces—the European ghetto and the Tunisian Hara—is not uncommon despite their significant disparities. The Italian ghettos of Christian Europe, as has been demonstrated throughout this edited collection, were sequestered community spaces away from the centers of political and social life in Italy, guarded by Christian soldiers. Though the Hara was the center of Jewish life in the city of Tunis from the thirteenth century until French colonialization in 1881, the boundaries between Jewish and Muslim life were more porous than in Western Europe.

As Fitoussi notes, the filming of *El Hara* in 2016 aligned with the five hundredth anniversary of the world's first ghetto, founded in Venice, Italy, which was circulating among global news outlets. When she spoke with Tunisian Muslims and Jews about the neighborhood, she was surprised by the way the concept of the ghetto bubbled up. Whether it was to compare or contrast, the link between Tunisian haras and European ghettos has been a feature of conversations and scholarly debates since the early twentieth century. Memmi himself describes the Hara as a ghetto—a designation Fitoussi and her codirector, Mo Scarpelli, must grapple with in their film. In the interview below, Fitoussi explains that what makes the ghetto present in the Hara is its connection to empire, to the European colonizer's efforts to transform the cultural landscape but also the colonial effort itself to inculcate the minds of the colonized. As Memmi explains, "the ghetto was equally interior."[1]

As we have seen through the essays in this collection, the psychic effects of ghettoization haunt and permeate the history of Jewish experiences from 1516 forward. The ghetto acts as a metaphor for containment that also exceeds its physical or temporal planes, pervading individual and collective memories from a variety of contexts and conditions. The ghetto as a memory space that travels reorients the conditions of possibility for communities that are ever aware that they can—in their present moment—"walk five hundred steps in [their] city and [see the] changing civilizations," the layered pasts that contribute to the present.[2]

Fitoussi and Scarpelli excavate these layered pasts for multiple audiences in their short documentary. The film becomes the medium to better understand the relationship of these (at times conflicting) pasts for a present audience grappling with a precarious future. Throughout his career, Memmi has insisted that events beyond our control or comprehension shape the course of our individual lives. University of California at Los Angeles professor Lia Brozgal, who interviewed Memmi, relays that Memmi mentioned "that he wouldn't have left Tunisia if history hadn't chased him out."[3] Seven years later, he explains to Fitoussi in an interview for the film, "I stayed until I was seventeen years old because my generation didn't have much luck." *El Hara* (2017), now available for streaming, raises important questions about the role of memory for a new generation now removed from the narrow streets, smells, and tastes of the Hara. These generational shifts exact a toll of their own, especially for those leaving the literal and figurative ghettos of minority enclaves for a better life. The film reminds us of the power of memory to name these losses, as well as presents a path forward for new audiences to understand and remember the memories that are not their own, carrying them to new contexts to help them reimagine places far removed.

Margaux Fitoussi is a filmmaker and anthropologist based at Columbia University in New York City. Her award-winning short film *El Hara* was shown at multiple venues, including the Atlanta International Film Festival, the Mountain Film Festival, the Film Society at the Lincoln Center, and the Musée d'Art et d'Histoire du Judaïsme; it was also released online as a Jewish Film Institute Short of the Month.

El Hara was first screened as part of an exhibition that Fitoussi curated at Harvard University and Dar Ben Achour Library in Tunis, Tunisia, about the Hara of Tunis. From 2011 to 2013, as a Judith Lee Stronach Scholar, Fitoussi was based in Central Africa developing an early warning system in communities affected by the Lord's Resistance Army. Before beginning at Columbia University as a PhD student in anthropology, she studied at UC Berkeley and at Harvard University as a Harvard Presidential Scholar. Her research analyzes transformations in social life and the built environment in Tunisia in the wake of colonialism, migration, and political authoritarianism. Her work also engages philosophical and political debates about materiality, temporality, and cultural memory.

INTERVIEW WITH MARGAUX FITOUSSI

AMANDA SHARICK:[4] *The film* El Hara *has been lauded by the* Huffington Post *in its review of the 2018 New York Jewish Film Festival as "one of the most eloquent sixteen minutes [audiences] will experience this year."*[5] *Others have noted that the film captures parts of Albert Memmi's story in a new way. Ella Shohat, for instance, explains that by "interlacing the quotidian sights and sounds of* El Hara *with Albert Memmi's texts, reminiscences, and commentaries about his formative years there, the film deftly captures the dissonances of a multi-layered Jewish-Maghrebian-French identity."*[6] *What inspired you to create a film about the Hara? And what were some of the reasons why you chose to revisit Albert Memmi's established connections to the Hara?*

MARGAUX FITOUSSI: *El Hara* (2017) was both an exploration of Tunis, the city my family left in the 1960s, and my long-standing interest in pasts that are both unsettled and unsettling. What happens when stories are not told, when people have been uprooted for one reason or another, when we no longer know nor remember what came before? The film juxtaposes images of Tunis's historic Jewish quarter with Albert Memmi's writings and a 2016 interview with him. Mo Scarpelli, my codirector, and I wanted to build on Memmi's analysis of the contradictory position of Tunisian Jews within the colonial order while also exploring the force (or lack thereof) of one's attachments to home.

Memmi told me he enjoyed exchanging ideas with students, and we met several more times after the film's completion. Our conversations ran the gamut—U.S. imperialism in the Middle East; why *The Colonizer and the Colonized* was popular in Québec; his concepts of *Judaïté* and *heterophobia*; and recollections about his friends, mostly philosophers, primarily Jewish, whom he met weekly in 1950s Tunis to discuss the events of the period and who were, he remarked, "all dead now." I learned a great deal from him even as our perspectives on late colonialism and Palestine differed.

With Memmi's passing in May 2020, I've returned to his work to help me think through the ways we are—and are not—beholden to place. I was struck by a discussion we had about how proper names can be shed, disavowed, and transformed but how more often they express—even essentialize—our relationship to places we may never have lived. Writing about Marcel Proust's relationship to names, Roland Barthes describes the proper name as the "linguistic form of reminiscence," a "semantic monstrosity" holding memory, usage, and culture together.[7] Names lie at the heart of this question of origins and home, the thread linking people through the labyrinth of time and space. With Memmi, my surname, commonly found among Jewish families from western Tunisia and eastern Algeria, served as a point of connection, signaling that we shared something despite our many differences. His surname, he explained, could signify Italian or Berber origins. He told me: "There are quite a few families with the name Memmi in Florence, but it could also mean 'little man' in Berber." "So perhaps," he added cheekily, "my ancestors were little." These two explanations of his surname, among others, indicated to Memmi that "his family doesn't know where they come from" and this, he said, "is the fate of Jews, more generally."

AS: *Thank you for offering this reflection on names and how they mark and remark on our relationship to our communities' pasts and present. Names have a metonymic function, in this way, and I am wondering if you found other literary forms helpful for the framing of your documentary or interview with Memmi?*

MF: Memmi is never quite at home in the world. The indeterminate state of being "this and that, and even more," has been a source of productive tension in his work.[8] *El Hara* explores this tension, the push and pull of overlapping identities, and draws on two spatial metaphors operative in Memmi's own work: the impasse and the sea. The impasse, as a narrative signpost of childhood, and the sea, as a diasporic metaphor of possibility. But this is not a hard-and-fast juxtaposition: one finds elements of loss in both. In a 2016 conversation, he said to me: "The 'paradox of the writer' is that of 'trying to escape, to leave their fate, but never succeeding in doing so.'"[9] In making the film, I wondered what I would find by shadowing Memmi through the architectural landscape of the Hara of Tunis, the Jewish quarter in the old city, or in repeating his journey across the Mediterranean. Would retracing his steps enable me to better know this writer's particular paradox?

The impasse remains the beating heart of Memmi's origin story, a place he returns to again and again.[10] The impasse is a dead end, a one-way street, a blind alley. His insistence on the architectural form of the impasse as a place of origin interests me. What did this symbolize for him? What kind of meaning accrued to it? He describes his impasse—real and imagined—as a borderland between the Arab and Jewish quarters, the European and Tunisian worlds. It's a familiar place. One can know the crevices of its walls and know *how* and *where* one is situated within it. Belonging in and to a place, a people, a heritage can be incredibly affirming. But as Memmi evocatively described in *The Pillar of Salt* (1953), breaking away from the impasse can also be crushingly alienating. The protagonist of his first semiautobiographical novel is a young Tunisian Jewish man who contends with how his French education changed his relationship to the impasse, and created distance between himself and his family and community. The novel seems to suggest that only by crossing the sea will the protagonist be free to live unbound by communal and colonial constraints.

When I asked Memmi about the impasse and about characterizing the Hara as a "kingdom of the poor" in a 1976 interview with Victor Malka,[11] he swiftly responded, "That was poetics. I don't really believe that. The poor don't have a kingdom, it's not true. I withdraw that statement. Simply, it was a poor neighborhood, very poor . . . If you came from this neighborhood, you cannot forget what you went through. Those who passed through the Hara were imbued with the Hara. We do not forget our origins." The double movement here—passing through the Hara as the Hara simultaneously passes through him—leaves an indelible mark. I went looking but never did find Memmi's impasse. But to say the impasse cannot be found on a map is not to say it doesn't exist.

Memmi's use of the sea as a metaphor is contradictory and hard to hold onto. The sea is a site of self-fashioning but also one of self-effacement. Its surface may be traceless, but its currents and its swells are familiar and nourishing. In the "Richness of Exile," an essay in the form of a letter written from somewhere in the Mediterranean, Memmi states: "I write to you from nowhere, which is to say from everywhere."[12] From the vantage of a ship afloat at sea, the northern and southern shores appear almost indistinguishable to him. To remain adrift, to claim all and nothing, can leave one feeling unmoored. However, the sea in its expansiveness, in its rootlessness, allows for a multiplicity of affiliations to exist simultaneously: Jewish, Tunisian, French, Berber, African. The sea is, as Memmi would have it, an exilic space par excellence. And exile, he confesses in the "Richness of Exile," may be as generative as it is painful.[13]

The sea voyage for the person in exile becomes a passageway between past and future as represented geographically, as well as a rite of passage. Nearly three quarters of a century after he and his family crossed the Mediterranean and settled in Paris, Memmi spoke of Tunisia and the Mediterranean in a nostalgic register.

"Tunisia was a country in blue, a sparkling blue," he told me. "When I see the 'western' sea in some ways perhaps, it doesn't inspire me in the same way. It is cold, glacial, there is a certain distance. While I need the warm Mediterranean Sea. My wife called it my lemonade." The seas—the cold French Atlantic of midlife and the warm Mediterranean of his Tunisian childhood—only become distinguishable once he's experienced both. Not all seas are created equal, according to Memmi. But it's also true that he didn't experience the Atlantic and the Mediterranean in the same way. He traversed the Mediterranean during a crucial period in his subject formation, and he's nostalgic toward the sea as viewed from Tunis before the crossing.

AS: *I was struck by Memmi's assertion that the built environment of the Hara imbues those who lived there with a sense of place that transcends the physical reality. Its affect has the power to shape the memory of the space in ways that evoke a historical relationship. How important is it that the built environment match an individual's memory of that place?*

MF: I am not sure how to answer your question except to say that there will always be a gap between life lived and life narrativized. Memmi frequently invoked the built environment in his work and created a strong sense of place through its sights, sounds, and smells. We have his and other novelists' descriptions of the Hara; we have sociological accounts, which characterize the neighborhood as poor and insalubrious; and we have photographs of and demographic statistics about its inhabitants. Yet so little is really known about people's lives. *El Hara,* a film made over half a century after the Hara's last Jewish inhabitants migrated, must necessarily veer into the speculative.

AS: *Yes, the enduring questions you name here point us toward the inability to ever fully recover the past of any particular moment. It's interesting that Memmi references Tunisia in the past tense. In the film, how did you navigate competing temporalities, those of the past (his memories) and images of the present-day Tunis and the time line that Memmi narrates in the documentary?*

MF: Memmi speaks in the past tense about a Tunisia that has receded from his view. Though the Hara of Memmi's childhood no longer exists, this place remains a living, vibrant neighborhood. It was important for us to include present-day images in the film. We hoped that knotting disparate temporalities and geographies, personal and collective memory, written and oral narrative, could help us glimpse forgotten connections to the past and, ideally, alternative futures. When I asked Memmi about the politics of present-day Tunisia, he responded, "But I don't feel Tunisian in regards to its institutions, politics, and all of that. Not at all. I have no desire to get involved in its political affairs, especially as a Jew, it would be very poorly received and it is not worth it." The "but," this simple conjunction, suggests both Memmi's sense of loss of the past and lack of hope in a present and future where Jews are integral to Tunisian society. To cross the sea is not only to discover *what might be* but also to resign oneself to *what has been* and what *will never be*.

Perhaps Albert Camus got it right when he described Albert Memmi in his preface to *The Pillar of Salt* as a "French writer from Tunisia who is neither French nor Tunisian" but simply, "we are tempted to say, a writer."[14] Ultimately, writing is where Memmi felt most at home, where he could work through the paradoxes of his experience. "It is," he stated, "something I have to do. You write first, and you don't know why, and then it comes slowly. It becomes clearer with time."

AS: *Memmi's reflection seems to apply to more than writing. The idea that meaning emerges through a creative process of remembering is a core focus of memory studies. This edited volume explores how these processes are and continue to be initiated through engagement with the Venice*

Ghetto as a model and metaphor for thinking about a range of Jewish experiences and the global discourses they have informed over the centuries. In your conversations with current or past residents about the Hara, were there any connections made between the two iconic Jewish spaces? Does the "ghetto" or its many histories show up in the physical spaces of the Hara?

MF: If meaning emerges through a creative process of remembering, then one of the challenges of remembering the Hara is the conflation of the historical experience of Jews in the Maghreb with Jews in Europe. The specter of European ghettos such as the Venice Ghetto does haunt present-day conversations about the Hara. During the opening night of an exhibition I curated about the neighborhood at the Dar Ben Achour Library in 2016, the same summer as the five hundredth anniversary of the Venice Ghetto, I explicitly asked the panelists of the round table about using the term ghetto in reference to the Hara. The question initiated an animated discussion about doorways: "Were the doors of the Hara closed at night to protect the Jews from external threats, to punish them, or as a symbol of respect during the sabbath?"[15] Unlike the two Jewish panelists who were more inclined to describe the Hara as a ghetto, the other panelists and audience members were resistant and strongly denounced it being characterized as such.

Though I am ambivalent about using the term *ghetto* to describe the Hara, it is the term Memmi uses, and it was difficult to bypass as our film draws directly from his texts. Twentieth-century Tunisian Jewish writers like Memmi and those who made up the "Tunis School," a generation before Memmi, used "ghetto" interchangeably with "hara." But as Lia Brozgal and the historian Sarah Abrevaya Stein pointed out in their introduction to *Ninette of Sin Street*, the term *ghetto* is rooted in medieval Europe and awkwardly deployed in predominantly Muslim, French colonial North Africa.[16] When I asked Memmi to define what "ghetto" meant to him, he drew parallels not with the Hara but between the Jewish quarters of Morocco, known as *mellah*, and the Venice Ghetto, which he used to visit from "time to time": "Jews felt in danger in Venice and so they chose a piece of land where they could live out their lives. This piece of land was not very large and had no room to expand, but at the same time they were happy to be sheltered from historical adventure . . . The ghetto is on the one hand a symbol that crushes Jewish communities and at the same time the sign of possible salvation, of a possible historical solitude."

He concluded by restating: "Life is paradoxical and ambiguous in that way."

AS: *With Memmi's recent passing (May 2020), I am sure you're reflecting on your conversations with him. Was there anything from those interviews that you see in a new light? And how, if at all, do you think the film might contribute to future understandings of Memmi's relationship to the Hara?*

MF: It's been five years since I returned to the transcript from our first conversation. I was surprised to recall what Memmi called his "pragmatic wisdom." He said to me: "We should not look to the past, we should look ahead. The past is not useful, look ahead of you, this is how we can move forward and do things." When I asked him specifically about the Hara and the role of the past in the present, he said, "You, we, have changed so much. We have changed so much. It helps to know [the past] in some ways, but it's not true, you're not a child of the Hara. I don't think so, you're not. There is one part of the Hara with you, of course, but also a part that is western obviously. You are more French or American than a child of the Hara. Therefore, on this point, I believe we must look ahead."

It's true that no matter how many stories I collect about this place, it will always remain opaque to me. But I don't fully agree with Memmi's insistence on looking ahead. Making *El Hara* provoked questions I would have never otherwise thought to ask my family. Screening a rough cut for my grandfather in 2016 (he died within weeks of Memmi in 2020) evoked stories I had never before heard, including that he used to pray in the synagogue that appears at the end of the film. It was an entry point into memories he'd long thought forgotten. What I am left with is the knowledge that within the larger story of the Hara are thousands of individual stories of people like my grandfather. Each story, like each wave, resembles but never mimics that which came before and that which will come after.

NOTES

1. *El Hara*, directed by Margaux Fitoussi and Mo Scarpelli (2017), HD video, 16 min.
2. *El Hara*.
3. "The Life and Legacy of Albert Memmi: A Conversation with Dr. Lia Brozgal," interview by Christopher Webb, November 6, 2020, in *NokokoPod*, podcast transcript, 4, https://ojs.library.carleton.ca/index.php/nokoko/article/download/2821/2490.
4. Margaux Fitoussi, interview by Amanda Sharick, December 21, 2019, Long Beach, CA; updated remotely via Zoom on May 25, 2020.
5. Brandon Judell, "So What's a Jew? Ask a Film: Checking Out the 27th Annual New York Jewish Film Festival," *HuffPost*, January 8, 2018, https://www.huffpost.com/entry/so-whats-a-jew-ask-a-film-checking-out-the-27th_b_5a53d236e4b0ee59d41c0d1e?fbclid=IwAR0iTle4Y9b4NeyQBTErSUYgK-mzk_NuOZQbGhrA28jLGbpsWjGwJ_MgMLw.
6. Ella Shohat, quoted on *El Hara*, Rake Films, https://rakefilms.format.com/el-hara.
7. Roland Barthes, *Marcel Proust—Mélanges*, ed. Bernard Comment (Paris: Seuil, 2020), 20–21.
8. Albert Memmi, "The Fecundity of Exile," trans. Scott Davidson, *Journal of French and Francophone Philosophy* 19, no. 2 (2011): 4–6. First published as "Fécundités de l'exil" in *Histoires de lecture: Lire en Fête, 17, 18, 19 Octobre 2003* (Paris: Ministère de la Culture et de la Communication, 2003).
9. Albert Memmi, interview by Margaux Fitoussi, June 4, 2016, Paris. All quotes from Memmi in this section come from this interview unless noted otherwise.
10. Memmi, "Fecundity of Exile," 4–6.
11. Albert Memmi, *La terre intérieure: Entretiens avec Victor Malka* (Paris: Gallimard, 1976).
12. Memmi, "Fecundity of Exile," 4–6. Fitoussi is translating the essay's title slightly differently from the published translated version.
13. Memmi, "Fecundity of Exile," 4–6.
14. Albert Camus, preface to *La statue de sel*, by Albert Memmi (Paris: Gallimard, 1966), 9. Translation by Fitoussi.
15. "Nostalgia, Memory, Place: Margaux Fitoussi on the Hara of Tunis," Center for Middle Eastern Studies, Harvard University, May 12, 2017, https://cmes.fas.harvard.edu/news/nostalgia-memory-place-margaux-fitoussi-hara-tunis.
16. Lia Brozgal and Sarah Abrevaya Stein, introduction to *Ninette of Sin Street*, by Vitalis Danon, trans. Jane Kuntz (Stanford, CA: Stanford University Press, 2017).

AFTERWORD

THE GHETTO AFTER THE PLAGUE

SHAUL BASSI

If you don't mind coming to the ghetto, then we can do it there. If the ghetto scares you, then I can come over to Lavington." It was 2012; I was living in Nairobi and interviewing various writers for my research project on Kenyan literature. It was recommended that I meet Stanley Gazemba, an author who lived in Kangemi, one of the overcrowded slums that skirt the original colonial quadrangle of the city center and the green pastoral suburbs of the colonial and postcolonial elites. "No problem," I replied to his kind message. "I come from the place where the ghetto was invented." Of course I had long been aware that the word "ghetto" had a separate and independent existence from its specific Venetian roots: Mitchell Duneier and Daniel B. Schwartz have more recently made important contributions to this surprising semantic and conceptual metamorphosis across time and space, in Jewish and non-Jewish contexts.[1] But never had it been so clear to me how far the ghetto had traveled away from that peripheral corner of my city, my familiar Jewish territory. That the local is the global is a cliché that has been around for a few decades now, but not many sites can make such a literal claim to it. Like most people who think through this lens, Gazemba was not aware he was using an originally Venetian word, and yet I argue he was adding yet another layer of meaning to a palimpsestic concept that, arguably, continues to reflect back on its eponymous site.[2] In other words, all world ghettos, real and metaphorical, potentially return and reconfigure their Venetian archetype.

There was something else that resonated with me in Gazemba's calling his own home a ghetto. He explained that his choice to live there was based on the fact that the teeming area of Kangemi, unlike the sleepy gated communities of the upper classes like the one I temporarily lived in or Lavington where he made a living as a gardener, provided the vibrant narrative matter that inspired his short stories and novels. That established an important parallel for me. When in 1516 the Jews of Venice were relegated to the Ghetto, not only did they negotiate some of the terms of their settlement (certainly with few palatable alternatives in Europe) but they also reacted with great creativity to the restrictions, making Venice a hotspot of Jewish culture and a capital of Hebrew book production. Gazemba does not celebrate the Nairobi ghetto any more than anyone wanted to celebrate the Venice Ghetto in 2016 (as someone claimed polemically), on the quincentennial of its foundation. But we recognize the power of resistance and imagination as part of a complex history that could not be reduced to the lachrymose paradigm criticized by Salo Baron in his famous essay on the Ghetto nor to the symmetric argument that the Ghetto was only one of many ethnic and religious enclaves in a tolerant and cosmopolitan early modern Venice.[3]

A few days before I started this afterword in March 2020, I walked to the Ghetto to buy matzos for Passover. Venice was on lockdown because of the coronavirus pandemic. A city afflicted by overtourism—too many people—was suddenly transformed into a ghost town by a modern plague. That happened only a few months after another exceptional event—a flooding of unprecedented magnitude and duration in November 2019—a forewarning of the climate crisis and a clarion call for urgent measures. When I reached the Ghetto in the middle of the morning, the square was empty, totally empty, except for the presence of a single, indispensable policeman. That uncanny scene (images of a deserted Venice have become iconic tropes of the global pandemic) evoked its mirror image: the Ghetto animated by the many events of the quincentennial, never so brimming with people as it was on the five nights of *The Merchant in Venice,* staged by Compagnia de' Colombari. In their introduction to this book, the editors ask, "After the five hundredth anniversary, what future possibilities emerge from interacting with the Ghetto of Venice? What is the value of memory studies frameworks for holding together competing pasts, layered histories, and contested futures?" A provisional assessment of what has been accomplished and a possible indication for the future would suggest that the anniversary has produced a lot in terms of scholarly outcomes and intangible heritage and has not had much effect in terms of tangible heritage. Or, in plain terms, we have many more books and artworks centered on the Ghetto (the studies by Donatella Calabi are exemplary in this regard), but the Ghetto itself has not changed much.[4] This is a painful conclusion to reach, albeit temporarily, for someone like myself who was fully committed to a milestone date and its potential. Clearly more temporal distance and critical detachment are needed for a more objective appraisal, but some provisional remarks can be offered here.

The quincentennial was a big, concerted effort coordinated by the historic Jewish community of Venice and aimed at planning the future of this site on the basis of a rich legacy that was perceived to contain important lessons for the present. Almost five years after the commemoration, the area has not changed much. The rich calendar of events had one main goal: to raise substantial funding for the restoration of the five early modern synagogues (an unparalleled concentration of extant ancient Jewish edifices) and a transformation of the Jewish Museum into a hotspot of international Jewish culture. However, famous international philanthropists who had gone public in offering support vanished into thin air. A foundation that will remain nameless because of the good work it has done elsewhere comically requested naming rights to the Ghetto as a condition of its donation. Even putting aside the fact that the toponymy in Venice has by and large remained unchanged for two centuries—and that I calculated that by the standards of that pledged donation, I could have traded the value of my one bedroom apartment for naming rights to my *calle*, the street where I spent my childhood—an offer of that nature showed a total lack of understanding and respect for the historical importance of the heritage it was meant to support. Other things went awry, and not only has the museum remained the same (with partial restoration under way), but smaller exhibition places have closed, as has the larger kosher restaurant. The fact that if you look up what used to be the anniversary's website today you will instead find a blog on drug addiction recovery suggests that the organizers themselves have decided to move on and, I would argue, that some form of *damnatio memoriae* is even at play.

In this afterword, true to the workings of memory, I feel the need to go back and forth. I would like to share a few episodes from the last two decades not only to suggest a possible narrative of the cultural memory of the Ghetto in the new millennium but also to offer some hypotheses for the future. In 2002, I visited the University of California, Santa Cruz, and thanks to Margaret Brose, I met Murray Baumgarten. I gave a talk on the Ghetto where I spoke too fast due to stage fright. Fortunately, I was also given the opportunity to turn the talk into an article in *Judaism*, which ends with "Coda 2010?": "It is then no utopia to imagine a Jewish-oriented academic program founded in the Ghetto, capable of restoring it to its most positive historical vocation. It would be a place where scholars and students, as well as artists and writers, can live in this unique historical environment, interact with the local community, and become a companion to it, always present, always different."[5] A year later I was back on campus teaching a global Jewish literature course and had further conversations on the Ghetto of Venice and its international significance. I recognized how relatively little I knew of its history. Like many, I took for granted my home turf. The Ghetto was a part of my childhood and I had read about it, but I became more interested in its many dimensions through the questions of friends and visitors. In the summer of 2006, thanks to Murray Baumgarten and the National Endowment for the Humanities (NEH), twenty-five scholars from the United States (which meant twenty-five colleagues from many different places with distinct languages, religions, and disciplinary backgrounds) were now studying the Ghetto while sitting in the Ghetto, for an immersive experience lasting five full weeks. It happened again in 2008, adding up to fifty specialists developing essays, books, poetry, fiction, syllabi; exploring new directions of research and creative engagement; and interacting with numerous local and international experts invited as guest speakers. We had created *temporary communities* of visiting scholars which, among other things, defied the dichotomy between permanent resident and tourist that typically monopolizes the debate over the future of Venice. The next question was: Could these academic initiatives be turned into a regular feature, perhaps even the signature of a new era for the Ghetto? That model depended on an active engagement with the main social and cultural players in the Ghetto: the historic and official Jewish community (lively but small and dwindling, active but nostalgic and inward looking) that also owned the library, archive, and museum;

Chabad, the most enterprising global force of Hassidic Judaism, itself pivoting its activities to religious tourism, part of the industry gradually becoming the main—if not the only—economic game in town; and the local scholarly community. As two essays in this collection testify, the library and archive house precious collections but remain underfunded and underutilized, and the museum, with its precious educational activities for schools, remains focused on the basic form of the quick guided tour. What was new about the Venice Center for International Jewish Studies (founded in 2009 in the wake of the NEH experiments and today operating as Beit Venezia to overcome the polysyllabic challenge posed by the original denomination) was its targeting of both local Jewish residents (including many unaffiliated Jews) and an international community of committed visitors as its audience, an attempt to create regular and long-term relationships that contrasted with the gravitational pull exerted by tourists. The mission was to think of the heritage of the Ghetto neither as a mere celebration of the past nor as an exclusive patrimony reserved for local use but rather as a dynamic living memory to be continuously elaborated on through an interaction between insiders and outsiders, even blurring the distinction between the two groups.

Back and forth. Recently I was in Florence and I heard a cantor engaged in the Shabat morning prayer. All of a sudden, I heard a sound that brought me back to my childhood—the pronunciation and intonation of a certain word that more recent cantors in Venice, while learning the traditional melodies under the severe scrutiny of older members, had not absorbed, probably because it was a mispronunciation that needed to be rectified. I felt the harrowing pain of nostalgia stemming from the voice of a Venetian cantor who had relocated to Florence, because that loss was a synecdoche for a larger loss. For many Italian Jews, prayer is a musical and aesthetic performance before anything else. I learned that ritual by heart as melody before I delved into its meaning, and this is why it strikes profound chords. This personal anecdote sums up the entanglements between individual memory, communicative memory, and cultural memory (to use Jan Assmann's categories) that relate to the Ghetto, all dimensions that need to be addressed to build for the future.[6] It is time to confess that it is a harrowing pain to see forms of life and culture fade away in front of your eyes, especially since they survived the utmost attempt at annihilation during the Shoah (a sentiment magisterially captured by Giorgio Bassani in the opening page of *The Garden of the Finzi-Continis*).[7] It is more of an empirical observation than a scientific analysis, but I have the impression that new approaches to the cultural heritage of the Ghetto find a more open-minded audience in older people, who have lived through the war and are perhaps more pragmatic about the past. Those more resistant to change are the generation born right after the war, who lived the trauma indirectly and felt the obligation and burden of reconstruction (which in Venice was more psychological and cultural than physical, since the Jewish sites of the Ghetto were left unharmed). It is this generation that has arguably been more past-oriented, bent on preservation, almost paralyzed by the anxiety of transformation (a syndrome that affects the whole of Venice, far beyond the specific Jewish case). You would need to understand the Venetian dialect to appreciate all the nuances of the phrase *se ga fatto sempre cussì*, "it has always been done this way," an impersonal statement that typically ignores the well-known fact that all traditions are invented and were invented at some point in time. It is no coincidence that the only conspicuous change in the outlook of the community has been a typical neo-Orthodox turn in which all the local rites that smacked of reform Judaism were gradually removed from the traditionally accommodating and flexible Italian Orthodox body, aligning this community with new religious protocols mostly imported from Israel by a younger generation of rabbis. Women started covering their heads, and the organ and women's choirs disappeared, as did, generally, that relaxed attitude to orthodoxy that had characterized Italian Judaism since the nineteenth century and had helped in fending off the official adoption of alternative forms of organized Jewish life. This is a necessary digression to frame any discussion of the role of memory in the Ghetto. The interaction with an international Jewish audience is perceived by many affiliated Jews as a threat to tradition. An irony deserving a more in-depth examination is that, on top of the generational factor, the most resistant are nonobservant Jews who tenaciously protect practices that they themselves do not engage in but see as forming the bastion of their communal identity (the influence of the Catholic matrix of Italian culture is a factor that can only be mentioned here).

Of all forms of resistance to the gradual but inexplicable decline of organized Jewish life in Venice, I would like to highlight the role of art in activating the memory of the Ghetto and mediating between the past and the present, using two examples that I would define, respectively, as an inside-out and an outside-in intervention. A project such as the Israeli artist Hadassa Goldvicht's *The House of Life* is based on a profound respect for the tradition and the feelings of Venetian Jews.[8] This multimedia installation, which has had exhibitions in Venice and Jerusalem, embodies a series of exemplary principles. It originated through the residency of an artist who, as an observant Jewish woman, had an intimate understanding of the dynamics of a small Modern Orthodox community. The fact that she neither spoke Italian nor had any specific background in Jewish Italian culture created a critical distance and cultural gap that she beautifully bridged through a series of video-recorded interviews over several stays that generated intimate relationships with many people. The project led her ultimately to concentrate on a specific site of memory, the Jewish cemetery (Bed A Haim, the House of Life, in local Judeo-Venetian terms), and a specific person, an eighty-five-year-old individual who, for four decades, has been the custodian of the place. Goldvicht turned the communal and individual memory of a very special individual into a delicate artwork, performed without any archiving impulse or pretension. The project is still in progress, with a great quantity of footage and interviews that may take future forms. Is turning memory into art a way of acknowledging that it has ceased to function through its normal channels of communication, from generation to generation? Is art singing the swan song of communal memory? Or is this work an additional way to revive that memory and to provide the same community (while simultaneously targeting a general audience interested in art) another tool to explore and understand its own tradition? I will leave it to art specialists to provide the necessarily nuanced answers, but commenting on the creative process, we can define it as one that started from an intimate immersion—experiencing the "inside" of the local Jewish community—and resulted in the production of an installation that then traveled successfully to the "outside."

The Merchant in Venice was a different model of engagement. Here the most famous representation of Jewish Venice by an absolute outsider—William Shakespeare, who never set foot in Venice—was brought inside the space. As the editors of this volume remark, "The space of the Ghetto compels us to consider the categories of insider/outsider; the authors' examination of these various theatrical productions likewise asks us to think through how the historical context supports a narrative of 'disruption'; the very structure of the Ghetto relies on the 'necessary other.' This is what drives the conflict in *The Merchant of Venice*."[9] In the Colombari production, the "necessary other," Shylock, was put to the service of that very disruption. The space of the Ghetto witnessed a massive interaction between all of its social and cultural actors. Bringing Shakespeare to the Ghetto under the auspices of the university, with the full support of the city authorities and especially the Jewish community, and with the help of local residents and cultural professionals, was a way to show that Jewish Venice could handle its spectral double without succumbing to the fiction and could instead use the philosemitic potential of a play against its undeniable antisemitic components. While the other chief events of the quincentennial took place away from the Ghetto—the main exhibition was held at Palazzo Ducale and the main ceremony at the Fenice Theatre because, ironically, the Ghetto is too small to host all those who wanted to commemorate it and it was important that the quincentennial be recognized as an event for the entire city—*The Merchant* was created for the space of the Ghetto itself. The fact that the production acquired an aesthetic autonomy that allowed it to travel to other European and North American venues bears witness to the fact that it was far from an occasional piece. The Ghetto generated it, but it also enabled its independent life, and the memory of the Ghetto continues to produce meaning far away from its original site.

As I complete my afterword, the lockdown is easing in Venice; we are returning outside and the *calles* and *campos* fill again with people gasping for air. The desire for normality is palpable, and although the masses of tourists are still held back, the economic system screams for them to return to make up for lost income. But many fear that returning to a pre-coronavirus Venice would mean trading one lethal blow for another and that this exceptional situation, unexpected and unwelcome as it has been, opens a unique window of opportunity to reimagine the city under different conditions: A city where the economy of knowledge and its beneficial social effects would regain critical space from that of mass tourism. A new system that would generate more residents and more qualified and respectful visitors against a system based on extraction and consumption. Salvatore Settis has defined Venice as "a thinking machine that allows us to ponder the very idea of the city, citizenship practices, urban life as sediments of history, as the experience of the here and now, as well as a project for a possible future."[10] If we took advantage of this unprecedented opportunity, and of course there are all sort of reasons not to be optimistic about it, the Ghetto could function as a paradigmatic site in terms of how its heritage could inspire new forms of experiential tourism, religious and cultural exchange, educational activities, and artistic reimaginings. In a renewed Venice, to quote the editors one last time, the Ghetto could really function as "a laboratory for thinking through the ways in which we consider how heritage sites 'do' memory work."[11]

I want to conclude by presenting three further examples of artwork that propels the memory of the Ghetto into the future. These are all examples of cultural practices and artistic projects where the Ghetto has been conceived as a future-oriented machine of multidirectional memory, to extend Michael Rothberg's definition beyond the boundaries of the Holocaust (which remains an unavoidable part of the discourse) and to suggest that remembrance of the Venetian Ghetto and the remembrance of other forms of ghettoization can nourish and enable one another over and above any false notion of competition, misleading analogies, or hierarchies of intolerance.[12] All of the pieces were also based on the experience of living in Venice and exploring the Ghetto over an extended period of time, with artists invited not only to visit all relevant heritage sites under expert guidance but also to live and understand its ordinariness, its daily dynamics and social interactions. Choosing examples from music, literature, and the visual arts is also a way to suggest the multiple forms and senses through and into which the Ghetto can be translated and made accessible across national, linguistic, and cultural barriers, having an impact here and elsewhere.

The composer and trumpeter Frank London, famous as an award-winning soloist and member of the Klezmatics, combined his vast expertise in adapting traditional Jewish musical repertoires to contemporary musical forms with the scholarship of Jewish Italian music scholars Gabriele Mancuso, Francesco Spagnolo, and Enrico Fink to produce both the soundtrack for *The Merchant in Venice* and a brand new program (now an album) titled *Ghetto Songs*. In this concert, which premiered in Hamburg in 2019 (outside the aura of the anniversary), London drew inspiration from the historical complexity of the world's many ghettos: "Songs . . . are a means for inhabitants of ghettos to express their humanity in inhuman conditions, to escape from harsh realities of subjugation, to give voice to their yearning and hope. Ghettos are historically complex phenomena. They offer both freedom and restriction, protection and imperilment. They isolate groups from the world outside, becoming cultural 'petri dishes' where the cultures of particular groups thrive."[13] His inventive and bold gesture of artistic freedom allowed for the juxtaposition, mixing, confusion, collapse of one ghetto into the other, showing how the old can influence the new and vice versa. Much of the music in the concert came from or was about Venice and Italy: boat songs, synagogue music, Italian poetry (by Sarra Copia Sullam and Primo Levi), biblical texts, and political songs, old and original text in Judeo-Venetian. It elaborated on the Venetian and Italian *nusakh* (the melody to which the liturgical texts are chanted in Jewish prayer service), Renaissance Venetian and Italian secular and sacred music by Bartolomeo Tromboncino (who was not Jewish), and Italian Jewish violinist and composer Solomone Rossi. London then moved to other European Jewish ghettos, from Warsaw to Budapest, and to his own Lower East Side in New York. Going beyond Jewish ghettos, he included music that came from the African American ghettos of Harlem, Watts, and Detroit (the classic "The World Is a Ghetto" by War and "The Ghetto" by Donny Hathaway) and Antônio Carlos Jobim and Vinícius de Moraes's famous song of the Brazilian Favela (ghetto), "O Morro Não Tem Vez." Crucially, the concert did not proceed in any chronological or geographic order, making the ghettos' temporalities and musicalities flow into one another, letting the memory of the Venice Ghetto reactivate the musical memory of other places. Music was able to perform a form of analogical thinking with less responsibility than any historical argumentation.

The literary project "reimagining the Ghetto," the framework for the texts by Marjorie Agosín and Rita Dove discussed in this volume, had a similar premise but a different outcome, focusing on essays, short stories, and poems.[14] It included Jewish and non-Jewish writers from five continents (Daniel Mendelsohn, Anita Desai, Arnold Zable, Moti Lerner, Molly Antopol, and Igiaba Scego, among others).[15] Ironically, Stanley Gazemba was invited but contributed in absentia: he was denied a visa from Italy because he lacked specific economic credentials. A prominent African intellectual was profiled as a potential illegal migrant because in the world in which we live, a credit card number takes precedence over any number of ISBN codes. The most unexpected output of that project, perhaps, has been Amitav Ghosh's novel *Gun Island,* a fast-moving and erudite narrative in which the cosmopolitan history of the Ghetto features prominently:

> Sitting on a bench, in a corner, I made an effort to imagine the square as it might have looked, three and a half centuries earlier, trying to envision it as it would have appeared to a traveller from Bengal. I tried to think of the Gun Merchant treading on those cobblestones, surrounded by people in red and yellow headgear—the colours enjoined on the inhabitants of the Ghetto by Venetian law, to mark them out as non-Christians. Warmed by the sun I began to daydream and suddenly the Gun Merchant seemed to appear before my eyes, tall, broad-shouldered, with a yellow turban, walking unhurriedly past on some errand. He glanced at me as he went by and his eyes were clear and untroubled. I could see why he would feel safe here, beyond the reach of Manasa Devi and the creatures and forces that she commanded. This, if any, was a place that would seem to be secure from non-human intrusion: apart from a few ornamental trees and plants there was almost nothing in sight that was not made by human hands.[16]

Ghosh, who had already addressed the cross-cultural entanglements of Jewish history in his magisterial *In an Antique Land*, revisits a key period of the history of the Venice Ghetto, the early modern period of the fictional Shylock and the historical Leon Modena and Sarra Copia Sullam, to insert an unusual presence, "a traveller from Bengal" whose yellow turban marks both a distance and a possible analogy with the Sephardic merchants of the Ghetto (described by Thomas Coryat, the adventurous English traveler who visited both the Ghetto and India). Ghosh highlights the cosmopolitan identity of the area, its role as a contact zone, as much an area of separation as a site of potential to generate ideas for our present. The novel makes historical memory global: its narrative sleight of hand is to make the Ghetto the place where the protagonist, a Bengali antique book dealer tracing the footsteps of the mysterious gun merchant, has an unlikely encounter (in a narrative punctuated with unlikely events) with a young Bangladeshi migrant employed as a construction worker. The scene of migration of the early seventeenth century becomes the scene of migration of the twenty-first century, the Jewish refugees of yesterday somehow aligned with the modern-day foreigners' welcome to Venice (and Europe) as a cheap labor force. The fact that the young man is an ecological refugee allows Ghosh to showcase the role of Venice as the battlefront of the climate crisis and a cosmopolitan city fully entangled in the flow of trans-Mediterranean migration.

Ghosh's writing was also the inspiration for the last Ghetto project I would like to mention: *Living Under Water.*[17] In October 2018, Beit Venezia invited to Venice five international visual artists—Andi Arnovitz, Lynne Avadenka, Meydad Eliyahu, Kenny Goldman, and Leora Wise—to provide a Jewish perspective on the environmental crisis. In *The Great Derangement*, Ghosh warns us that "the climate crisis is also a crisis of culture, and thus of the imagination," and identifies Venice as a focal point for our necessary reflections, a city uniquely vulnerable to sea levels rising and uniquely stimulating with a glorious past of equilibrium between human achievements and environmental sustainability.[18] The project title was inspired by a famous Jewish joke that illuminates the creative (and humorous) Jewish response to crisis, adversities, and catastrophe.[19] As the essays of this book confirm, the Ghetto of Venice embodies this historical condition: limited by harsh restrictions in a partially segregated area, Venetian Jews reacted by forging a vibrant community, blending diverse Jewish, Italian, and European elements, becoming a focal point for Jewish communities by disseminating texts and ideas throughout Europe and beyond. The artists examined the role of climate change as it relates to Venice, explored the city, met with the local Jewish and Venetian community, and engaged and conversed with both biblical and environmental scholars. The final output was a printed and digital zine launched alongside the original artworks at an exhibition in Jerusalem with the aim of raising awareness about climate change in Jewish circles and beyond. The pandemic has slowed down this project, but it has also paradoxically reiterated its relevance, since the spillover of the coronavirus from animal to human is but one of the many symptoms of our perilous environmental condition. Restoring and renewing the synagogues and Jewish museum—the most tangible sites of memory—remain necessary and desirable actions. However, the multifaceted memories of the Ghetto have shown that they come alive through new art forms and idioms, confirming that the space, rather than being a site for melancholic pilgrimages to a fading tradition, can still be a vital hub for rethinking urgent problems in the present moment. For that potential to be activated, a renewed interaction between insiders and outsiders is indispensable.

March–May 2020

NOTES

1. Mitchell Duneier, *Ghetto: The Invention of a Place, the History of an Idea* (New York: Farrar, Strauss & Giroux, 2016); Daniel B. Schwartz, *Ghetto: The History of a Word* (Cambridge, MA: Harvard University Press, 2018).
2. Stanley Gazemba, *Dog Meat Samosa* (Venice: Cafoscarina, 2017).
3. Salo Baron, "Ghetto and Emancipation," in *The Menorah Treasury: Harvest of Half a Century*, ed. L. W. Schwartz (Philadelphia: Jewish Publication Society of America, 1964), 50–63.
4. See, especially, Donatella Calabi, ed., *Venice, the Jews, and Europe: 1516–2016* (Venice: Marsilio, 2016), and Donatella Calabi, *Venice and Its Jews: 500 Years since the Founding of the Ghetto* (Milan: Officina Libraria, 2017).
5. Shaul Bassi, "The Venetian Ghetto and Modern Jewish Identity," *Judaism* 51, no. 4 (2002): 478.
6. See Jan Assmann, "Communicative and Cultural Memory," in *Cultural Memory Studies: An International and Interdisciplinary Handbook*, ed. Astrid Erll and Ansgar Nünning (Berlin: Walter de Gruyter, 2008), 109–18.
7. Giorgio Bassani, *The Garden of the Finzi-Continis*, trans. Jamie McKendrick (New York: Penguin, 2005), 9.
8. Hadassa Goldvicht, *The House of Life*, 2017, multimedia, http://www.thehouseoflifevenice.com.
9. Amanda K. Sharick and Katharine G. Trostel, introduction to this volume, 11–12.
10. Salvatore Settis, *If Venice Dies* (New York: New Vessel, 2016), 170.
11. Sharick and Trostel, introduction to this volume, 9.
12. Michael Rothberg, *Multidirectional Memory. Remembering the Holocaust in the Age of Decolonization* (Stanford, CA: Stanford University Press, 2009).
13. Frank London, *Ghetto Songs*, liner notes, Felmay, 2021, compact disc.
14. See Katharine G. Trostel, "The Poetry of Marjorie Agosín," this volume, chap. 8, and Sharick and Trostel, introduction to this volume.
15. Shaul Bassi, ed., *Il cortile del mondo. Storie dal Ghetto di Venezia* (Firenze: Giuntina, 2021).
16. Amitav Ghosh, *Gun Island* (London: John Murray, 2019), 166.
17. Living Under Water: A Jewish Exploration of Climate Change, Beit Venezia, accessed February 12, 2021, http://www.livingunderwater.org.
18. Amitav Ghosh, *The Great Derangement* (Chicago: University of Chicago Press, 2016), 9.
19. A rabbi, a priest, and an imam receive a message from God. He's had enough of mankind's sins and intends to punish them with a flood more lethal than Noah's. The priest goes to his people, reports the message, and asks them to repent, appealing to Jesus for their admission to heaven. The imam goes to his people, reports the message, and tells them to accept the will of Allah. The rabbi goes to his people and says, "Jews, we have a few days to learn how to live under water."

Contributors

MARJORIE AGOSÍN, professor of Spanish, Wellesley College, is an award-winning poet, memorialist novelist, and scholar. Agosín has received important awards for her literary career and also for her human rights activism, among them the Pura Belpré Award by the American Library Association and the Gabriela Mistral Medal of Honor. At Wellesley College she holds the title of Andrew W. Mellon Professor in the Humanities.

SHAUL BASSI is professor of English literature and director of the Center for Environmental Humanities at Ca' Foscari University of Venice. He is the cofounder and president of Beit Venezia: A Home for Jewish Culture and was the coordinator of the cultural projects related to the 500th anniversary of the Ghetto of Venice (1516–2016), where he spearheaded the production of the first performance of Shakespeare's *The Merchant of Venice* in the Ghetto. His books include *Visions of Venice in Shakespeare* (coedited with Laura Tosi, Ashgate, 2011), *Experiences of Freedom in Postcolonial Literatures and Cultures* (coedited with Annalisa Oboe, Routledge, 2011), *Essere qualcun altro: Ebrei postmoderni e postcoloniali* (Palgrave Macmillan, 2011), and *Shakespeare's Italy and Italy's Shakespeare: Place, "Race," and Politics* (Palgrave Macmillan, 2016).

MURRAY BAUMGARTEN, Distinguished Emeritus Professor of English and Comparative Literature, University of California, Santa Cruz, has taught modern imaginative literature at the Santa Cruz campus of the University of California for over fifty years, working with novels, poems, and essays and their interpretive responses as well as their cultural, historical, and geographic contexts. In recent years he has explored the literature of the ghetto, invented in Venice in 1516 as a political and governmental instrument for the social control of the Jewish people in their European exile. The Venice Ghetto is one of the dark secrets of the Renaissance that brought past knowledge into the present to help reimagine a new European future but also sought to control and even close off Jewish life. How to see around the Ghetto's high walls and reclaim Jewish experience continues to center his thinking, writing, and teaching.

CHIARA CAMARDA completed a PhD in Asian and African studies (Hebrew Department) at Ca' Foscari University of Venice in 2017, with a dissertation titled "Tracing the Hebrew Book Collection of the Venice Ghetto." She then worked on a research project sponsored by the Catholic University Center of Rome and by the Memorial Foundation for Jewish Studies of New York cataloging the early Hebrew books kept in Sicilian libraries. Camarda is also a librarian specializing in Hebrew book cataloging and is currently working at the I-tal-yah national cataloging project managed by the Union of Italian Jewish Community, the National Library of Israel, and the National Central Library of Rome. Publications include "Il patrimonio bibliografico ebraico in Sicilia," *Materia giudaica* 25 (2021): 303–20; "Il Sefer Or ha-Śekel di Avraham Abulafia e i commenti aggiunti nel Ms 12 della Biblioteca Fardelliana di Trapani," *Materia giudaica* 24 (2019): 101–16; and *Ha-sefarim shel ha-Geṭo. I libri del Ghetto: Catalogo dei libri ebraici della Comunità Ebraica di Venezia (secc. XVI–XX)* (Padua: Il Prato, 2016).

MARGAUX FITOUSSI is an award-winning filmmaker and a PhD candidate at Columbia University in New York City. She is currently completing fieldwork funded by the Wenner-Gren Foundation for Anthropological Research. Prior to her doctoral work, Fitoussi received her master's degree from Harvard Divinity School, where she was named a Presidential Scholar, a prestigious grant.

ANDREA YAAKOV LATTES has taught at Bar Ilan University at Gratz College in Philadelphia and currently teaches at the Yaad Academic College in Tel Aviv. Lattes has published four volumes on the history of Jews in Italy, including the critical edition of the Rome Community Registry of the 1600s and that of the Lugo Jewish Community. In addition, he has published about fifty scientific papers concerning historical and sociopolitical analysis of Italian Jews and their communities. In 2008 he was one of the founding members of the Israeli Association for the Study of the History of Italian Jews and has been its president since.

DARIO MICCOLI is assistant professor of modern Hebrew and Jewish studies in the Department of Asian and North African Studies, Ca' Foscari University of Venice. He is the author of *Histories of the Jews of Egypt: An Imagined Bourgeoisie, 1880s–1950s* (Routledge, 2015) and *La letteratura israeliana mizrahi* (Giuntina, 2016). He has conducted research and published on the history of the Jews of modern Egypt, Jewish memory and heritage in the Mediterranean, and Israeli literature.

FEDERICA RUSPIO, freelance archivist, holds a PhD in European social history from the Middle Ages to the Modern Age from the University of Ca` Foscari in Venice, with a thesis on the Portuguese nation in Venice between the sixteenth and seventeenth centuries. She also worked on Jewish demographic sources in Italy, dated seventeenth to nineteenth centuries, with a research grant from the same university. From 2011–12, she received a diploma from the Scuola di Archivistica, Paleografia e Diplomatica within the State Archive of Venice. Since then she has worked as an archivist in many Venetian cultural institutions, including the Renato Maestro Library and Archive of the Venetian Jewish Community. She published *La Nazione portoghese: Ebrei ponentini e nuovi cristiani a Venezia* (Silvio Zamorani editore, 2007).

MICHAEL SHAPIRO is professor emeritus of English and was founding director of the Program in Jewish Culture and Society at the University of Illinois at Urbana-Champaign, where he was also artistic director of the Revels Players, an acting troupe devoted to early modern drama. He has been a visiting professor at Loyola, Cornell, Reading (England), and Tamkang (Taiwan) Universities. Shapiro is author of *Children of the Revels* (Columbia University Press, 1977) and *Gender in Play* (University of Michigan Press, 1994), as well as articles, notes, and reviews in early modern English literature and drama and in modern Jewish secular literature. He is the coeditor of *Wrestling with Shylock*, a collection of essays about Jewish responses to *The Merchant of Venice* (Cambridge University Press, 2017). His current project, "Shylock after the Shoah," is a book-length study of the influence of the Holocaust on productions and adaptations of *The Merchant of Venice*.

AMANDA K. SHARICK received her PhD in English from the University of California, Riverside. She specializes in late nineteenth-century British and related literatures, Victorian media and visual culture, Jewish studies, gender studies, and immigrant literature. Her research project traces the transatlantic networks of Anglo and American Jewish women writers from 1880 to 1923. Currently, Amanda is the associate director of the Harvard

University's Graduate Commons Program and is a founding member of the Venice Ghetto Collaboration.

CLIVE SINCLAIR was born in London in 1948 and was winner of the Somerset Maugham Award, the PEN Silver Pen, and the Jewish Quarterly Award and was selected in 1983 as one of Granta's original Best of Young British Novelists. He was a fellow of the Royal Society of Literature and held a doctorate from the University of East Anglia. He taught there, at the University of Uppsala, Sweden, and at the University of California, Santa Cruz. Sinclair lived in London until his death on March 5, 2018. His final collection of short stories, *Shylock Must Die*, published posthumously, was a series of reincarnations of Shakespeare's most alluring antihero. Through these stories, Shylock—as a man, a ghost, and an idea—travels through time and across continents, through comedy and tragedy, awaiting that final judgment between mercy and revenge.

EMANUELA TREVISAN SEMI is senior researcher of modern Hebrew and Jewish studies at the University of Ca' Foscari in Venice. She has published books, essays, and articles in international journals on the topics of Jewries at the margins, Karaites, Jews of Ethiopia, issues of memory among Moroccan Jews, movements of conversion to Judaism, and the literature of the Mizrahim.

KATHARINE G. TROSTEL completed her PhD in literature at the University of California, Santa Cruz, and is assistant professor and chair of English and the humanities at Ursuline College in Pepper Pike, Ohio. She is cofounder of the Venice Ghetto Collaboration (www.veniceghettocollaboration.com) and coauthor (with Amanda K. Sharick and Erica Smeltzer) of the chapter "Reading-in-Place and Thick Mapping the Venice Ghetto at 500" in *Doing Memory Research: New Methods and Approaches* (Palgrave, 2019).

JAMES E. YOUNG is Distinguished University Professor Emeritus of English and Judaic and Near Eastern Studies at the University of Massachusetts, Amherst, and founding director of the university's Institute for Holocaust, Genocide, and Memory Studies. Young is the author of *Writing and Rewriting the Holocaust* (Indiana University Press, 1988), *The Texture of Memory* (Yale University Press, 1993), *At Memory's Edge* (Yale University Press, 2000), and *The Stages of Memory* (University of Massachusetts Press, 2016) and editor of *The Art of Memory* (Prestel Verlag/Jewish Museum, 1994).

Index

Page references in *italics* refer to figures.